JOHN McINTOSH KELL

of the Raider
Alabama

JOHN McINTOSH KELL OF THE RAIDER *ALABAMA*

by
NORMAN C.
DELANEY

THE
UNIVERSITY OF
ALABAMA PRESS
Tuscaloosa

For Linda

The University of Alabama Press
Tuscaloosa, Alabama 35487-0380
uapress.ua.edu

Cover image: John McIntosh Kell (from *Two Years on the* ALABAMA by Arthur Sinclair, 1895)

Cataloging-in-Publication data is available from the Library of Congress.

ISBN: 978-0-8173-1268-8 (paper)
ISBN: 978-0-8173-9624-4 (electronic)

CONTENTS

LIST OF ILLUSTRATIONS

PREFACE

In presenting a biography of John McIntosh Kell, my object is, first of all, to spotlight the man. Secondly, I have tried to present a new look at the cruise of C.S.S. *Alabama*, aboard which Kell served as first lieutenant and executive officer. My study covers all of Kell's naval career (1841–1865), including the California phase of the Mexican War and the Perry Expedition to Japan. However, it was not until the Civil War that Kell attained a position of authority as first officer under Captain Raphael Semmes on C.S.S. *Sumter* and *Alabama*. Since the *Alabama* was the most successful of the Confederate raiders, I was interested in learning how Kell contributed to her success. Although my special interest has been the war years, I have also attempted to fill the gaps in Kell's life—episodes mentioned only superficially in his *Recollections of a Naval Life*. For example, he had little to say of his court-martial and dismissal from the navy in 1849, yet this period was significant in shaping Kell's later career and was directly related to his association with Raphael Semmes. The official record of the court-martial proceedings helped in understanding the background of a major crisis for the young Kell.

I have written of the *Alabama-Kearsarge* battle off Cherbourg in detail in an effort to present an objective account of the fight as seen by both sides. A researcher invariably turns up conflicting sources, and this has been particularly true with material relating to the *Alabama*. One author of a book on the *Alabama* was James Young, alias "Philip Drayton Haywood." Although "Haywood" was easily proven to be a fraud who never sailed on the Confederate raider, many secondary works on the *Alabama* still cite his yarns as authentic.

For my sources, I have relied chiefly on the large collection of primary material at Duke University. This includes the correspondence of Kell, his wife, mother, and sisters—the basis of the John McIntosh Kell Papers. Blanche Kell saved practically every letter that ever came into her hands. Fortunately, the habit of preserving these letters continued into a later generation. Munroe d'Antignac of Griffin, Georgia, a grandson of Kell, is the present caretaker of his family's heritage.

This biography is the result of the encouragement and assistance of many people. I owe my greatest debt to Dr. Robert H. Woody of Duke University. Dr. Woody suggested Kell as a subject worthy of study and has provided valuable suggestions during months of researching and writing. Two grandchildren of John McIntosh Kell have generously given of their time and made available important material; they are Munroe d'Antignac of Griffin and Mrs. Evelyn (Kell) McLemore of Darien, Georgia. I am also grateful for assistance from staff members of the following libraries and depositories: Duke University; Southern Historical Collection at University of North Carolina; Georgia Department of Archives and History; National Archives; Library of Congress; Boston Public Library; Peabody Museum at Salem, Massachusetts; G.W. Blunt White Library at Mystic Seaport, Connecticut; Confederate Museum at Richmond, Virginia; Georgia Historical Society at Savannah; Free Library of Philadelphia; and the United States Naval Academy Museum.

My thanks and appreciation to my wife, Linda, for her painstaking work in typing the original manuscript. She has also given assistance in innumerable other ways, as well as being a constant source of encouragement and inspiration.

I wish to thank Mrs. Beverly Baggett, who did the typing of the revised manuscript.

Corpus Christi, Texas N. C. DELANEY
August, 1972

With all the strain upon his energies that body and mind can endure, he must be even of temper, and infuse good humor and cheerfulness in the atmosphere around him. A high moral character, united with an indomitable courage, bold and daring, quick of wit, and slow of passion, he must seek to cultivate and embody in himself the graces of a *gentle life*, the generosity of a knight, the gallantry of a sea-officer, and the cool, cutting discernment, and judgement, with all the polished graces of a gentleman.

Lieutenant Commander Francis A. Roe, U.S.N.
on the duties of an Executive Officer (1865)

Captain John McIntosh Kell

1

McINTOSHES AND KELLS

Visitors to the attractive one-story white house perched above the railroad track at Sunnyside, Georgia, during the early 1880's, could hardly fail to be impressed by the commanding appearance of the tall, bronzed, heavily bearded farmer. Indeed, he was no ordinary farmer: He was John McIntosh Kell—"Captain Kell" to his neighbors—former first lieutenant and executive officer ("luff" in sailor language) aboard the Confederate cruisers *Sumter* and *Alabama*. Moreover, he was a veteran of twenty years service in the United States Navy, during which he had seen action in the Mexican War and participated in the Perry Expedition to Japan. But to those who knew him, Kell was most of all associated with Raphael Semmes and the *Alabama*.

During the postwar decades, veterans and nonveterans alike were reading and contributing to the growing accumulation of books and articles on the war. The campaigns and battles were refought as fiercely with the pen as they had been with musket, saber, and cannon. Nor was the war at sea overlooked. Readers of Raphael Semmes' *Service Afloat* were introduced to the lieutenant to whom he gave his highest praise:

> [He is] a tall, well-proportioned gentleman, of middle age, with brown, wavy hair, and a magnificent beard, inclining to red. See how scrupulously neat he is dressed, and how suave, and how affable he is, with his associates. His eye is now beaming

> gentleness, and kindness. You will scarcely recognize him, as the same man, when you see him again on deck, arraigning some culprit, "at the mast," for a breach of discipline.[1]

The lieutenant described by his captain was still an impressive figure twenty years after he had walked the decks of the *Alabama*. A visitor to Sunnyside in 1883 observed that Kell looked twenty years younger than his sixty years. He wrote further:

> In manner he is somewhat nervous. His voice, clear and ringing, indicating that he was born to command, can express in his very tones the utmost kindness and the most genial hospitality. Although most of his life has been spent upon the sea, where self-assertion is absolutely a necessary qualification to success, Captain Kell is a very modest man, and shrinks from the public gaze.[2]

Another observer noted that the "clear blue eyes, aquiline nose and strong cheek bones betoken quickness of perception and resolute determination." Yet, the voice had the "peculiar musical softness most frequently heard on the Southern coast of Georgia."[3] To still another visitor, the reddish hair and "broad Scotch face" resembled those of a Highland chieftain.[4]

To most Northerners Kell of Georgia was just another "Rebel," yet the term was to him more compliment than insult. While he would have objected vehemently to the appellation "pirate," which had been hurled at the officers of the *Alabama* by Yankee enemies during the war years, to be a Rebel was in the tradition of Kells and McIntoshes and went back to the remote glens of Scotland. Kell knew about his McIntosh forebears; he also knew that he was a descendant of Scottish heroes, including William Wallace and Robert Bruce. The seacoast county of Georgia where he had been born and raised was named in honor of his Scottish ancestors, the Borlum McIntoshes.

McIntosh County, Georgia, is well named. Its boundaries include the lands pioneered by sturdy Scots, most of them veterans of the unsuccessful Stuart Uprising of 1715. The leader of one hundred and seventy-seven Highlanders (including families and servants) was John Mohr McIntosh (1700–1745),[5] who had forfeited his estates after the 1715 rebellion. The group was specially recruited by General James E. Oglethorpe, who wanted hardy and resourceful men willing to face dangers imposed by nature, hostile Indians, and the Spaniards to the south. Arriving in Georgia in early 1736, the Scots made their settlement, New Inverness, on a twenty-foot high bluff overlooking the Altamaha river, about sixty miles south of Savannah; the surrounding district was named Darien to commemorate the unsuccessful Scotch settlement on the Isthmus of Darien in 1698.

The progeny of John Mohr placed the McIntosh name upon the rolls of subsequent American wars, beginning with the Battle of Bloody Marsh (1742), where a young son, William, fought. In January, 1775, a District Congress was held in St. Andrew's Parish, Georgia, for the purpose of "opposing the execution of the several arbitrary and oppressive acts of the British Parliament. . . ."[6] The first signature on the petition is that of Lachlan McIntosh, another son, who served in the Continental Army as a major general directly under George Washington.[7] William McIntosh became a colonel of cavalry. When the British compiled the names of leading Georgia rebels for their Disqualification Act of 1780, Lachlan and William were included; Lachlan had the "honor" to be third on their list, following the two "rebel governors." Near the bottom of the list of one hundred and fifty-one rebels is the entry "John Kell, Gentleman."[8]

The origins and early background of this John Kell are not given in available records; many years after his death, his daughter-in-law and grandchildren came to the conclusion that he had emigrated to Georgia from Wales.[9] Records show that Kell was an early settler of Sunbury, Georgia, who took up the Patriot cause in 1775. During the war years he was a Savannah merchant and auctioneer and was also appointed to several influential positions.[10] He was one of the first members of the Midway Congregational Church in Sunbury,[11] where he held a pew at the time of his death. His death in 1784 came unexpectedly, and his wife, Elizabeth (Senior) Kell, was left with a daughter, Mary, and a newborn son, John. The estate left by John Kell indicates that he had prospered in his professions.[12] Three years later, his widow married David Reese, a lawyer friend of her husband.

The second John Kell, born November 3, 1784, was raised in Sunbury and probably received his early education at Sunbury Academy, which at the time was the best school in the region.[13] He attended Yale College, receiving his B.A. in 1807.[14] The following year he studied law in Savannah.[15] At that time, the legal profession was attracting some of the best minds of the South, and Kell's legal contemporaries were men of ability, wealth, and influence. Some would later gain national renown, including James Moore Wayne (1790–1867), who would rise in state and national politics until, in 1835, he would be appointed an associate justice of the United States Supreme Court. There was also John Macpherson Berrien (1781–1856), already a well known Georgia figure in 1810. And there were other Savannah lawyers who, in 1810, were among the best in the country.[16] That John Kell could compete with them successfully is evidenced by his appointment as solicitor general for the Eastern District of Georgia[17] and his later appointment as judge of the same district, a position he held at the time of his death.[18] In December, 1808, Kell married Barbara McIver of Sunbury, but the young wife died less than three years later. Not long after his loss, beginning January 1, 1812, Kell and George W. Owens formed a law partnership in Savannah.

During this time—perhaps on his circuit journeys—Kell became acquainted with Margery Spalding Baillie (1794–1870) of Darien, only daughter of Alexander and Hester (McIntosh) Baillie. Margery, a child when her mother died, had been reared by her aunt, Margery Spalding, for whom she was named. As a member of the "first family" of Darien, she had received a fine education at a French school in Charleston, South Carolina, and was a highly desirable bride for the up-and-coming Sunbury lawyer. Years later, her daughter-in-law would say of her: "She painted beautifully, was quite a musician, and a very cultivated woman."[19] John and Margery were married at Laurel Grove in Darien on May 30, 1816. Margery brought to the marriage an estate of her own: twenty-one Negroes and two hundred and forty acres of the land originally granted to her grandfather, William McIntosh. This was "Laurel Grove"—the place of her birth.[20] It was here, a mile north of Darien, that the couple spent most of their married life. The early years of their marriage were marred by the death of one child, a daughter, at the age of fifteen months. However, there were three daughters who lived—Mary, Evelyn, and Hester—and on January 23, 1823, a son was born. The boy, born at Laurel Grove, was named John McIntosh Kell to honor both his Kell and McIntosh forebears. A second son—Alexander—was born five years later.

Between Darien and Sunbury, and on the coastal islands, lived many of the friends and relatives of John and Margery Kell: McIntoshes, Holmeses, Gouldings, Kenans, Wyllys, Troups, Wards, Sadlers, and Brailsfords. By far the most distinguished of these neighbor-relatives was Thomas Spalding (1774–1851), whose main estate was on Sapelo Island. He had another fine tabby house—Ashantilly—built on the mainland, north of Darien, in 1815. Although he was to gain a national reputation as a defender of the Union, Spalding was recognized in the South for his interest in promoting the agricultural development of his region. He tried to instill into his fellow Southerners the virtues "which would make them love their locality, their section, and their nation."[21] Spalding, more than any other man, helped to promote the town of Darien, which became incorporated as a county seat in 1818. But despite his great hopes for its future after the War of 1812, a period which saw several large sawmills contributing to its economic prosperity, Darien (like the more extreme case of Sunbury) was unable to develop its potential as a great seaport. Benefiting from new railroads, Savannah and Brunswick were able to forge ahead of Darien, and soon left her behind. In 1828 an English lady traveling through Georgia noted that Darien "looks like a city of the dead."[22] In 1839 the critical eye of English actress Fanny Kemble, sophisticated wife of Pierce Butler, the wealthiest plantation owner in the county, was also unfavorably impressed with Darien:

> The abomination of desolation is but a poor type of its forlorn appearance, as, half buried in sand, its straggling, tumble-down wooden houses peer over the muddy bank of the thick slimy river. The whole town lies in a bed of sand: side-walks, or mid-walks, there be none distinct from each other; at every step I took my feet were ankle deep in the soil, and I had cause to rejoice that I was booted for the occasion. . . .The houses seemed scattered about here and there, apparently without any design, and looked, for the most part, either unfinished or ruinous.[23]

For all that, the Kells and their growing family were contented with their comfortable two-story home facing the Altamaha river. A description of the Kell home as it appeared in the early 1820's is found in the writings of a Kell cousin, the Reverend Francis Robert Goulding, who gained a reputation as a writer of adventure stories for young people. Goulding (who was thirteen years older than his Kell cousin, John) spent enjoyable boyhood days at the home of "Aunt Kell."[24]

> It was about a mile distant from Darien, with a wide lawn between the house and the river, while on every other side, for more than a furlong, extended a forest of live-oaks, with long drooping branches gracefully hung with moss, under which were occasional clumps of evergreen, with here and there a rustic seat, the work of one of her tasteful daughters. Her court-yard was crowded with flowers and shrubs, some of a tropical and some of a semi-tropical character—sagoes, bananas, guavas, and oranges of every ornamental variety, from the little dwarf and myrtle oranges the size of a walnut to the shaddock, a Malay variety of pear-shape, large as the head of a two-year old child. But the chief attraction . . . was not so much the beautiful forest around the house, nor the beautiful lawn before it, nor the beautiful court-yard beside it, as it was the large and beautiful orangery adjoining it, from whence the place derived its names of "The Grove," or rather the large and beautiful orange-*room* above-stairs. . . . During the whole winter the floor of that room was kept covered with delicious oranges, to which we young folks had free access, and where we were permitted to eat as many as we pleased . . .[25]

Judge Kell, respected leader in the community, had become an Elder in the Darien Presbyterian Church.[26] Managing the plantation and other property took most of his time when not traveling the circuit. But, without warning, at a time when life had much to offer him, Kell died,[27] leaving a pregnant wife with the enormous responsibilities of managing a plantation and its slaves[28] and raising five young children. Margery had little time to grieve for her husband. She would have to be content with memories, while concentrating on her children during forty-three years of widowhood ahead. Fortunately for the Kell children, their mother was a woman of strong will, despite her small size and fragile appearance.

From his mother, doting sisters, and little brother, Johnny Kell—"Donny"—received lavish attention. Years later he would recall his boyhood as one spent "in the healthful, manly sports of hunting, riding, boating, and fishing, varied by school attendance [and dancing lessons] in Darien." His best friend and almost constant companion was his cousin Randolph Spalding (1822–1862), son of the renowned Thomas.

The education received by Donny Kell, although irregular, was the best that could be provided south of Savannah. His first teacher was a Mr. Bradwell, whom he later recalled as "a teacher of great merit and ability." In 1835 he was at Perry's Mills, Georgia, attending a school run by a Mr. Musgrove. However, the teacher's absences, caused by his fondness for alcohol, soon brought an end to classes, and the students returned to their homes.[29] In late 1838 Kell, with his cousin Henry K. Reese, was sent to the highly reputable Chatham Academy in Savannah; Margery Kell wrote him that she hoped God would enable her to raise the money needed to keep him in school, and added, "You must be very attentive to your lessons and your behaviour too—now is the time for your character to be formed." The devoted mother believed that if only Donny would "study hard and turn out a smart good man," she would have no regrets for her sacrifices.[30] She made a practice of noting her son's spelling errors, then correcting them in her answering letters.

Having finished his formal schooling at sixteen, Kell spent

the winter of 1839–1840 in Savannah as an apprentice at the counting house of Andrew Low and Company. A few months of this work convinced Kell that a business profession was not to his liking, and in the spring of 1840, at a most opportune time, he returned to Darien. The brig *Consort*, Lieutenant James Glynn commanding, was anchored at Sapelo harbor engaged in surveying the coast. Some of the *Consort's* young bachelor officers began to call at the home of the now blossoming Kell girls, Mary and Evelyn, and their visits aroused the enthusiasm of young Kell. The tall, well-built teen-ager visited the *Consort* repeatedly, making friends with the officers and sailors aboard. Eventually, he reached a decision: he would serve his country as a naval officer. Kell's decision was not a hasty one. His experience as a clerk, which had brought restlessness and dissatisfaction, strongly influenced his choice. Then, too, he recognized his love of the sea:

> I think being born almost within sound of the billows and in sight of the "deep blue sea," I had an innate love for it which grew with my growth and strengthened with my strength. . . .[31]

Kell was one of many young men contemplating a naval career in 1841. Of these, however, only those with political influence had any chance of receiving the coveted midshipman warrants. As it was, over two hundred youngsters—far more than were needed—were appointed, for it was a year of two new national administrations, that of William H. Harrison and his successor, John Tyler. Kell's appointment was among those approved by George E. Badger, President Harrison's Secretary of the Navy.[32] It had been necessary to use influence. Margery Kell had been a friend and classmate of wealthy Anna Matilda Page, who in 1824 married Thomas Butler King. In 1841 King was a United States congressman whose district included McIntosh and other Georgia coastal counties. Whether or not to write King must have been a difficult decision for the widowed mother, who had told her son when he was twelve: "My son, always remember that . . . you are God's highest gift of love to me." If her appeal to King was successful, it would mean Donny's absence from her for many months, even years, at sea. But she finally wrote the letter, appealing on the basis of her friendship with Anna King.

Congressman King had a special interest in naval affairs at the time Margery Kell's letter reached him. His first major legislation, introduced and passed in 1841, called for the establishment of a Naval Home Squadron.[33] With letter in hand he approached Secretary Badger, who was a strong supporter of King's bill.

The impatient youth at Laurel Grove must have shouted for joy when the long-awaited letter arrived. There would have been no mistaking the official-looking envelope. The good news was soon read and re-read:

> After many and repeated efforts I have at length obtained a midshipman's warrant for your son; he now belongs to his country.[34]

On September 27, 1841, the new acting midshipman appeared before the Justice of the Peace in Darien to take the oath of allegiance:

> I, *John Kell*, appointed a *Midshipman* in the Navy of the United States, do solemnly swear to bear true allegiance to the United States of America, and to serve them honestly and faithfully, against all their enemies or opposers whomever, and to observe and obey the orders of the President of the United States of America, and the orders of the Officers appointed over me; and in all things to conform myself to the rules and regulations which now are, or hereafter may be, directed, and to the articles of war which may be enacted by Congress for the better government of the Navy of the United States, and that I will support the Constitution of the United States.[35]

During the twenty years of his service, Kell would face two separate conflicts between this pledge and his conscience. Each would be caused by completely different circumstances; both would have a profound effect upon his life. On that day in 1841, however, the young Georgian had thoughts only of adventures ahead.

2

YOUNG REEFER

Herman Melville, who spent fourteen months aboard an American man-of-war, the frigate *United States*, exposed in his novels the hardships and cruelties he observed and warned that innocent boys who chose a sea life would soon become "cabined and cribbed in by all manner of iniquities."[1] Melville and Richard Henry Dana (whose *Two Years before the Mast* was published in 1840) aroused public indignation against the abuses and tyranny they had witnessed. Throughout the 1840's, beginning under Secretary of the Navy Abel P. Upshur, increased attention was given to naval reform. This was due partly to the occurrence—in 1842—of one of the most controversial events in American naval history. Philip Spencer, an immature nineteen-year-old midshipman, was accused by his commander of plotting a mutiny aboard the brig *Somers* and, with two seamen, was hanged. Their judge and executioner, Commander Alexander S. Mackenzie, became the center of a controversy which rocked the nation, for not only was Spencer extremely young, he was the son of Secretary of War John Canfield Spencer and nephew of Navy Captain William A. Spencer.[2] Although Mackenzie was acquitted by a court-martial and by a court of inquiry, repercussions continued for many years, striking into the very "system" itself. One of many questions raised asked why a boy with such an unstable record had been allowed to continue as a midshipman. Generally only midshipmen with ability survived at their profession for very long. For example, of the two hundred and twenty-four midshipmen appointed along with Kell in 1841, only one hundred and thirty-six eventually were promoted to passed midshipmen.[3] The old navy was tough, and only those equally tough survived.

With his appointment secured, John Kell began to consider the future. He was not the first of his family to embark upon a naval career; a cousin, James McKay McIntosh (1792–1860), was a thirty-year veteran of the service and had risen to the rank of Commander.[4] Kell had only a vague memory of having met him years before, but his name was often mentioned at Laurel Grove. Margery Kell's worries about Donny would be greatly reduced if he were in the capable and presumably sympathetic hands of his cousin. Kell himself agreed; it would be important that his first cruise go well.

Commander McIntosh was then living in Bridgeport, Connecticut, waiting to take command of the sloop *Falmouth* then being fitted out at the Brooklyn Navy Yard. When he received the news that his cousin had been made an acting midshipman, he wrote to Kell, suggesting that he apply to Secretary of the Navy Upshur for orders to the *Falmouth.* Kell was prompt in making this request, but no reply came.[5] Impatient, he decided to go to Bridgeport without orders and report to Commander McIntosh, rather than miss a chance to sail aboard the *Falmouth.*

The passage from Savannah to New York took ten days and gave Kell "a little touch of what I am going to have on board ship." A storm hit them with such force that the mainsail was blown away, and it took a full day to rig up another. Kell wrote about the experience in a letter to his family:

> I staid [*sic*] nearly all the time on deck with the Captain and I can tell you it is not such a pleasant thing to be on deck in a hail storm when it is blowing a gale. I staid on deck with the Captain so that I might feel a little of what I was going to feel.[6]

After a brief stay in Bridgeport, Kell returned to New York, accompanied by his Cousin James. Here the Commander made arrangements for him to eat with the officers aboard the *North Carolina* so as to learn some of a midshipman's duties. He also took Kell to his own tailor to be measured for an overcoat and undress naval jacket. (The regulations of 1841 called for a dark blue double-breasted coat with a double row of buttons and an anchor of buff cloth inserted in either side of the collar. For undress wear, midshipmen were instructed to wear short jackets while on duty.) Later, Kell secured the regulation head-gear—a cocked dress hat and a cap (dark blue with an anchor over the vizor) for undress.[7] He was also required to purchase a sword and a quadrant. Kell was fortunate to be in the company of an experienced officer since he was apparently apprehensive about New York; he wrote home that he had to be "very particular" how he went about.[8]

November was slipping away, and still Kell had not received orders. He again wrote to Secretary Upshur;[9] this time a reply soon reached him. Midshipman Kell now had a ship—the *Falmouth*. This vessel, which had been first launched in 1827, was recommissioned in December, 1841, and assigned to the newly organized Home Squadron. The *Falmouth* was a sturdy vessel, one hundred and twenty-seven feet long, with a thirty-four foot beam; she could accommodate a crew of one hundred and ninety men. Her armament consisted of twenty cannon: four eight-inch and sixteen thirty-two pounders.[10] To young Kell, she appeared to be a "fine comfortable ship," and he was optimistic about the pending cruise: "I think we shall have a very pleasant time of it."[11]

While the *Falmouth* was delayed in port until her full complement of seamen could be enlisted, Kell became ill, seriously enough to be sent to the hospital. On the first day of the new year—1842—he wrote cheerfully to his family that he was in a "fine room with a large fire and everything comfortable with servants to wait on me."[12] On February 9, a week before the *Falmouth* was to sail, Kell boarded her but remained on the sick list. He and the eleven other "reefers" (as midshipmen were commonly called) were quartered in the steerage, an uncomfortably crowded place made foul with the stench of bilge water and smoky lanterns. Each reefer had his own campstool and a locker about two feet square.[13] The washing arrangements were "two rude wash-stands" with tin basins, into which water was poured from a deck bucket. Each reefer had his own hammock man ("cot-boy"), chosen from the crew, who lashed and stowed the hammock in the morning, got it from the nettings at night, and scrubbed it at intervals. For this he received an extra glass of grog or, after the grog ration for midshipmen was abolished (August 29, 1842), a small sum of money, saltwater soap, and plug tobacco. The hammocks of the reefers were similar to those of the crew but had a mattress and more bedding. When they were swung in their places, they were extended by cross-sticks or spreaders, making them into comfortable beds. Sailing ships were unheated even in winter and cold latitudes, hence the steerage contrivance for warmth was usually a bucket of sand with a heated shot buried in it; reefers could place their feet in the bucket.[14]

Two days after coming aboard the *Falmouth*, Kell may have seen his first flogging. A man of sensitivity had good cause to be sickened at the sight. Melville provides a vivid description of this punishment:

> The captain's finger was now lifted, and the first boatswain's mate advanced, combing out the nine tails of his *cat* with his hand, and then, sweeping them round his neck, brought them with the whole force of his body upon the mark. Again, and again, and again; and at every blow higher and higher rose the long, purple bars on the prisoner's back. But he only bowed over his head, and stood still. Meantime, some of the crew whispered among themselves in applause of their shipmate's nerve; but the greater part were breathlessly silent as the keen scourge hissed through the wintry air, and fell with a cutting, wiry sound upon the mark.[15]

On February 11, 1842, Kell noted in his journal that two seamen were punished with twelve and ten lashes each for desertion.[16] Young reefers often fainted when first witnessing corporal punishment, but they soon "grew callous to it, and correspondingly demoralized."[17] Yet flogging of seamen was a routine part of life at sea (until 1850, when it was abolished).

John Kell was hardly in the mood of a reformer as he sat writing a letter in the steerage of the *Falmouth*, away from the "confusion" on deck. It was February 14, 1842, and his ship was leaving port. With eleven reefers as steerage-mates, Kell anticipated a "pretty mess."[18] He was best off where he was. Another "green" reefer, Thomas S. Phelps, has left a record of his own confusion while his ship, the *Preble*, was leaving port:

> Somebody told somebody else to "Sheet home"; then the first lieutenant ordered some one to sharpen the after-yards, and to put the head-yards in a box. Bodies of men would rush forward, and bodies of men would rush aft. Then there was a shout of "broken ground," when "young gentlemen" [midshipmen] were told to clap men on ropes, of which there appeared to be a million. The second lieutenant, on the forecastle, was ordered to "let the cat and fish have the anchor." I was run over and nearly knocked down a dozen times, and crawling under the poop ladder out of the way, became conscious that I knew nothing of what was transpiring, and, in my opinion, neither did any one else.
>
> All hands seemed to have gone crazy, and I felt that if this was sailoring, a whole lifetime would be required to gain a knowledge of it.[19]

This same green reefer had had his feelings of "greatness" removed at first encounter with a lieutenant on the quarter-deck of the *Preble*. At that time ("Who the devil are you, sir?" "Here's another damned young cub for me to lick into shape, a sucking Nelson for me to nurse!" "Get off the quarter-deck and touch your hat, sir, and don't stand gaping at me!") "he realized that among creation's atoms he was the smallest."[20]

In addition to this lesson, young midshipmen had much else to learn. Aboard warships at this time it was customary to have a professor assigned to instruct them in seamanship—entering and leaving a harbor, shortening and making sail, tacking, and handling the ship in all kinds of weather. Aboard the *United States* in 1843 the reefers assembled every other afternoon on the gun deck; a drum head served as the professor's desk, students sat on shot-boxes and match-tubs, the blackboard was supported by three boarding pikes, and a cutlass was used as a pointer.[21]

The professor aboard the *Falmouth* was William S. Fox. Kell considered him "a very smart Professor. . . . I get him to show me everything that I want and he is very kind."[22] The duties of Kell and the other reefers allowed them to absorb the fundamental principles of seamanship. It was required that each midshipman keep a daily journal (called a "checkerboard"), in which he copied from the ship's log accounts of the wind and weather, reckonings of latitude and longitude and distance sailed, statements of provisions received and issued, ports made, ships passed, and punishments administered. Journals were periodically examined by the ship's captain. Although they hardly make exciting reading, the keeping of a journal (usually considered an unhappy chore) acquainted the reefer with nautical terms and improved his spelling and penmanship.

Midshipman Kell had not made a satisfactory recovery from his illness; when the *Falmouth* arrived at Hampton Roads, Virginia, he was sent to the Naval Hospital in Norfolk. By early June, however, he was well enough to resume the many duties of the reefer. Midshipmen, Herman Melville wrote, were like college freshmen and sophomores, who made the steerage buzz, hum, and swarm like a hive. In describing them, Melville presents a sailor's less-than-complimentary view of the reefers:

> These boys are sent to sea for the purpose of making commodores, and in order to become commodores, many of them deem it indispensable forthwith to commence chewing tobacco, drinking brandy and water, and swearing at the sailors. As they are only placed on board a sea-going ship to go to school and learn the duty of a Lieutenant, and until qualified to act as such, have few or no special functions to attend to; they are little more, while midshipmen, than supernumeraries on board. Hence, in a crowded frigate, they are so everlastingly crossing the path of both men and officers, that in the navy it has become a proverb, that a useless fellow is "as much in the way as a reefer."

In a gale of wind, when all hands are called and the deck swarms with men, the little "middies" running about distracted, and having nothing particular to do, make it up in a vociferous swearing; exploding all about under foot like torpedoes. Some of them are terrible little boys, cocking their caps at alarming angles, and looking fierce as young roosters. They are, generally, great consumers of Macassar oil and the Balm of Columbia; they thirst and rage after whiskers; and sometimes, applying the ointments, lay themselves out in the sun, to promote the fertility of their chins.

As the only way to learn to command is to learn to obey, the usage of a ship of war is such that the midshipmen are constantly being ordered about by the lieutenants; though, without having assigned them their particular destinations, they are always going somewhere, and never arriving. In some things they almost have a harder time of it than the seamen themselves.[23]

Midshipman Kell considered his duties important, however, and would have disagreed strongly with anyone who thought otherwise:

Our pay is 40 dollars a month. We pay our mess bill out of that—from 10 to 15 dols—I find it plenty to clothe me and gives me some pocket money in the bargain. Our duty in port and at sea is very different. At sea we have four hours watch to keep, except the dog watches so we are 4 hours on duty and 12 hours off. You may judge that the mid-watch is the most disagreeable of all. I mean the midnight watch. On shore we do not have dog watches but have all of the day's duty to keep from 8 in the morning till 8 at night. They keep four hours at sea. Then we have 2 liberty days and one boat duty. Then comes the days duty again.[24]

By the end of July, 1842, a short Caribbean cruise had ended, and the *Falmouth* was at the Pensacola Navy Yard, with Commander McIntosh awaiting further orders. The town of Pensacola, when first seen from the ship, disappointed Kell. He was, however, excited by the accounts he had been hearing of the beautiful Pensacola girls. "I am sure," he wrote, "there can be nothing more pleasant than to be in pretty young ladies [*sic*] society." Kell's first impressions of Pensacola remained the same ("not much of a place"), but there were pleasant ways to spend one's free time. On the evening of August 19, a theatrical performance, attended by local citizens and a number of young ladies, was held aboard the *Falmouth*. On some days visitors would come aboard the ship; otherwise, the officers not on duty could make up fishing parties, taking their dinner and returning late in the evening.[25]

In late September, 1842, Commander McIntosh received his orders, and after a week's cruise the *Falmouth* was anchored off the island of Sacrificios, the port of Vera Cruz, Mexico, three miles to the south. McIntosh's orders were to pick up a quantity of silver specie as cargo and convey it to New Orleans for delivery to merchants there. Kell was allowed to visit Vera Cruz, but he found it unattractive. He was far more impressed with New Orleans, which he saw while assigned to the party delivering the silver.

By April the *Falmouth* was once again at Pensacola, and Kell proudly reported that he was performing the duties of a master's mate. "The oldest Midn. generally demands it," he wrote, "but as we are all forty one's and only a few months difference in our date, it was given to me." As master's mate, he was responsible for bringing provisions and supplies aboard ship and submitting daily reports on the water supply to the master. Midshipman Kell had learned a great deal about seamanship during his months aboard the *Falmouth*. Also, he was in excellent health and made a fine appearance, standing just over six feet in his stocking feet. He took pride in his ship, which he considered "the fancy ship of the Squadron."[26]

During April and May, 1843, the *Falmouth* made another cruise to the Caribbean, stopping at St. Mark's and Port au Prince in the West Indies. From there her course was directed toward the Georgia coast, and on June 18 she dropped anchor off Tybee Roads, Savannah.

Donny Kell had been away from his home for nineteen months and could hardly have been recognized as the same boy of two years before. Now he was an experienced naval officer who looked the part, dressed in a smart uniform and accompanied by his commanding officer. With family, friends, and familiar servants around him, he must have relished that week. He felt a "great importance" in his position, he admitted, "though only a midshipman!"[27]

After a week, Kell and McIntosh boarded the stage for Savannah and were well on their way when the careless driver dozed off. While going over a causeway the coach overturned. Kell, who was seated next to the driver, managed to jump clear and thus avoided injury. Soon a sputtering and fuming Commander was lifting his rotund figure through a window of the overturned coach. When he had succeeded and given the driver a tongue-lashing in the best tradition of a sea captain, the coach was righted and the journey resumed, Commander McIntosh marveling at the risks involved in land travel.[28]

During the *Falmouth's* trip to New York, where she would be re-fitted for her next cruise, Kell thought about requesting a transfer to another vessel, an idea he intended to discuss with his cousin. The *Franklin* and *Savannah* were at the Navy Yard, and there might be an opportunity to sail aboard one of them. Kell had decided that a three-year cruise would be preferable to staying on the *Falmouth* and "running into port every day or two along our coast."[29] Commander McIntosh concurred with his cousin's decision, and on August 25, 1843, Kell and four other midshipmen of the *Falmouth* received orders to report to the recently launched frigate *Savannah*.

Kell had the satisfaction of having made a successful first cruise and did not fear the future. When he saw his Cousin James several weeks later, he received a letter of recommendation that strengthened his hopes for a bright career ahead:

> With great pleasure I bear testimony to your correct, moral and gentlemanly deportment during your service of twenty one months under my command in the U.S. Sloop of War Falmouth. I never had the slightest complaint made against you, and your conduct never failed to meet my approbation. You cannot doubt the deep interest I take in your welfare, and the hope I entertain of your passing on your return from your present cruise a creditable examination.[30]

The commander of the *Savannah*, Captain Andrew Fitzhugh ("a large corpulent man"), was, like Commander McIntosh, a thirty-year veteran of the Navy. His midshipmen were under strict discipline and, as was customary, received specific instructions on their duties:

> [The midshipmen] are each required to obey all orders of their Superiors and are to be "watched" as I may direct and must never leave the deck until regularly relieved, except by permission of the Officer of the watch. They are required to produce their Journals every Sunday for my Inspection in which they will be particular in noting their day's work. They will also keep correct copies of all "Station Bills" and international "rules and regulations" and send them to me on the first day of every month to be examined.
>
> They are forbidden to strike the men and are to avoid cursing and abusing them. If they have cause of complaint against any person on board, they will inform the officer of the Deck, First Lieutenant, or myself as the case may require.
>
> When in charge of boats on shore or elsewhere they are never to leave them or suffer the men to do so. Nor are they to give them or suffer them to receive any Spiritous Liquors while absent from the Ship on duty without permission from a Superior Officer.[31]

On the first day at sea three seamen were punished with nine lashes each, an example of what was ahead.

Midshipman Kell had reason to be grateful for his *Falmouth* experience, which would be of the utmost value aboard a strict man-of-war. The frigate *Savannah* was one of nine warships authorized by Congress after the War of 1812. Launched in 1842, she was more than twice the size of the *Falmouth*, having an armament of forty-four guns.[32] She required a complement of four hundred and eighty officers and sailors.

The Savannah remained in New York until the middle of October, 1843, receiving men and supplies for her three-year cruise. Kell had his tailor make up two dozen shirts for him, with "linen bosoms, wrist bands and collars." When he learned that several of his messmates were deeply in debt to tailors, he congratulated himself on having no debts. He was able to send his mother an allotment ticket, which he instructed her to use whenever she needed funds. He was also determined that his sixteen-year-old brother should receive "the best college education."[33]

The destination of the *Savannah* was Callao, Peru, the station for the American Pacific Squadron.[34] This trip would be Kell's first crossing of the equator, customarily an occasion for the visit of "King Neptune" and his attendants. However, the comic and often wild ceremony had been dispensed with, having been deemed "an infraction of discipline."[35] Thus, Kell—a "pollywog"—became a "shellback" without undergoing the traditional hazing.

It took two months for the *Savannah* to reach Rio de Janeiro, where she remained for ten days. Kell and other officers were given opportunity to visit the city, and Christmas of 1843 was spent at that port.

Once again at sea, the *Savannah* plowed steadily southward. There were the customary off-duty diversions such as catching porpoises and, on at least one occasion, an albatross, caught with a baited hook. ("It cut his mouth a little but when we threw him overboard he swam bravely away.")[36]

Late in January the *Savannah* reached Cape Horn, where she encountered the heavy gales and wild seas for which the Horn is well known. As the ship pitched and rolled, Captain Fitzhugh lost balance and fell heavily against a cannon. He was badly bruised and severely injured his shoulder. During the raging storm, Kell had the experience of keeping the morning watch, from 4 to 8 a.m., in the midst of driving hail. Icebergs were always a potential danger here, but—much to his disappointment—he saw none. In January the Horn experienced only two hours of darkness, and Kell was amazed to see "hammocks slung and all hands turned in when the sun was two or three hours high."[37] Finally the *Savannah* was in safe open seas, and Fitzhugh set her course northward.

A week short of Callao, the *Savannah* spotted the store ship *Erie,* flying the pennant of Commodore Alexander J. Dallas. Several months earlier Dallas had been sent to relieve Commodore Thomas ap Catesby Jones, but he had thus far been unable to locate him or the frigate *United States*.[38] He was headed for Callao, where he hoped to find the object of his search. When Dallas came aboard the *Savannah*, Captain Fitzhugh, still disabled by his injury, formally turned over his ship to the Commodore. Fitzhugh asserted that the ship had on board "as fine a set of officers as he had ever sailed with." Kell observed Commodore Dallas to be "quite small" and a pleasant-appearing man. The new commander made an inspection of the *Savannah*, seemed pleased, and gave directions for making the officers' quarters more comfortable.[39]

On February 17, 1844, the *Savannah* arrived at Callao, "a collection of low, dingy dwellings, occupying the rippling verge of a vast sand plain."[40] The *United States* was there, but the elusive Commodore Jones had left a week before on the *Constellation*. Kell was surprised to find an acquaintance aboard the *United States*—Chaplain Theodore B. Bartow of Georgia.

A week after his arrival in Callao, Captain Fitzhugh departed for the United States, after receiving three hearty cheers from the crew of the *Savannah*. Before he left, he gave the midshipmen excellent letters.

There was little to do in Callao, and at the Marine Hotel gambling was the principal pastime. "Around the table could be seen, almost any night, officers of the Navy of all nations, from Midshipmen up well into the higher grades."[41] Lima, six miles away, was far more interesting. There Kell, with officer friends, witnessed the "wild excitement and great brutality of a bullfight."[42]

At the great Cathedral of Lima, Kell paid a dollar to be shown the alleged remains of Pizarro in a dim, candle-lit chamber below the altar. A few years earlier Navy Chaplain Fitch W. Taylor had been deeply impressed by the same spectacle:

> The edge of the box was broken, and the top gone, showing the dusty and crumbling skeleton, said to be the remaining bones of the conqueror of Peru. The flesh had gone.... His hands lay crossed upon his breast, exhibiting the skeleton of a remarkably small hand—and his feet corresponding in size. Quicklime,

that covered parts of the body, had hardened into white lumps, and was dry. . . . Parts of a dingy linen shroud still wrapped portions of the relics, and a knotted button clasped a worked thread-lace wristband around the ulna bone of the skeleton. It was a dark place, that depository of the olden dead; and the unlabelled boxes bore the dust of centuries upon their crumbling slabs. I now held in my hand a small relic from the shroud of Pizarro, which lay loose in the skeleton box.[43]

The sight of "Pizarro" seems to have had a mesmeric effect on a number of visitors to the vault. Probably the eerie surroundings, the silence, and the candlelight created a sense of history. In any case, the urge suddenly came over Kell to seize a relic—part of the body itself. (The guides could be bribed.) He broke off a finger of the skeleton, placed it in his pocket, and brought it away with him. Kell was not the only visitor who felt the spell of "Pizarro." Robbing the body of fingers and toes was a common practice at the Lima Cathedral.[44]

Kell remained aboard the *Savannah* until April 9, when he was ordered to temporary duty aboard the schooner *Shark* of the squadron, commanded by Lieutenant Neil M. Howison. While the squadron was at Callao, the *Shark* made short trips to Valparaiso and to Panama, carrying passengers and delivering or picking up dispatches. She was the smallest vessel in the squadron (one hundred and seventy-seven tons), and could best be used for these missions. Kell was aboard her for just over a year, during which he relished his new responsibilities:

I am allowed all the privileges of a Lieutenant, have a watch to keep, a fine Captain, and a nice set of Officers. Our vessel is small but comfortable. I would not change places with any Midshipman in the Squadron. I have had several offers, but I prefer remaining six or eight months longer, for by that time I will feel that confidence in myself that I certainly want and which is requisite for every young officer. On board a Frigate or any larger vessel while I would do Midshipman's duty I would never hold any very responsible office but here I sail the vessel at my own discretion and I think it benefits me a great deal.[45]

On April 26, 1844, the *Shark* left Callao for Panama with two lieutenants as passengers. Although Kell had been in the service for two and a half years, he still had much to learn about running a ship. Once, while the *Shark* cruised off the Lobas (Seal) Islands of Peru, Kell was left in charge of the deck. A group of seals began to frolic in the wake of the schooner, and Kell, amused by their antics, called down a hatchway to Lieutenant Howison. Another officer appeared and was amazed to see that the ship was dangerously close to the rocks. He shouted for Howison, who immediately ordered Kell to "put the helm down and haul on the wind," adding, "Mr. Kell, you must think you are in a coach and four, driving round a street corner."[46] Although he had kept the schooner on course, Kell had not considered the action of the current. It was a lesson he would not forget.

When they arrived at Panama on May 12, they found letters and dispatches which had been sent across the Isthmus. Seventeen- and thirteen-gun salutes were fired to honor the late Secretary of the Navy and the Chief of Naval Construction, both of whom had been killed by the explosion of an experimental ten-ton cannon aboard the steamer *Princeton*.[47] On May 24 the *Shark* began her return to Callao, stopping at convenient ports for hunting, fishing, and sight-seeing. At Huanchaco, Peru, where they arrived on June 25, they learned of the death of Commodore Dallas aboard the *Savannah* on June 3. This loss of "a popular officer" was cause for sorrow. Kell had found him to be "of mild and pleasing manner, a perfect old gentleman." When the *Shark* arrived back at Callao, they found that the death of the Commodore had "turned everything upside down."[48] Captain James Armstrong of the *United States* was now temporary commander of the Pacific Squadron, and even Kell admitted that Captain Armstrong (Herman Melville's "Captain Claret") was a "rough old customer."[49]

The next three months at Callao were enlivened by an occasional pleasure trip. Kell made friends with a wealthy planter and his three daughters but had little success with attempts to communicate:

> One of the girls was quite a beauty and very pleasing in her manners, and played beautifully on the guitar, but could not talk English, so she and I could not be interesting to each other. I hope before we leave the Coast I shall be able to speak the language tolerably well.[50]

On October 31, 1844, the *Shark* left Callao for Panama to pick up Commodore John D. Sloat (1780–1867), the new commander of the Pacific Squadron. Kell was now performing the duties of master aboard the *Shark*. "There are so many men in my class older than I am, when they hear of my being Master they will be terribly put out," he wrote.[51] At Callao Commodore Sloat transferred to the sloop *Levant* and, on March 24, 1845, raised his pennant aboard the *Savannah*.

In April Kell made one more short cruise aboard the *Shark* to Valparaiso. Captain Armstrong and Professor of Mathematics Henry H. Lockwood were aboard and would take passage on another vessel to the United States. Kell found Valparaiso to be "a very flourishing place," where "everyone moves as if he had his hands full of business."[52]

On May 11, 1845, the *Shark* had returned to Callao, and three days later Kell was back aboard the *Savannah*. He was glad to be again under the "strict . . . discipline and etiquette" of a man-of-war,[53] and pleased with the letter Lieutenant Howison had given him. ("Midshipman Kell . . . has eminently displayed . . . all the qualities necessary to form a good officer.")[54] He now had three letters to submit to the Naval Examining Board after his return to the United States.

Callao had become dull and monotonous to Kell, and he yearned for the Pacific Islands. On the day when the shrill sound of the boatswain's pipe signalled "All hands, up anchor," Kell felt that he had never heard a more welcome sound. He may have felt almost as strongly as the navy chaplain who wrote: "Farewell, Callao! I have seen quite enough of your destitution and dirt, your pickpockets and parrots, your fish and your fleas, your brats and your buzzards."[55]

After four weeks of pleasant sailing, they arrived at Byron's Bay on the island of Hawaii. "A most luxuriant spot it is!"

wrote Kell.[56] The ship was promptly visited by natives in outrigger canoes, bringing fruits, vegetables, animals, and poultry to sell or barter. Whenever Kell had the opportunity, he went ashore. He found the natives to be a "kind hearted people and some of the girls . . . actually beautiful. . . ." "I really fell in love with the place," he wrote home, "and never yet was so sorry to leave a foreign port."[57]

The *Savannah* then sailed for Honolulu, where she remained for four weeks. Here was the center for American whaling ships in the Pacific, and there were far more American settlers than at Hilo. Kell was surprised and disappointed to observe the "drunkeness and debauch" which so contrasted the natives of Honolulu with the "innocence and purity" of those at Hilo.[58]

Rumors of pending war with Mexico were rife when the *Savannah* sailed for that country's port of Mazatlan. The sloops *Portsmouth* and *Levant* also rendezvoused there. Kell, who doubted that there would be war—"I expect it will all blow over"—was surprised to find the Mexicans on shore "rather troubled" at seeing them.[59] He was still looking forward to visiting other Pacific islands before the end of the three-year cruise, but because of the war threat, Commodore Sloat remained at Mazatlan for seven and a half months—until June of 1846. By then Kell had concluded that the cruise was a great "disappointment." Since he expected never again to make a Pacific cruise, he regretted "very much our making such poor use of our time, for had we visited more among the Islands it would have been a more interesting cruise."[60] His main consolation was knowing that before long he would be home.

It was during the long stay at Mazatlan that Kell witnessed for the first time the punishment of "flogging through the fleet." So numerous were the cases of desertion, disobedience, and drunkenness on the vessels of the squadron that for three weeks the court-martial flag was raised above the *Savannah*. Two cases of extreme punishment were witnessed by Kell, who—until then—had seen only the maximum number of twelve lashes authorized by the law for the usual offences. On March 2, 1846, a sailor was sentenced to one hundred and eighty lashes with the cat-o'-nine-tails and discharged from the service. Commodore Sloat remitted the sentence to one hundred lashes—fifty to be administered on board the *Savannah*, twenty-five on the *Levant*, and twenty-five on the *Portsmouth*.[61] Midshipman Franklin, who may have witnessed the same "severe punishment," considered it "very painful to be an unwilling witness to this kind of torture."[62]

On May 17, 1846, Commodore Sloat received an unofficial report that hostilities had begun between Mexico and the United States. Earlier, he had been instructed by Washington, in the event of war, to seize San Francisco and other California ports. It was hoped that, by securing the good will of the Californians, armed conquest could be avoided. Two weeks after receiving his first report, Commodore Sloat sailed on the *Savannah* for Monterey. Midshipman Kell was about to have a taste of war.

3

A TASTE OF WAR

During 1845 the strong possibility of war with Mexico led the Polk administration to inform Commodore Sloat that, when he had ascertained "beyond a doubt" that Mexico had declared war, he was to occupy San Francisco and such other California ports as his forces would permit. However, since dispatches from Washington usually took three months to reach the Pacific (via Panama), Sloat received no further instructions until long after war had been declared by Congress on May 13, 1846. Despite rumors of hostilities, he remained indecisive, hoping to receive more positive information. Therefore, when he arrived at Monterey on July 2, 1846, he entered the harbor as a friend, paying such customary courtesies to the California authorities as offering to fire a salute to the Mexican flag.[1] After five days of deliberation, however, three factors prompted Sloat to act: first, he learned from Thomas O. Larkin, American Consul at Monterey, of military operations in the north led by John C. Frémont; secondly, he was under orders to act without unnecessary delay; and finally, he feared that the British Pacific fleet would arrive at any time and raise their own flag over the town. (Her Majesty's Ship *Collingwood* had been closely watching the *Savannah* while at Mazatlan.) Thus, he chose to seize Monterey, preferring to be "sacrificed for doing too much than too little."[2]

On the morning of July 7, Captain William Mervine of the *Cyane* went ashore to deliver an ultimatum to the local military commander. The town, its forts, and environs were to be immediately surrendered. While Mervine was on shore, the officers and crew of the *Savannah* were called to muster, and Sloat's General Order was read:

> We are about to land on the Territory of Mexico, with whom the United States are at war. To strike her flag, and to hoist our own in the place of it, is our duty.
>
> It is not only our duty to take California, but to preserve it afterwards as a part of the United States, at all hazards. To accomplish this, it is of the first importance to cultivate the good opinion of the inhabitants, whom we must reconcile.

The men were to avoid the "detestable crime of plundering and maltreating unoffending inhabitants."[3]

Captain Mervine returned with the reply from Captain Mariano Silva: Silva had no authority to surrender Monterey.

A half-hour later a force of eighty-five marines and one hundred and forty sailors, all under Captain Mervine's command, rowed across the harbor to the Custom House wharf. They immediately advanced to the building, where Purser Rodman Price read a proclamation of Commodore Sloat, addressed to the "inhabitants of California":

> The central authority of Mexico having commenced hostilities against the United States of America . . . and the two nations being actually at war . . . I shall hoist the standard of the United States at Monterey immediately, and shall carry it throughout California.[4]

Sloat's proclamation assured the Californians that the Americans came as their "best friend" and would bestow the same rights and privileges as were enjoyed by all American citizens. Civil officials would be allowed to retain their offices, and all property rights would be respected. An American flag (from the *Cyane*) was then raised over the Custom House by two midshipmen, amid cheers of the sailors and marines present and those aboard American ships in the harbor. A twenty-one-gun salute was fired from both the *Cyane* and *Savannah*.

At 11 a.m. the boats returned to the ships, leaving a detachment of marines stationed in the town. It was a bloodless victory; not a hostile shot had been fired.[5]

Commodore Sloat next sent ultimatums to General José Castro, Commander of the Mexican forces in California, and to Don Pio Pico, Governor of California, demanding immediate capitulation. From Castro came the reply that he intended to fight "so long as I can reckon upon a single individual to join me in this cause, as just as it is natural."[6] But by the middle of July, the American flag, in obedience to Sloat's orders, had been raised—without opposition—at Yerba Buena (San Francisco), Sutter's Fort (Sacramento), Sonoma, Bodega, and San Jose, thereby bringing an end to Captain Frémont's Bear Flag Republic movement.[7]

Another threat suddenly seemed near when, on July 17, the English ship of the line *Collingwood* appeared. Sloat ordered the *Savannah* and *Cyane* prepared for action. Fortunately, though, Admiral Sir George Seymour had no intention of getting his country embroiled in war, although he allegedly said: "Sloat, if your flag was not flying on shore I should have hoisted mine there."[8]

Captain Frémont, who had been ordered by Sloat to report to him at Monterey, arrived there on July 19, accompanied by one hundred and twenty-five riflemen and six Delaware Indians. The English sailors were intrigued by the sight of "this wildest wild party,"[9] dressed in deerskins and recently acquired sailor shirts. Kell, too, must have been fascinated by the sight of Frémont and his men. The "rough and travel-worn" backwoodsmen made a strong contrast with the "fresh looks of the uniformed officers and men in their clean sailor dress."[10]

When Frémont went aboard the *Savannah* to call on Sloat, he found an "aged, sallow, nervous little man," uncertain of himself and greatly concerned over the legality of what he had done.[11] Sloat believed that Frémont had been acting under "written authority," which would justify his own seizures of Monterey and Yerba Buena; he was shocked to learn that no such authority had been given. Ill and unsure of his responsibility, Sloat made it clear to Frémont that he would undertake no aggressive plan of action. Earlier in the year he had submitted his request for a replacement, and he intended to turn over the Squadron to Commodore Robert F. Stockton, then return to the United States. Frémont could expect no action as long as Sloat remained in command.[12]

On July 28 Walter Colton, Chaplain of the *Congress*, was appointed *alcalde* (chief magistrate) of Monterey by Commodore Stockton. Colton had a high opinion of the officers of the *Savannah*, whom he had come to know through his services aboard that vessel. Colton had learned that, although lacking a chaplain, "they have had during a three year's cruise, their religious services regularly on the Sabbath."[13] Four *Savannah* officers had told Colton that they were professing Christians. (Since these did not include any midshipmen, it can be assumed that Kell at this time was not overly concerned with religion.) Colton had a great concern for public morality; as co-publisher of *The Californian* (first issued August 15, 1846), he attacked card playing, fandangoes, and horse racing.[14]

On July 23 the departing Sloat appointed Commodore Stockton as his successor. Stockton promptly brought Frémont and his force into the service of the United States as the "Battalion of California Volunteers." On July 26 the California Battalion boarded the *Cyane* and sailed for San Diego to cut off the escape of General Castro. The new Commodore was as "ambitious, smart and headstrong" as Frémont.[15] Together they planned a land campaign calculated to capture Castro or drive him and other officials into Mexico. Stockton issued a violently worded proclamation on July 29, in which he blamed Castro for "rapine, blood, and murder" and announced his intention to march against those who "keep this beautiful country in a state of revolution and blood."[16] (Later, Kell merely noted in his journal that the proclamation "was not at all popular, for various reasons.") Little wonder the Californians were confused. Sloat's earlier proclamation had expressed friendship. Now—for no apparent reason—his successor, Stockton, had adopted a bellicose position.[17] On August 1 Stockton sailed in the *Congress* from Monterey to San Pedro, to launch his campaign to aid Frémont in capturing Los Angeles.

The chief officer aboard the *Savannah* since Commodore Sloat had left was Captain Mervine. On August 14 he had all hands mustered, and the war message of President Polk—dated May 15, 1846—was read. The men must have felt the irony of the situation.[18]

The crew of the *Savannah* had every reason to be weary of ship and cruise; nearing the end of their three-year enlistment, they found themselves in the middle of a war, and there was no knowing when it would end. When Stockton returned to Monterey on September 15, he came aboard the *Savannah* to encourage the crew. The ship, he acknowledged, was in no condition for the return cruise, and there was no way of repairing her at present; however, as he was "a *living man*," they would return home soon. Kell himself felt optimistic that the war in California was almost over: "Castro is driven out of the country and we only hear now and then of a brush with the Indians, which is of very little importance. The inhabitants are getting more reconciled to us.[19] Kell also knew that he would soon be ordered to return to the United States to take his naval examinations. He could not become a career officer until after he had passed the qualifying examinations before the Board of Examiners.

On August 31 Commodore Stockton had appointed Captain Archibald H. Gillespie (a marine officer and secret agent of President Polk) as commandant of the southern department of California. A diplomat was needed to fill the position, for Los Angeles already had the strongest anti-American sentiment of any California community. Gillespie, however, extended rigid controls over the Spanish residents of Los Angeles. A revolt broke out, and soon several hundred Californians were in arms. Lacking fortifications, equipment, and supplies, Gillespie and his small force capitulated, thereby giving the Californians their first military victory since the occupation. At San Francisco Stockton learned of the insurrection and Gillespie's defeat. The *Savannah* being close at hand (since September 27), he ordered Mervine to sail for San Pedro to aid Gillespie in retaking and subjugating Los Angeles.

When Chaplain Colton watched the *Savannah* sail for San Francisco a week earlier, he had felt a strong sympathy for her sailors:

> She goes with a heavy heart. The time of her crew is out; they are almost half the circuit of the globe from their home, and have now, seemingly, as little prospect of reaching it as they had a year since. Commodore Stockton went on board a few days since and addressed them, but even with his happy tact in inspiring enthusiasm, it was difficult to arouse their despondency [*sic*], and make them cheerful in a resignation to their lot. The war being against a power unarmed at sea, is with them a mere bubble. . . .

Colton felt confident, however, that the *Savannah's* officers and crew would do their duty: "They are a body of brave, unflinching men and are commanded by officers of great firmness and force"[20]

Captain Gillespie was awaiting reinforcements aboard the *Vandalia* at San Pedro when the *Savannah* arrived. Early on the morning of October 7, Captain Mervine landed over three hundred sailors and marines who, with Gillespie's marines, would march against Los Angeles. Kell was not assigned to the expedition, but two of his midshipmen friends, Robert D. Minor and Robert C. Duvall, were. The expedition was marred from the beginning by Mervine's alleged ineptness. He refused to take a field piece, extra ammunition, and provisions, as urged by Gillespie. When the company descended into a narrow valley to approach the enemy, Gillespie ordered his skirmishers to charge and clear the hill; Mervine cried out: "Captain Gillespie! You are wasting ammunition! We can't spare the caps!" When they met the enemy, Mervine (according to Gillespie) acted like an "insane man." After dark, when the enemy began firing into the American camp, Mervine called the entire company to arms, then ordered out uncoordinated patrols, which began shooting at one another in the dark. At daybreak they encountered fifty of the enemy, armed with a light cannon. One shot fell in the midst of the tightly grouped seamen and marines, wreaking a "dreadful havoc." However, Gillespie's volunteers pressed hard upon the Californians and were about to capture their mobile gun, when Mervine decided to abandon the effort and retreat. Gillespie later commented that the expedition was "one of the most disgraceful defeats our arms have ever sustained. . . ."[21] Commodore Stockton concurred: "Being in the habit of calling things by their right names, I have in all my letters called it a defeat, and a very bad defeat."[22]

The *Savannah* was at San Pedro awaiting Stockton. On October 22 Midshipman Kell was assigned to deliver dispatches by cutter to San Diego. On the day of his return, four days later, Stockton arrived aboard the *Congress*. The next morning a command landed on shore against only token opposition, seized two strategic buildings, and raised the flag over San Pedro.

Early in November Commodore Stockton sailed to San Diego, determined to advance upon Los Angeles. Mervine was sent with the *Savannah* to convey provisions to the California Battalion at Monterey. On November 19 the *Savannah* returned to San Francisco, where she stayed through the remainder of 1846. Minor duties occupied Kell during this period. Lieutenant Titus Craven, an officer aboard the *Dale*, was ordered by Mervine to take the *Savannah's* launch to Santa Clara to pick up a supply of bread. On the night of December 17, Craven, Kell, and another midshipman, with thirty sailors and marines, all well armed, set out in the launch. Since Craven was a new arrival to the theatre of war, he was filled with the "expectation of an adventure." He wrote: "I determined at all events not to *be taken* alive, and to bring off the bread if possible." Six hours after they left the ship, Craven allowed his "worn out crew" to sleep, and the "tired Midshipmen, soon added their harmonizing snores to the rest of the party. . . ." At the first grey light of morning he awakened them, and—after a breakfast of coffee, cold meat, and bread—they continued.

The next afternoon "the slow moving oxen came along, dragging a rude wagon with the bread, and drawn by three or four noisy Indians." They made quick work of loading the bread in the launch and, by early the next afternoon, had returned to the *Savannah*, "after the shortest trip that had been made to the Santa Clara landing and without having seen an enemy."[23] The bread expedition was more of an adventure to Craven than to Kell. After being in California for six months, Kell had still not seen combat, although several expeditions which included midshipmen had left the *Savannah*. Other reefers were winning glory commanding sailors and marines. Before 1846 ended, however, Kell had his opportunity.

On December 29 Acting Master William F. DeJongh and Midshipman Kell were detached from the *Savannah* and assigned to an expedition commanded by Captain Ward Marston of the marines.[24] The expedition (consisting of one hundred and one sailors, marines, and rangers) was to be sent against a force of California insurrectionists led by Francisco Sanchez. Most of these Californians had been living quietly on their farms until stirred to action by the depredations committed by irresponsible local American authorities. They foresaw a worsening of their situation when American forces withdrew, leaving them under a despotic *alcalde*, Washington A. Bartlett. Therefore the Californians made a prisoner of Bartlett and several other Americans, hoping to bargain for a treaty to protect their rights. According to Walter Colton, these Californians were "men of the better stamp—men who had a permanent interest in the soil, and who had refused to join the rash spirits of the south."[25]

DeJongh and Kell, commanding ten sailors, were in charge of the only cannon with the expedition. On December 30 they learned that the enemy had been seen riding toward Santa Clara. The Americans advanced slowly because of difficulty in moving the cannon. The beauty of the country was not lost on anyone: oak-covered hills, mountains darkened with evergreens, and a distant range of snow-capped peaks.

On the morning of January 2, on the road to Santa Clara, they discovered that the enemy was near. Captain Weber, with twenty armed and mounted men, left the main body to follow their trail. Kell, being on horseback, accompanied this scouting party. They proceeded through thick early morning fog, Kell and two others riding abreast and somewhat ahead of the others. Suddenly, each of the three—thinking that he had spotted the enemy—cocked and raised his carbine. The next instant the fog cleared, revealing not enemy cavalry but a clump of bushes![26] Soon enough, however, the enemy appeared, mounted and in force. The Americans regrouped and the battle began. Lieutenant Marius Duvall later wrote of the encounter in his journal:

> The riflemen were dismounted and ordered on each flank into the wood to clear it of any lurking sharpshooters of the enemy, and the marines and cannon advanced along the road—the enemy kept beyond the reach of shot and retreated as we advanced. When we had emerged from the woods we saw their line on the plain between us and Santa Clara Mission. As our party pursued the road, the Californians were seen to cross the road ahead of us and in a short time surrounded us, each one of them keeping a considerable distance from his neighbour to lessen no doubt the chance of the effect of our fire. When about midway between the woods and the Mission, our cannon became immoveable on account of the mire, and the Californians seeing that we were embarrassed here, made their attack. They rode down upon us from all sides but were compelled to turn their backs by the discharge of our cannon loaded with grape, and by the fire from the marines and riflemen. They repeated these attacks but were always repulsed. The cannon was fired three times, twice with grape and once with a round shot which last ended the affair.[27]

Kell was directing the field piece to great advantage, "training the gun on the point from which came the greatest discharge of the foe." Flushed from their cover, they would mount their horses and ride to a safer distance. As the enemy retired to the woods, the Americans reached the Mission, where they were greeted by cheers from the emigrants. The "battle of Santa Clara" had ended with no serious casualties on either side.[28]

That night a messenger with a white flag appeared with

a request from Sanchez for a truce. During the meeting held the next morning, Sanchez explained why his followers had taken up arms: they had opposed the outrages of individual Americans, not the United States government. An armistice was agreed to, and the Californians were allowed to come and go as they pleased. Terms agreeable to both sides stated that the Californians should deliver up their arms and munitions (ancient and largely ineffective fowling pieces), retain their saddles, and return to their homes. All horses with the brand of the United States or of any American were to be delivered up immediately. Kell sympathized with the "enemy," who seemed to him "peaceful people, who cared more for tending their flocks and herds . . . than they did for warfare."[29] It must have seemed ironic to him that, when the Americans returned to San Francisco on January 11, they were praised by Captain Mervine for having so "effectually entrapped" the "unrivalled California cavalry.[30]

In late February the *Savannah* was once again in Monterey, preparing for the long cruise to the United States. During these weeks the officers and crew participated in no other expeditions but followed with interest the course of events in California. Commodore W. Branford Shubrick had succeeded Stockton, and in March of 1847 Commodore James Biddle assumed command of the Squadron. On March 25 the *Savannah* was in San Diego, ready to sail. The next morning she raised anchor and, in passing the *Congress*, fired a parting salute to Stockton. Fearing recall by the "capricious" Stockton, Mervine suggested to his Quartermaster that he "need not look too attentively" at the Commodore's ship. Finally in open sea, an officer could write: "The Savannah is homeward bound at last. May God speed her in her passage."[31]

The ship sailed directly for Valparaiso, which she reached on May 18; some of the crew were by then beginning to contract scurvy, and fresh fruit was a welcome addition to their mess. As Surgeon Duvall had anticipated, "we are all long-faced, and anticipating a horrible passage." Chess became "the rage and one only amusement."[32]

For Kell, the passage around Cape Horn was "the most disagreeable time I have ever experienced at Sea." It being winter at the Horn, they encountered freezing weather and constant gales. The snow fell so fast that sailors were kept busy shoveling it from the deck.

At Rio de Janeiro on July 28, they learned good news: General Zachary Taylor had won a brilliant victory at Buena Vista.

As September arrived and the *Savannah* came closer to New York, Kell would hardly believe that he would soon see his family. He was embarrassed to admit that he had no money for the train fare to Georgia. In explanation he wrote: "It is invariably the case with Midshipmen . . . to spend all of their money into whatever port they go as they are always sure of a home on board ship." Reluctantly, he wrote to Margery Kell requesting a loan of two hundred dollars, as "I see no other chance of visiting you without your assistance."[33]

On September 8 the *Savannah* arrived in New York harbor, and several days later, with leave in hand and money which his mother had forwarded, Kell boarded a train.

4

NAVAL SCHOOL

On November 2, 1847, Midshipman Kell reported to the superintendent of the new Naval School at Annapolis, Maryland. The school, replacing the inadequate facilities in Philadelphia, had been established two years earlier through the efforts of Secretary of the Navy George Bancroft. Fort Severn (built in 1808) was transferred to the Navy Department and became the site of the new school; it was administered during its first two years by Commander Franklin Buchanan and—after 1847—by Commander George P. Upshur, a brother of the late Secretary of State. Lieutenant Sidney Smith Lee served as Executive Officer. Its staff included William Chauvenet, former head of the Naval Asylum school, who had been the prime force in persuading Secretary Bancroft to establish a school which provided two years of training for newly appointed midshipmen.[1] The buildings of the old army post, which were converted into classrooms and dormitories, overlooked Chesapeake Bay and the Severn River.

Kell found that many students of his division—the "date of 1841," as they were known—had already arrived. There was much to talk about. The years had taken their toll among the original members of their date: approximately forty had been lost to the service, most by resignation or dismissal. The most unusual case was that of Philip Spencer, the alleged mutineer who had been hanged aboard the *Somers*, but two of the dead were recognized heroes: Thomas B. Shubrick had been decapitated by a cannon ball while serving the naval battery before Vera Cruz, and J. Wingate Pillsbury had drowned off that same coast while trying to aid one of the sailors of his capsized launch.[2] Although reduced considerably, the "date of 1841" was still too large—at one hundred and eighty-six—for the facilities at the Naval School. Therefore, it was divided into two sections, each to spend eight months at the school, after which examinations would be given in June of 1847 and 1848. (A third group, which included repeaters, was examined in 1849.) Kell, having been appointed in September of 1841, was one of the second division of ninety-four reefers. He was typical of the members of his division. Most were well along in their twenties and unprepared for formal studies and onshore discipline. In the years since their appointment, they had already seen much of the world, had gone through a war, and considered themselves seasoned veterans. The "date of 1841" soon established a reputation for mischief-making and escapades. Samuel Franklin, who was at the Naval School with Kell (although they did not become close friends), considered his "date" to be "an unruly set of devils to manage. . . ."[3] Superintendent Upshur, an "amiable, gentle, quiet man, of the type that inspires affection rather than fear," admitted: "I cannot govern you, young gentlemen; so if you will only govern yourselves I shall be delighted."[4] Although a poor disciplinarian, Upshur was later remembered for his "gentle manner" and a "pure character." William A. Parker recalled: "If *example* counts for anything we had it before us in him. . . ."[5]

Kell was delighted with his three roommates, veterans like himself of the Pacific cruise and former shipmates aboard the *Savannah*. They were Robert D. Minor of Virginia, Robert C. Duvall of North Carolina, and Alexander R. Abercrombie of Maryland. The four friends were housed in the building (formerly the Fort Severn hospital) known as "Rowdy Row," "the scene of the most hilarity and general uproariousness."[6] (Other buildings used as dormitories were "The Abbey," "Brandywine Cottage," "Gas House," and "Apollo Row.")

The professors at the Naval School were: Chauvenet,

Instructor in Mathematics and Navigation; Henry H. Lockwood, Instructor in Natural Philosophy; Arsene N. Giraud, Instructor of French; Surgeon John A. Lockwood, Instructor of Chemistry; and Chaplain George Jones, Instructor in English Branches. There was no instructor in Seamanship, as it was assumed that in this the reefers were already well prepared. Midshipman Parker, who was one of the top students at the Naval School, considered Chauvenet's classes "very good" ("as an instructor he stood second to none"), Professors H. Lockwood's and Giraud's "fair," but those of Surgeon Lockwood and Chaplain Jones below standard.[7] Franklin considered Chauvenet the best teacher he had ever known, with the "peculiar faculty of discerning whether a man at the blackboard knew what he was talking about or not."[8] The students were divided into four sections, arranged alphabetically at first, but later according to proficiency in their studies.

For seven months (interrupted only by Christmas and Easter vacations), Kell prepared himself for the all-important examinations. Although the pressure became intense as the date of examinations drew near, life was far from being all "grind," especially at "Rowdy Row." Late at night slumbers were frequently interrupted by the noise of 32-pound shot being rolled along the end of the second floor piazza, where "they would go thumping down the stairs with the noise of thunder. . . ." And Kell, too, was not above breaking regulations. Article 16 of the Rules and Regulations (1846) stipulated: "No midshipman shall bring, or cause to be brought, within the limits of the institution, any wine, porter, or other intoxicating or spiritous liquors." However, before Christmas of 1847, when Kell received a fruitcake from home, he decided to stage a festive occasion for his friends. After smuggling in some bottles of wine, they indulged themselves until late that night. Next morning Kell was too ill to leave his bed, and he sent for Surgeon Lockwood. After confessing to his "violation of all school discipline," he was relieved to learn that he was suffering only from "violent and acute dyspepsia."[9] The doctor kept his silence, and Kell was not disciplined. (Or, if reported, Upshur did not consider the incident serious enough to act upon.) At any rate, Kell's caper was not unique. Franklin, a resident of "Apollo Row," recalled that on Saturday nights it was customary to assemble at someone's room for what were referred to as "reform banquets." Here the reefers were "regaled with whiskey and cigars, and crackers and cheese, and swapped yarns and sang songs until midnight." Blankets were placed over the windows to prevent detection, and by midnight few of the revelers were sober. Next morning Executive Officer Lee would raise his hands "with an air of intense disgust" on finding the empty bottles, half-smoked cigars, and overturned furniture, which indicated a "rollicking dissipation."[10] There were also the "nocturnal revels" of the "Owls" and "Crickets," which "gave the citizens of the quiet old town something to talk of."[11] Once, nearly the entire class —armed with pokers and other weapons—rushed to town when word spread that a fight had broken out between reefers and local "roughs."[12]

There was one breach of discipline, however, which Upshur would not tolerate—dueling. During the session two duels were fought by reefers, one within school boundaries and the other at nearby Bladensburgh. In both cases a reefer was wounded, and the infraction of discipline was discovered; those involved, including seconds, were dismissed from the service.[13]

During the spring of 1848, attention concentrated on Navigation, Gunnery, Steam, and French; drill was considered "rather an amusement than otherwise."[14] After John A. Dahlgren, briefly Instructor of Gunnery, left the school, Professor Lockwood, a West Point graduate, took charge of drilling. The reefers treated these exercises as a farce, likening them to "pig-driving"; they would slouch, stand on one leg, or "roll about aimlessly in calm disregard of orders." They also frustrated Lockwood's efforts to teach them gunnery; they stole the linchpins, dismounted the guns, and hid the parts. Finally, accusing him of trying to give them more gunnery than the "date of 1840" had been required to learn, they hanged Lockwood in effigy from the school flagstaff.[15]

Far away in Georgia, Margery Kell was doing her utmost to persuade her son to resign from the service. His long absences were depressing her, and she hoped that he would turn to a vocation that would bring him nearer home. Her other son—Alexander Baillie—had entered the College of New Jersey (at Princeton) in the fall of 1847, and she needed a man at home. Kell had his own ideas on the subject:

> I have ever made it a rule never to be too determined on any of my future movements in the service but always to be contented till the time arrives, when it will be soon enough to decide upon it. I am happy in the belief that should I ever become dissatisfied with my profession or meet with any ill treatment by the Navy Dept. I can at that moment resign and return to my dear home. This is saying a great deal for after being in the service as long as I have, and therefore unfitted for any business on shore, it would be a most serious step to take, to give up my appointment.[16]

In June (or early July) of 1848 the Board of Examiners arrived at Annapolis. The service of these five veteran officers dated no later than 1810. Commodore Charles W. Morgan presided, with Captains Thomas W. Wyman, Isaac Mayo, Bladen Dulany, and John Gwinn.[17] The reefers were required to take written tests in Mathematics. Then each captain took a student and gave him a "long, exhaustive" oral examination in Seamanship. According to Franklin, however, Seamanship was not too difficult, "for there were but few questions with which an intelligent Midshipman was not more or less familiar."[18] The standing for each reefer was finally determined from the average of their accumulated grades, along with the rating given by the Board of Examiners. The failures ("bilgers") would, if recommended, be allowed to repeat the eight-month course and try again the next year. Kell and his friends Bob Minor and "Duvy" passed, but poor Abercrombie had the mortification of being a "bilger."[19] The class standing of each member of the "date of 1841" was not announced until all the members had had a chance to take the examinations. Kell ranked forty-eight[20] in a class of one hundred and thirty-six—the total of those who finally passed.

On July 10 Kell was notified that he had passed his examinations and was given a three-month leave of absence.[21] He immediately returned to Georgia, where for the rest of the summer he enjoyed the company of his family and friends. He had every reason to be satisfied with himself.

A few days before his leave was over, Kell wrote to the Navy Department, requesting that he be ordered to the Mediterranean Squadron, "as my former cruising have been [*sic*] long and tedius [*sic*] in the Pacific, and Gulf of Mexico." He preferred to be kept on waiting orders, "should there be no vessel fitting for that cruise and my services not required." But it was too late. In the Department a notation was made on his letter: "Already ordered to the Albany."[22]

5

COURT-MARTIAL AND DISMISSAL

When Passed Midshipman Kell arrived at the Gosport, Virginia Navy Yard (October 28, 1848), he learned that three messmates from the Naval School would be sailing with him on the *Albany*. They were Passed Midshipmen Francis A. Roe and Francis G. Clarke, both Northerners, and fellow Georgian Charles F. Hopkins. All four proudly wore a star on their collars, over the anchor, which signified their new rating.[1] Kell learned that the *Albany*, under veteran Commander Victor M. Randolph of Virginia, would cruise the West Indies, "among the Islands and on the Spanish Main," and not, he regretted, the Mediterranean.[2] The *Albany*, launched in 1846, had an armament of twenty-two guns and a complement of two hundred and ten officers and crew.[3] The ship appeared "very pretty"; she sat low in the water and looked much like a clipper. (She was rated a first-class sloop-of-war.) However, an officer who sailed on her considered that the *Albany* "was of a character which would necessarily send her to the bottom, unless carefully watched and properly handled."[4] He compared her construction to the ill-fated brig *Somers*, which had capsized in a gale off Vera Cruz two years earlier. (It so happened that one of the *Albany's* new officers, Passed Midshipman Clarke, had served aboard the *Somers* during her final cruise.)

To the two young midshipmen assigned to the *Albany*, their senior shipmates in the steerage were models to be emulated. One reefer—seventeen-year-old John R. Eggleston of Mississippi—was promptly nicknamed "Youngster" by the four passed midshipmen. Sixty years after his *Albany* cruise, "Youngster" Eggleston could still remember the beginning of his association with "dear old Kell":

> Kell was a man of splendid physique, well formed in every respect, his face the mirror of his character, filled with benevolence and goodness, but stern to all that was mean and unprincipled. Of the many people with whom I have been associated in the course of a long life, for what may be good in me I owe more to Kell than anybody else. All loved him. . . .[5]

Despite such admiration, their new ratings, and qualifications for responsible duties, the passed midshipmen soon faced the disturbing fact that they were treated as ordinary midshipmen by their superior officers. These middle-aged lieutenants had been in the navy for most of their lives. If they recalled their own frustrations as passed midshipmen, some nevertheless considered the duties they had performed as part of that rating. For practically all of these men, promotion to the grade of lieutenant had taken more years than they cared to remember. It was now assumed that the passed midshipmen would accept their lot, regardless of how they felt. The status of passed midshipmen in the old navy has been described by Park Benjamin as "a sort of purgatory":

> He was still a warrant officer, and therefore not entitled to the consideration and privileges of the bearer of a commission, although he had become qualified for one. . . . He continued to mess in the steerage. He lived in a state of expectancy, waiting for the making of a vacancy on the lieutenant's list which would permit him to don the single epaulette, and as this sometimes took years, he found himself the associate of small boys long after his beard had fully grown and his natural desire to put away childish things had changed into a disgust for his surroundings and the life they entailed.[6]

Passed Midshipman Roe, especially, resented his status. An officer with an impeccable record, Roe had been one of the few men who left the Naval School without a single mark against him in Superintendent Upshur's conduct book. Serious and ambitious, he had brought with him aboard the *Albany* a number of books on steam, navigation, and gunnery. As it turned out, however, there were few free moments for study. The only "privilege" granted the passed midshipmen was exemption from keeping a journal. In every other respect, their duties were still those of the "greenhorn" reefers with whom they shared the steerage. It was a deflating experience for proud young men.

From the middle of November until February of 1849, strained relations developed between Roe and two senior officers, Daniel B. Ridgely, the first lieutenant, and James H. North, the second lieutenant. Events seemingly trivial at the time they occurred would later be used by the lieutenants and Commander Randolph to "prove" that Roe was a "Mischief-Maker" and a "Sea-Lawyer."[7] Roe had protested to Ridgely, for example, against doing boat duty and working chronometer sights. In the latter instance, Roe believed that he was singled out for the duty after he had asked to be excused in order to test new theories of navigation. On December 2 Roe approached Ridgely with a proposal that the midshipmen do all the boat duty, while the passed midshipmen keep all the watches. Irritated by the request, Ridgely refused, contending that he knew of no distinction in the duties of the two grades. He then reported to Commander Randolph that Roe seemed inclined to avoid duty at the expense of the two midshipmen.

The issue that finally brought tensions to the breaking point occurred off the town of Fredericksted, on the Danish Island of Santa Cruz. Here, an order was issued that while in port the passed midshipmen should keep their watches on the quarter-deck, thereby making it necessary for them to call the reliefs at the expiration of their duty. On reading the order, the four officers became furious. They were now degraded, they believed, to performing duty that had customarily been done by a quartermaster. The duty included the indignity—as they considered it—of lighting the candle for the relief lieutenant. The immediate suspicion of Kell and the others was that the order had been issued in a spirit of vindictiveness. Although the order was unsigned, Roe had no doubt that Ridgely was responsible. After conferring, the four decided to bring the matter before Commander Randolph. On February 13, Kell, Roe, Clarke, and Hopkins entered Randolph's cabin to protest the order. Kell, as senior in appointment, was spokesman. He explained to Randolph that the duty of calling the reliefs had heretofore been done by the quartermasters and stated that they could see no reason why the passed midshipmen should do it: "It is very disagreeable at our age to be running into the ward-room and doing this quartermaster duty." Randolph replied that he knew nothing of the circumstances but would inquire of Lieutenant Ridgely why the order had been given. He saw nothing degrading in the duty, which, he said, he himself had performed uncomplainingly when a passed midshipman. Randolph added, however, that he felt they should not be required to call the officers to "all-hands" and that he intended to speak to the first lieutenant about it. Kell replied that he had never objected to calling the officers to "all-hands" but merely begged to be excluded from calling the relief at the expiration of each watch. The Commander promised to protect the four passed midshipmen from "caprice and oppression" but reminded them that he would expect of them "such duties as the usages of the service and his own experience taught were right and proper." They then left Randolph's cabin, looking, as he later stated, "evidently displeased." He believed that they had "a strong disposition to resist the order." However, Clarke later claimed that when he left Randolph he believed that the order would be revoked.

Summoned to Randolph's cabin, Lieutenant Ridgely explained that at sea he always assigned an officer to the quarter-deck during one of the watches; that officer, he claimed, was required to summon his relief. Now that they were in port, he argued, the passed midshipmen had no reason to protest the same duty that the two midshipmen had been performing while at sea. Ridgely's assumption—that there was no difference between the duties of the midshipmen and the passed midshipmen—was not challenged. On this point the two officers apparently agreed. Randolph felt that Ridgely's order was a proper one and assured him that he would enforce it.

The next night Hopkins, at the expiration of his watch, was ordered below to summon the reliefs. However, he brought with him a sailor to light the senior officer's candle. Lieutenant North, waking to find a common seaman in his cabin while Hopkins stood outside, became furious; he angrily dismissed the sailor. Later, he told Ridgely that the passed midshipmen had no intention of lighting the candles for the lieutenants. Ridgely then decided to settle the issue once and for all; he put in writing the order that the passed midshipmen when on quarter-deck watch were to call the lieutenant's relief by taking a lantern with them, lighting his candle, calling their own relief, then returning the lantern to the deck. The first lieutenant informed Randolph of his action and also suggested making a test case of Roe, who ordinarily performed his duties on the berth-deck, but could be ordered to keep watch on the quarter-deck. It should be done, Ridgely contended, in order that Roe be "taught his duty." Randolph agreed.

That night Roe was on the quarter-deck, as ordered, during the 8:00 to 12:00 watch. (Midshipman Eggleston was on the same watch, but was excused early, after boat duty, apparently to insure that Roe would be obliged to call the relief.) The four passed midshipmen had earlier reached an agreement between themselves regarding Ridgely's order: they would accept their assigned duty on the quarter-deck and would summon their reliefs without protest. However, they would refuse to light anyone's candle so long as it came as an order. At midnight Roe started below to summon Lieutenant Washington Reid, Lieutenant North's relief. North asked him where he was going, then stated that it was requisite for him to take a lantern. Roe replied that he would call the relief but would not take a lantern. North insisted: "If you do it at all it must be done in a proper and *usual* manner. Do you refuse to obey the order?" "No, sir," answered Roe, who then repeated that he would summon the relief but would not take a lantern. He continued below, but North ordered a quartermaster to perform the duty instead. North then went to awaken Commander Randolph, and—soon afterward—Roe was summoned to his Commander's cabin. Enraged, Randolph shouted at him: "You are *arrested*, sir—*arrested! arrested!*"[8] Roe returned to the steerage but was sent for by Lieutenant North, who was then informed by Roe of the "arrest."

Lieutenant Reid and Passed Midshipman Kell were the reliefs for North and Roe. Before he turned over the watch to Reid, North gave him the written order relative to summoning the reliefs. Reid was also summoned to Randolph's cabin and told to advise Kell to obey the order at the expiration of their watch.[9] Reid was no friend of Commander Randolph,[10] but he liked Kell, whom he considered "a very mild and courteous man—a prompt and obedient officer." Moreover, he saw no point in Kell's disobeying the order. During their watch together, Reid argued that it would show a lack of respect for the navy to disobey an order before appealing it to the Department.[11] Kell replied that respect for the Department caused him to believe that it would not require him to obey an improper or illegal order, or to serve as a menial. They discussed the problem in abstract fashion, leaving Reid uncertain as to how Kell would respond to the order.

At 4 a.m., as Kell began to descend the ladder to summon the relief, Reid stopped him and read the written order. Kell replied: "I will call the relief, sir, but I cannot carry a lantern or light."

"Mr. Kell, I give it to you as a positive order, and you must obey it."

Kell repeated that he would not carry a light, and was told: "I must then report you to the captain."

When summoned to his Commander's cabin, he was asked: "What is this I hear, sir? Do you refuse to obey an order?" Kell replied that he did not refuse to obey an order but that he was not employed by the government to do menial duty and that he would not do it.

"I will *break* you, sir! I will dismiss you from the navy!" stormed Randolph.

"Very well; you can do as you please."[12]

Kell returned to the quarter-deck to inform Lieutenant Reid that he had been suspended from duty and was ordered to report to Lieutenant Ridgely immediately.

The next night Passed Midshipman Clark refused the order to take a lantern or candle below and was also suspended from duty; the night following, Hopkins did likewise. When Hopkins was brought before Randolph, the Commander tried to reason with him to make him acknowledge his "error." If the passed midshipmen would have the "moral courage" to admit their mistake, Randolph urged, he would overlook what had occurred. As Hopkins was the youngest of the four, Randolph hoped to reach the others through him, but found him "obstinate and his manner somewhat offensive."

As the *Albany* continued her cruise through the islands of the Antilles, the suspended passed midshipmen were given no duties and were confined to steerage. The ship remained at St. Thomas for two weeks, but they were refused permission to go ashore; nor were they allowed ashore at Ponce (Puerto Rico) or Santo Domingo. They had little to console them except the hope of vindication by a higher authority. Randolph and Ridgely, their duties made more difficult by the suspension of the four young officers, were now in no mood for conciliation. Lieutenant North contended that unless the four passed midshipmen were dismissed from the service, all discipline would come to an end. In North's opinion, they were "guilty of wilful and premeditated insubordination."[13] Randolph was gathering evidence for his case against the four, since he intended to be the prosecutor at their court-martial. Information gleaned from the memories of his lieutenants strengthened his belief that Roe had been an evil influence upon the others, that he had been a troublemaker from the very beginning of the cruise. On March 21 Randolph wrote to the Secretary of the Navy:[14] "I . . . hope that no clemency may be extended to him. It is every way desirable that the Service should be rid of all such Mischief-Makers, vulgarly called 'Sea-Lawyers.' "

On April 7 the *Albany* arrived at Pensacola, but remained there only a day or two. Roe sent a message for permission to go ashore, but this was denied. A few days later, Roe wrote to Secretary Preston, explaining why he had refused to obey an order given in "a spirit calculated to wound and injure my feelings as an officer and a Gentleman. . . ." Roe had learned of the additional charges and specifications being brought against him by Randolph, who, he contended, was "collecting together circumstances that took place at different periods and which were unworthy of notice at *that* time, but now [was] combining them in charges against me, apparently to sustain the prior report." Roe would later be astonished to learn that his letter, sent to Randolph by the Secretary, would be used as evidence against him in the charge "conduct unbecoming an officer."

The passed midshipmen were beginning to show the effects of their "rigorous confinement." Roe was in the worst condition of the four. He had become emaciated from loss of sleep and appetite and was suffering from facial neuralgia due to nervous strain. Kell tried to be cheerful, but it was difficult. There was little to do, and inactivity made him increasingly despondent. The ship's library contained a few "dull works" of history; the rest were mostly novels, "often very great trash." Kell nevertheless read the histories, commenting, "had I pleasant books I could manage very well." Despite everything, he wrote his family that the cruise was "pleasant . . . much preferable to going down in the Gulf." Kell had one important satisfaction:

> I am very much indebted to my family, especially my dear Mother for upholding me in disobeying that most outrageous order. I cannot think of it without feeling injured that a man should dare give me such an order! I sincerely wish it was the spirit of our service for an officer to allow no imposition but it is too often the case that a Captain is allowed to do as he chooses, and younger officers are afraid to protest against his conduct on account of his being court martialed. Of course a young officer gets the worst of it in disobeying an order, but I do not think this should influence one to allow such persecution, and it is an injury to the service. The grade of Passed Midshipman is such that there is no duty allotted to them, and a narrow minded Captain may enforce an officer of 25 and even 30 yrs. of age

the same duty that was required of him when he entered the service a mere youngster. I think it an ill contrived law of our navy that gives to a Commander despotic sway and such is my case. It has long been customary for Midshipmen to take a lantern below, certainly as a favor, but never as a duty required, for it cannot be a duty of one officer to be a menial of another, and it is nothing less in getting a light for him to dress by. I have done it as a favor. I never will as an order, unless the Navy Dept. decides it is my duty, then I think the matter should be referred to higher authority still and Congress made to decide if one officer shall be menial to another. I am confident that such is not the spirit of the Country.[15]

By mid-June an exasperated Commander Randolph had been unable to make contact with the *Raritan,* Flagship of the Home Squadron, and Commodore Foxhall A. Parker. However, at Aux Cayes (Haiti) he received a communication from Parker and left immediately for St. Iago de Cuba. Kell was "delighted" that they had not met the *Raritan,* as he did not want his court-martial to be held aboard that ship.

At St. Iago, the ship's surgeon, Dr. William A. W. Spotswood, a kindhearted Virginian, insisted that the passed midshipmen be allowed ashore. To Kell, being on land after the long confinement made him feel "quite a new being." After walking until tired, he entered an ice cream shop and treated himself to a variety of sweets. He returned to his confinement at sunset.[16]

From St. Iago Randolph sailed for Vera Cruz, found the *Raritan* there, and was ordered immediately to Pensacola; they arrived on July 10. There each of the suspended officers received a letter from the Navy Department containing the charge (or charges, in Roe's case) against him:

Upon the receipt of this order you will consider yourself under arrest.

A Naval General Court Martial has been ordered to convene on board the U.S. Ship Albany, at Pensacola, on Friday, the twentieth instant, at which time and place you will appear and report yourself to the presiding officer of the Court for trial.

The Judge Advocate will summon such witnesses as you may require for your defence.[17]

Secretary Preston had also sent orders to the nine officers —either stationed at Pensacola Navy Yard or there on waiting orders—who would comprise the Court. They were: Captain John Thomas Newton, Commander of the Yard, as presiding officer; Commander George N. Hollins; and Lieutenants Thomas W. Brent, Raphael Semmes, John R. Tucker, George M. Totten, William A. Parker, Henry P. Robertson, and Thomas B. Huger.

During the days preceding the court-martial, Commander Randolph allowed the passed midshipmen to go ashore each day and return at sundown. At the Navy Yard, Clarke was surprised and pleased to find Lieutenant Raphael Semmes, on temporary duty as Inspector of Provisions and Clothing. Clarke had served under Semmes on the *Somers* three years earlier, and the two men had shared an unforgettable experience. When the *Somers* had capsized off Vera Cruz,[18] Clarke had been fortunate in bringing off a boat before the ship sank and was able to reach shore. Most of those in the water, unable to keep afloat, were lost—thirty-nine in all. Fortunately, Semmes was able to keep himself from sinking. He later wrote:

> Midshipman Clark, after he had landed the officers and men under his charge, at Verde Island, shoved off a second time, in obedience to the order I had given him, at the imminent peril of his life—for the gale was now blowing with much violence, and the sea running so heavily, that it seemed impossible that so small a boat could live—and skirted Verde Island reef to see if it were possible to rescue any of us from the waves. His efforts were rewarded with partial success, as he picked up Lieutenant James L. Parker and myself, and one of the seamen. As soon as I had landed, I sent Midshipman Clark out again; who ventured as far from the island as he thought the boat would live; but this time he returned unsuccessful, having been unable to descry any floating object, whatever.[19]

Since Semmes owed his life to Clarke, he could hardly be an objective member of the court. Equally important, he supported the contention of Clarke and the others that they had acted correctly in disobeying an "illegal" order. A "maverick" himself, Semmes welcomed the chance to attack a system of which he had long been an ardent critic. The forty-year-old Marylander, a veteran of twenty-three years in the navy, was the ideal person to defend the accused; among his many talents, he was a self-educated lawyer. The accused passed midshipmen asked Semmes to serve as their Counsel, and he agreed. It was not the first time he had championed junior officers. For example, as commander of the *Somers*, he had used his influence to have a midshipman "under hatches" on another vessel restored to duty and transferred to him. That officer found Semmes to be "brave, well instructed, scholarly, and a keen observer and thoughtful analyst." He had also found in Semmes "the rare un-American quality of an economy or parsimony, of speech":

> Indeed he was a silent man. I have seen him, almost daily, standing aft, clinging to a back-stay, looking in a fixed direction, and then with that blending of his eye on vacancy, as if he either "with the incorporeal air held discourse," or as if in reflection or introspection. He would remain for hours in that Carthusian closure of the lips.[20]

In addition to Semmes, two of the other officers ordered to the Court openly stated their views on the case of the passed midshipmen. Commander Hollins, with whom Kell had sailed on the *Savannah*, stated that he "gloried" in the conduct of the accused officers, whom he believed had acted correctly in refusing to obey an "illegal" order. Lieutenant Huger, on the other hand, let it be known that he favored "breaking" them from the service. At the commencement of the trial, the seating of Hollins was objected to by the Prosecution and that of Huger by the Defense, and both withdrew.

The Court convened on board the *Albany*, and the signal cannon was fired at 10 a.m. on July 20. During the next two weeks, witnesses were presented, examined, and cross-examined by Raphael Semmes for the Defense, and by Commander Randolph, Prosecutor. The case of Passed Midshipman Roe required ten days, as three charges and six specifications had been cited against him. For Kell, Clarke, and Hopkins, there was only the one charge: "Wilful disobedience of a lawful order from his superior officer," the specification being the refusal of each to carry a light.

Several of the *Albany's* officers, on being questioned by the Defense, agreed that Commander Randolph was "a man of strong feelings," but only two—Lieutenant Reid and Dr. Spotswood—would admit to having experienced difficulty in their official relations with him. Spotswood was chief witness to the allegation of the Defense that Roe had been subject to "rigorous confinement" after his suspension. Kell, Clarke, and Hopkins, in addition to other officers, testified in Roe's behalf. At the conclusion of his case, Roe was allowed a day in which to prepare his own defense. On July 30 he read his lengthy brief, based on the contention that "any officer of the Navy has a right to disobey all illegal orders, come from what source they may. . . ." Roe's supporting arguments had been reinforced by legal principles suggested by Semmes. However, his bitterness in attacking the system of which he believed himself an innocent victim could not have helped his cause. After due deliberation, the Court announced their verdict of guilty on two charges and their specifications. On the charge "Disrespect to a Superior" he was found not guilty, since it had been determined that the date cited in the specification was incorrect. Roe's sentence was dismissal from the service.

On July 31 it was Kell's turn. He pleaded "guilty" to the specification and "not guilty" to the charge, but the plea was overruled; he then pleaded "not guilty" to both charge and specification. Lieutenant Reid, the first witness for the Prosecution, related the circumstances of the disobedience of his order and admitted that he was a "particular friend" of the accused. Reid testified that when he himself was a passed midshipman he had never been ordered to take a light below to call the reliefs. Randolph then introduced Lieutenant William A. Parker, a member of the Court, as a witness. Parker contended that as a passed midshipman on the *Ohio* he frequently had been given and obeyed the order. No officer had any complaint to make against Kell other than what was specified in the charge. On the contrary, Lieutenants Ridgely, Reid, and James A. Doyle testified that they held a high regard for him "both as an officer and a gentleman." Dr. Spotswood confirmed the fact that Kell, like Roe, had been subject to "rigorous confinement" during the four months after his suspension.

On August 1 Kell was allowed to read to the Court his own carefully prepared defense. First, the letters of recommendation written by his first five commanders were read. Then he delivered his defense.

> Mr. President and Gentlemen of the Court:
>
> There is but a single question presented by the charge and specification under which I have never contraverted any of the facts material to the issue which has been raised between my Commander and myself and would, if I had been permitted, have saved the Court the labor of an investigation by my plea. I did disobey the order of Lieut. Reid directing me to take a light below and light the candle of the relief. . . . If I have committed an error at all the most that can be said of it is that it is an error of judgement. Acting upon the principle which is unquestionably a sound one, that an officer of the Navy has the right to disobey any and every order which he may judge to be illegal, I have resisted obedience to the order in question on my responsibility to the Government, believing this to be the proper means of bringing the issue which has been raised between my Commander and myself, before a proper tribunal for adjudication.
>
> . . . I trust you will bring to the decision of the question, minds free from any prejudice of rank or station. I desire that each one of you will place himself in imagination in my position and ask himself the question whether if at my age such duty had been required of him specifically and peremptorily, under an order, he would not like myself have felt bound to decline obedience in defence of his self-respect. I do not pretend to say whose fault it is—whether it is the fault of the Government or of the Superior officers of the Navy, that the Passed Midshipmen find themselves in the anomalous position they at present occupy, but certain it is there is a fault somewhere. I have now spent the best years of my life in the Service. I have been examined and found qualified for promotion. I have reached

the age of mature manhood. I belong to an honored and honorable profession all the members of which are or should be gentlemen, and what is my position? Have I any of the rank or authority which should belong to my years, to my social standing in the community, or to my attainments, poor as these are? None. Whilst nature proclaimed me a man and at the age when man in such a profession as ours is or should be most useful—with all of my faculties developed both physical and mental—the position which I am still constrained to occupy denies me any of the privileges which should belong to my time of life. I am still confined to the steerage, regarded as a mere messenger and required to perform acts which would shock the ideas of propriety of any one in civil life who has passed beyond the leading strings of boyhood. Now that I have the most capacity to be useful to the Government, I am rendered by the Government of least use to it. Instead of performing the duties which I have been declared competent to perform—instead of handling a ship of war as an officer of the deck, I am degraded into a bearer of messages and a lighter of candles. This is a wrong system whoever may be the author of it. It may not be in your power, Mr. President and Gentlemen of the Court, to change this system, but you may do much towards ameliorating it. You should not hold the reigns of authority too tightly. Whenever it is possible to relax them without injury to the Service, you should do so. The more you release the Passed Midshipmen of the Service from the drudgery which in former years has been required of them, the more you will increase their self respect and the better officers you will make of them. Employments, like associations of men, have a powerful influence upon their characters. You do not find the high toned gentleman as a rule under the leathern apron of the mechanic any more than you can draw an accomplished officer from before the mast. Men who are made menials of soon learn to feel and act as menials and it is well worth the consideration of the Government and of every officer of the Navy whether Passed Midshipmen should not be removed from the false position in which they are at present placed. I do not wish the Court to infer from these remarks that because I regard my position as a hard and unnatural one, that therefore I would array myself in opposition to undoubted authority, for the sake of ameliorating it. This not only would not answer the end in view, but no officer could be justified in such a course.

He should rather appeal to the sympathies of his brother officers and to his government for the removal of the grievances under which he lives, than undertake to redress them in this manner. But what I mean to say is, that my position should be regarded as a sufficient justification of any attempt on my part to resist by legal and proper means any restraint put upon me, or compliance with the well settled laws and customs of the service. Instead of being regarded *a priori* as a wrong doer, I should on the contrary have the sympathies of my brother officers, and this Court instead of seeking industriously for ground on which to convict me, interpose if possible to save me harmless. It is no part of my intention, Mr. President and gentlemen of the Court, to argue my case over again to you today, since it is only day before yesterday that it was argued at great length in another trial. All the arguments that were then used, I adopt as a part of my defence and respectfully refer you to them.

It will be sufficient for me to state briefly the several points on which I rest my case. First. The illegality of the order. I insist that the order is illegal on the two following grounds, to wit: First. It is not sanctioned by any law. Secondly. It is not sanctioned by any custom, for although it be admitted that custom requires Passed Midshipmen to call the relief, it does not *require* them to light the candles, the latter act never having been demanded of them heretofore, but always performed *ex gracia* as a piece of politeness, and acts which men perform not under the obligation of an order, but freely and of choice, can never in justice be cited against them to saddle them with a duty. Secondly. The charge is defective, it not stating that the Superior whose order was disobeyed was in the execution of the duties of his office—which words are essential to describe the kind of disobedience punished by the act for the better government of the Navy. Thirdly. The act of refusing to take a lantern below, the only act of disobedience stated in the specification, was not the act objected to by me on any fair interpretation of my motives. My object in declining to take the lantern was to decline lighting the relief's candle, which was the real order given to me—the taking of the lantern being merely an incident of the act of lighting the candle.

The Court should therefore acquit me under the specification, since it does not raise the issue which was raised in fact between the officer of the deck and myself. Reminding the Court of my

> long confinement on board a small ship in a tropical climate and of the very exemplary character as an officer and a gentleman which it has seen I have borne from my entry into the Service to this time, a period of eight years, I submit my case with all confidence to their hands believing they will do equal justice to their government and myself.

The Court, after "mature deliberation," found the Accused guilty of both charge and specification. The sentence was that "Passed Midshipman Kell be dismissed from the Navy of the United States."

The cases of Clarke and Hopkins were soon disposed of with the same result, and on August 4 the Court was dissolved. Roe, Kell, Clarke, and Hopkins did not entirely give up hope, however, since their sentence would be sent to the Department and the President before becoming final. At Pensacola, soon after the trial, a banquet and reception were held in their honor at the home of Commander Hollins and attended by the fellow officers and friends who supported them. Kell would later say, "I had the full sympathy of . . . most of the officers and all the crew."[21]

From Pensacola Kell traveled north to Roswell, Cobb County, Georgia, where his family was spending the summer with Cousins Henry and Matilda Reese. It was not until fall, after arriving in Darien, that Kell received the letter dated November 3, 1849, that made his dismissal official. On October 23 President Zachary Taylor had approved the sentence of the Court.

In later years Kell admitted to his wife that the period following his dismissal was "a very trying time of his life." He tried to be "cheerful and brave but there often came over him an irresistable longing for the sea and his lost profession, but never a consciousness of having done wrong."[22]

It was only many years afterward that Kell could take lightly this period in his naval career. When asked about it in his old age, he replied: "I was not only as a youngster would be a little proud of my rank, but I had in my veins also a little of the rebel blood that made my ancestors, the Mackintoshes [*sic*], fight against the house of Hanover. . . .[23]

Although Kell may not have realized it during the trying year of 1849, he had made a favorable impression on a man he would not meet again until 1861. Raphael Semmes would one day recall:

> The relation of counsel, and client, as a matter of course, brought us close together, and I discovered that young Kell had in him, the making of a man. So far from being a mutineer, he had a high respect for discipline, and had only resisted obedience to the order in question, from a refined sense of gentlemanly propriety.[24]

6

EASTERN ADVENTURE

Although a court-martial had found Kell "guilty," he was still a hero to his family and friends, a "traveled officer who had seen . . . a great deal of the outside world."[1] Early in fall the Kells returned to Darien, where Donny received the official notification of his dismissal. He now had to confront the future.

With no immediate prospects of employment or reinstatement, Kell made himself useful on the plantation. Typical of the rice plantations in the region, with 160 acres under cultivation in 1850, the Grove also produced cotton, sweet potatoes, peas, and beans.[2] Baillie, who had returned to Princeton for his third year, had already shown some interest in planting, and it was hoped he would eventually assume the responsibilities long borne by Margery Kell.[3] As for Donny Kell, he was happy to be with his family and to bask in their attention and good will; however, any life other than that of a naval officer offered little permanent satisfaction. He was "filled with a restless discontent for the service."[4]

The year 1850 was one of great national crisis. Slavery and sectional issues threatened a dissolution of the Union and civil war. Many men of national prominence believed, however, that through compromise the Union could be saved. The adoption of the compromise measures of Congress by the Georgia Convention would be due largely to the efforts of its presiding officer, old Thomas Spalding. It would be Spalding's final, and greatest, contribution to his country. Before this, however, he had aided his young cousin in his difficulty. Well aware of Spalding's important connections, Kell had gone to him for advice. To Spalding's query why he had not obeyed an order which "could only degrade him that gave it," Kell replied that he had disobeyed only because of respect for the service. The answer satisfied Spalding, who was familiar with his cousin's career; during the past eight years he had read with interest the letters shown to him by Margery Kell. He had been especially impressed by Kell's having set aside a portion of his pay for Baillie's education. Spalding did not hesitate now to offer assistance. He realized that the man best able to help Kell was U.S. Senator John Macpherson Berrien,[5] a former friend, but one with whom he had had a falling-out in 1841. Now, at age seventy-six, Spalding was willing to forget past differences in order to help his cousin. With a reminder of past friendship, he wrote Berrien: "I ask you to read the evidences given on the court martial of these young gentlemen, and if they have been wronged, and if a remedy is within reach, you will best know after such examination."[6]

Fortified with the letter, Kell journeyed to Washington. He was courteously received by Berrien, who probably remembered Kell's father from the years when both men had practiced law in the Eastern Circuit of Georgia. He was pleased with Spalding's letter and agreed to assist Kell. In addition to Berrien's seniority and great influence at the Capitol, there was another factor which favored a review of the sentence: a new administration—that of Millard Fillmore—had brought in William A. Graham of North Carolina as Secretary of the Navy. Kell remained in Washington after Berrien began his investigation,[7] but he had returned to Georgia by the time he received official notice that he had been reinstated to his former rank and salary.[8] (Roe, Clarke, and Hopkins were also reinstated.)[9] Berrien forwarded Kell's warrant, along with a letter of congratulations, and when Kell wrote the good news to Thomas Spalding, he acknowledged that his "present success" was due entirely to the efforts of the Senator.[10]

Early in December of 1850, Kell received orders to proceed to Philadelphia and report aboard the steam frigate *Susquehanna*, the flag ship of Commodore John H. Aulick. The new commander of the East India Squadron was under orders to negotiate a treaty of commerce and friendship with Japan, which for more than two centuries had successfully asserted its right to seclusion; only the Dutch were permitted to bring in one ship a year and to operate a trading post at Nagasaki, Japan's most western port.

Kell missed his ship in Philadelphia,[11] and when he arrived at Norfolk he learned that it would be several months before she would be ready for the cruise. The *Susquehanna*, launched in April, 1850, was one of the finest of her type—a steam frigate, with two large paddle wheels.[12] Because of new features, she would be under close observation during this, her maiden voyage.

Finally, on June 8, 1851, the *Susquehanna* left Norfolk bound for the Asiatic Station. Aulick's instructions were to deal with Japan indirectly. He had several Japanese castaways on board, who were to be conveyed to Japan to show the good intentions of the Americans. If things went satisfactorily, Aulick was to suggest negotiating a treaty. They sailed first to the island of Madeira, which Kell found to be the "garden spot of the world."[13] Here he purchased several quarter casks of wine, enough to provide for a number of special occasions in his life during the next five decades.

After reaching Rio de Janeiro, a number of defects in the ship's engines and spars caused a two-month delay while the *Susquehanna* was in dry dock. Kell was delighted to find Captain McIntosh, now commanding the frigate *Congress*, at Rio; the two cousins enjoyed walking on shore, "talking . . . about home and our relatives."[14] One of the highlights of the stay at Rio was a reception given the officers of the *Susquehanna* by Brazilian Emperor Dom Pedro II. Kell found him "indifferent and ill at ease," but the Empress was "peculiarly graceful and charming in manner."

Eighteen days from Rio found them at Cape Town, where Kell delighted in the hospitality of a "fine looking" old Boer, whom he met while riding on horseback from Cape Town to Table Bay. This was the beginning of an admiration for the Boers which would continue throughout Kell's life.

The *Susquehanna* sailed around the Cape of Good Hope

and—after several brief but interesting stops—reached Hong Kong, where Commodore Aulick took formal possession of the Squadron. The city was a "gay and pleasant place to visit," as there were many English and American families to entertain the naval officers. From Hong Kong they sailed to Canton and up its river as high as "Blenheim Reach." The officers, armed against river pirates, went ashore to sight-see and purchase souvenirs. In addition to the articles he purchased for himself and his family, Kell selected a "very handsome Chinese punch bowl" for his "esteemed friend Judge Berrien."[15]

Aboard ships and especially during long cruises, friendships (and enmities) were deep and enduring. Bob Minor and "Youngster" Eggleston were two of Kell's shipmates from earlier cruises who remained lifelong friends. Aboard the *Susquehanna* was a man who, likewise, would be a devoted friend. He was Charles F. Fahs, Assistant Surgeon. Fahs, an affable Pennsylvanian, five years younger than Kell, was on his first cruise. He had a wide variety of interests and talents; some of his reports and observations of the Japan Expedition would later be used in Perry's official narrative.[16] Kell said of him:

> He has one of the purest hearts and one of the most noble intellects a man was ever gifted with. He is highly cultivated and scientific, an ornament to his profession and the Navy.[17]

Together Kell and Fahs visited the Chinese ports of Canton, Hong Kong, Macao, and Shanghai, learning a great deal about the people and their customs. As both men had a natural curiosity and a love of adventure, they made ideal companions. There were ample opportunities for danger and excitement during this period in China; the Manchu Dynasty, unable to cope with Western imperialism and internal unrest, was faced with a dynamic challenge in the Taiping Rebellion (1850–1864). Hung Hsiu-ch'uan, a Christian convert who led the movement, preached the doctrine of a new Trinity, in which he was the younger brother of Jesus Christ. His Taiping ("Great Peace") movement promised a new era of prosperity and a return to native rule. In March of 1853, Nanking was captured and became the capital of the Taipings.

Throughout 1852 the officers and sailors of the squadron were uncertain of their future movements; Commodore Aulick had been relieved of the command and, it was learned, would be replaced by Commodore Matthew C. Perry.[18] On March 24, Perry—in the United States—was given formal command of the Japan Expedition. He was expected to co-operate with American authorities in protecting American rights in China, but his first object would be to secure a treaty with Japan. After numerous delays, in November of 1852, Perry left the United States aboard the steam frigate *Mississippi*.

While the *Susquehanna* was anchored at "Cumsing Moon" (Kunhsin Men) awaiting the arrival of Commodore Perry, Kell mulled over the pending expedition to Japan. His mother had written of her concern over the possibilities of a war with Japan, and he tried to reassure her:

> We would rely more on the formidable show of such a Squadron of Steamers, to a half civilized race of people who have no idea of steam or the size of our ships, than coercing them by force of arms. Should we be obliged to act in a hostile way it does not follow that we must invade their country for that would be madness. As you say, they have millions to bring against us, who would fight perhaps to desperation but with our single steamer we could sink and destroy every fishing boat and trading vessel they possess. They have no vessels of any size so that with a Squadron we could batter down their Seaport towns, cut off their fish trade which is very great, thus annoying their Coast without their being in any way able to do us the least harm. They would soon be reduced to come to terms and make such reasonable treaty as our Government could desire, but I apprehend nothing of the sort. I do not for a moment believe there will be a hostile gun fired, should the Expedition come out for I know it is the earnest desire of the Government to obtain peaceably a depot for coal for our Steamers running between California and China. It needs [to] be on one of their uninhabited Islands and thus by establishing on, or near the coast of their Empire, leave time, and intercourse to effect their civilization.[19]

At Hong Kong on November 10, 1852, Captain Franklin Buchanan, who had arrived from the United States, took command of the *Susquehanna*. Strict discipline was immediately imposed in obedience to Perry's warning: "We shall be obliged to govern . . . by *moral suasion*."[20]

At Hong Kong again after a brief cruise to Manila, there was more recent and reliable news concerning the Japan Expedition, and Kell could affirm its "peaceful nature." Presents were being brought from the United States to show the Japanese the "improvements of the age." There was still speculation, however, whether or not Perry would resort to force, although Kell had "yet to learn what right we have to force them to have intercourse with us." He had seen an English cartoon which showed an army of missionaries landing in Japan under the guns of the American squadron, armed with a Bible in one hand and a revolver in the other. The idea of missionary coercion was repugnant to Kell, who conceded that there was "a popular party . . . Northern fanaticks [*sic*] principally, who would have us enter in the cause as defenders of the Faith, and convert the Japanese to Christianity whether or no."[21] He speculated that if the expedition proceeded peacefully, their work would be finished by fall; however, a blockade of the Japanese coast and destruction of their fishing vessels would require at least another year.

On March 16 Bayard Taylor,[22] a reporter for the New York *Tribune*, arrived at Hong Kong and was invited by Captain Buchanan to sail aboard the *Susquehanna*. Taylor was designated as an attaché of the American embassy. The gifted writer became popular with the officers of the *Susquehanna*, and the feeling was reciprocated. The journalist found Captain Buchanan to be "all that his reputation as a gentleman and a brave and gallant officer led us to anticipate; while the officers under his command justified the high opinion I had formed of our naval corps. . . ."[23]

The ship was placed at the disposal of Humphry Marshall, United States Minister to China, who intended to visit Shanghai, and possibly Nanking, to investigate the internal situation there. The entire coastal region of southeastern China was in chaos, and Nanking had already fallen to the Taiping rebels. Three days after reaching Shanghai, Commissioner Marshall ordered Buchanan to sail the *Susquehanna* up the Yangtze River to Nanking, and the attempt was made. However, due to either the incompetence or treachery of one of their Chinese pilots, the ship ran onto a shoal, and—after getting her afloat—they gave up the attempt. They returned to Shanghai, the city which Bayard Taylor considered "the most cheerful, social and agreeable community in China." It was perhaps the only Chinese city where the cries of "Fan-kwei!" (foreign devil!) were unheard, and the "faces of the populace are turned towards you with an expression of good will."[24]

Early in May of 1853, the *Mississippi* arrived at Shanghai, bringing Commodore Perry. Kell remembered at least two of her officers from the Naval School—Captain Sidney Smith Lee and Chaplain George Jones. It was Perry, however—"Old Matt" or "Old Bruin" to his officers and sailors—who was the fascinating figure.[25] In later years Kell compared him to General Winfield Scott, only without the "fuss and feathers." Another officer who served under Perry described him:

> He was a bluff yet dignified man, heavy and not graceful, something of a martinet; a duty man all over, held something in awe by junior officers, and having little to do with them; seriously courteous to others. The ship seemed to have a sense of importance because he was on board.

A seaman said of him: "So long as ye walk a chalk line there couldn't be a fairer man than the Commodore, but God help ye if ye slip off that line!"[26] President Fillmore and Secretary Graham had chosen well in selecting Perry for the delicate mission ahead. Aristocratic and haughty, Perry knew how to impress the Japanese by using their own techniques. In addition, he had brought with him a cargo of gifts, wines and liquors, ammunition, small arms, cutlasses, and an embossed letter of friendship from President Fillmore to the Emperor of Japan. He was prepared for any response to his mission to "open up" Japan to America.

Perry imposed a policy of censorship on his officers and crew; all journals, notes, sketches, and observations of any kind were to be turned over to him and reclaimed "as it may suit the convenience of the government." As a result, few journals were kept, but impressions and observations were often recorded in letters.[27]

On May 9 the Commodore transferred his pennant to the *Susquehanna*, and soon afterwards four ships of the squadron sailed for the Ryukyu Islands, the first to be explored by the Americans. These islands were tributary to the Japanese Prince of Satsuma. After careful observations, the Americans sailed to the Bonim Islands, five hundred miles south of Japan, to determine their suitability as a coaling station. They then returned to the Ryukyu Islands and on July 1, 1853, sailed for the Japanese mainland. They sighted the coast on the morning of the 8th, and soon Japanese fishermen were gazing in astonishment at the "Fire-vessels of the Western Barbarians" as they moved into Yedo (now Tokyo) Bay. (Because their hulls were black and they belched black smoke, the Japanese called them the "Black Ships.")[28] Perry ordered that the decks be cleared for action, and by late afternoon they were at anchor off Uraga.

During the next crucial days, both sides tried unsuccessfully to impose their own terms. Perry made it known that he would receive only a high official, and that the Vice Governor of Uraga was unacceptable. The Japanese, however, insisted that Nagasaki was the proper site for negotiations. Perry remained firm. To the Japanese response that it would take many months before they would have an answer to the President's letter, Perry answered that he would take his ships to the China coast and return the following year. It was implied that he would return with an even stronger force.

While at Yedo Bay, Perry made only one official appearance before the Japanese. On July 14, while his four ships took station in line to guard against treachery, three hundred and fifty men went ashore aboard fifteen cutters and launches. In addition to the Commodore, his staff, and the sailors and marines, there were two bands. Captain Buchanan was the first American of the squadron to set foot on Japanese soil. Kell was one of the officers on Perry's staff, and thus was a witness to the historic occasion.

Facing the Americans as they formed into line stood about five thousand Japanese soldiers, behind them women and peasants. Escorted to a reception hall built for the occasion, Perry and his suite were seated opposite two imperial princes and their retinue. Two giant Negro sailors, especially chosen for the occasion by Perry, bore the decorated boxes containing President Fillmore's letter and other documents and placed them before the Japanese. The purser of the *Susquehanna* later recorded his reaction to the landing:

> The effect as we approached the shore was beautiful and exciting: a mere handful, less than four hundred Americans, were landing in the face of five thousand troops, whose Eastern dresses and silken banners were imposing, whose character for cunning and duplicity was well known, and who were supported by countless multitudes covering the neighboring hills. But the moment we came near enough to compare ourselves with them, all ideas of treachery vanished; for there was not a Yankee who did not feel that one broadside, one war-whoop, and a rush upon them with the cold steel we could scatter as many as could stand before us. Their unsoldierlike dresses, their antiquated arms, spears, and cross-bows, match-locks, and about sixty old Tower muskets, and four or five two-pound brass fieldpieces. Their officers, dressed in silk and seated on camp-stools, in front of the soldiers under umbrellas, made us feel confident that we could drive any number of them like pigeons before our eagles.[29]

By having familiarized himself with their customs, by anticipating and understanding their moves, Perry had been able to meet the Japanese on his terms. After his departure the Japanese had to decide whether—on his return—to fight or submit to Perry's terms. Uncertain what to do, the shogun's council temporized in the hope that the Americans would become discouraged and return home.

After a brief stay at the Ryukyu Islands, the *Susquehanna* sailed for Macao, where Perry made his plans for returning to Japan. These were weeks during which Kell gained additional knowledge of China:

> I have seen much to interest me and improve my knowledge of the world in these years. China and its inhabitants are certainly of peculiar interest and can not be appreciated by one who has not visited this country, for although we may be familiar with the written accounts of their manners and customs yet there is something so peculiar and foreign in them it is quite impossible to convey it to the mind.

Kell was aroused to pity and disgust at the "barbarous custom" of binding women's feet (begun when children) as he observed them "hobbling along on their crippled feet, wearing shoes not over three or four inches in length and working so hard for a mere subsistence."[30]

Through the fall and winter of 1853–1854, the *Susquehanna* remained at Canton and Hong Kong. Early in 1854 Commodore Perry received orders to place a ship at the disposal of the new American minister to China—Robert M. McLane. The ship would be the *Susquehanna*, but first she would return with Perry to Japan. In February (earlier than he had originally intended because of apprehensions concerning French and Russian warships) Perry was again off Japan, this time with eight ships. Off the headlands of Yedo Bay, he ordered his squadron to enter the harbor in a line to emphasize their number and precision.

During the next weeks, Perry and the Japanese (through their agents and interpreters) discussed the terms of the treaty, which the Japanese commissioners—fearing hostilities—were already prepared to accept. In the Treaty of Kanagawa Perry obtained what were most essential to American interests: two open ports (Shimoda and Hakodate), coaling rights, the appointment of consuls at the two ports, and guarantees for the protection of American castaways.

A viceregal ceremony at Yokohama on March 8 marked the opening of regular relations between the two nations, amidst an exchange of presents and courtesies. As examples of Western civilization, Perry had brought a miniature railroad (one-fourth normal size), complete with engine, passenger cars, tracks and sidings; he also brought a telegraph, daguerreotype equipment, a printing press, agricultural implements, rifles, clocks, and numerous other items.[31] The Japanese presented unspectacular items, including symbols of the Shogun's esteem—rice, dried fish, and three small spaniels. The Americans were entertained by an exhibition of sumo wrestling, and they reciprocated with a minstrel show which delighted the ordinarily staid Japanese.

While the negotiations and ceremonies were still in progress, the *Susquehanna* was detached from the squadron for special service under Commissioner McLane, now at Hong Kong. McLane was anxious to obtain firsthand information about the Taipings. With the Commissioner aboard, the *Susquehanna* arrived at Shanghai on April 29. This was Kell's favorite Chinese city, but not for the reasons which had attracted Bayard Taylor. To Kell and other officers, the city offered the companionship of American missionaries, including a number of ladies. As one officer put it: "The ladies of the mission are not beautiful or fashionable but good and solid, and associating with them revives homely feelings. They feel flattered by our attention."[32] All the major denominations were represented. The head of the American Episcopal Mission at Shanghai was Bishop William J. Boone, a South Carolinian.[33] Boone's second wife was a sister of Bishop Stephen Elliott of Georgia, and this association with his native state was cheering to the homesick Kell. Bishop Boone had recently returned to China and had brought with him a new recruit to the mission field. She was twenty-seven-year-old Emma Wray of Augusta, Georgia, who had taught art at Bishop Elliott's school for girls in Montpelier (Georgia).[34] Miss Wray was undergoing "culture shock" and extreme homesickness and could see the Chinese only as a "cunning, lying, merciless and treacherous people, not for a moment to be relied on."[35] Her most intimate correspondent was a former pupil at Montpelier—Julia Blanche Munroe—a daughter of banker Nathan C. Munroe of Vineville (a suburb of Macon), Georgia. To her eighteen-year-old friend and confidante, "Sister Em" poured forth her loneliness and bitterness from the "land of heathen darkness."

It was natural that Kell (whose cousin, Henry K. Reese, was

an Episcopal minister) would seek out the Episcopal mission station and the Boones. Bishop Boone was a "fat and jolly" man, troubled with gout, while his wife was "fat and awkward in figure, but gentle in her manner and pleasant in her conversation."[36] But far more important to Kell's future was Miss Wray.

Soon after her arrival in Shanghai, Miss Wray attended a wedding at the mission church. The *Susquehanna* was in the harbor, and Captain Buchanan had allowed the ship's band to play at the wedding. While listening to "Katie Darling" being sung by a sailor, Miss Wray was overwhelmed by homesickness. She was pleased, therefore, to meet Thomas T. Hunter, the second lieutenant of the *Susquehanna*. Lieutenant Hunter had a wife and children in Virginia, and the lady from Georgia reminded him of familiar society and home. As for the lieutenant, Miss Wray found him "very agreeable.... He is a fine looking officer, a gentleman and a Christian."[37] Learning that Miss Wray was from Georgia, Hunter mentioned that Passed Midshipman Kell was from Darien and promised to bring him on his next trip ashore. Hunter returned with Kell three days later. Miss Wray was completely charmed with the young officer and began to consider what a fine husband Kell would make for her "Bannie" Munroe. She had been a matchmaker before, having brought together Harriet, Bannie's older sister, and her husband. The day after her meeting with Kell, Emma wrote:

> Bannie, Darling, I have at *last*, seen the man, whom I should like to see, and know, possessed your heart and hand. *Mr. Kell*, or rather, his family is well known in Savannah, and I have frequently heard of them. Bannie, Darling, keep your heart free until you can see this worthy, excellent young man, for I intend you shall see him when he returns to America.... Mr. Hunter in speaking of him to me, told me that "he was an honor to his country," and his native state, that "well might his country be proud of him," and with such high praise from his superior officer I was *not* disappointed when Mr. Kell was introduced. He is not what many persons would call *handsome*. The word would not apply to his face. Therefore do not picture an Apollo,

> but you would be struck with his fine, manly, frank and open countenance, and calm, dignified, *pleasant* expression. He may be twenty three, four or even five years of age, but not more.[38] I rather think he is younger than his lofty bearing and self-possessed manners would convey. . . . He does not wear a mostache [*sic*], and has light brown hair, and now Darling, I am going to leave him to your imagination for the rest, only please don't give your heart away until you have at least had a look at him. He sat by me most of the time during his visit, talking of home, and I assure you I was pleased with him, and could not help feeling proud of him and comparing him with another young Middy, from Ohio, who had called a week before, who, poor *little* fellow, had tried to be fascinating, but was surfeiting. I dubbed him little cock sparrow, as soon as he was fairly out of the room.[39]

Emma was already planning to give Kell a letter of introduction to Nathan Munroe, as well as to Bannie and her younger sister, twelve-year-old Sarah ("Tadie"): "Oh if he is only fortunate enough to win one of you, he will be blessed indeed." When she learned that Kell had been on Perry's Expedition to Japan, Emma warned him of his being a celebrity when he returned to the United States. She wrote: "He seems modest, and it strikes me, would bear such discomforts, with dignified and affable composure."[40] Not long afterward, when the ladies of the mission were invited to visit the *Susquehanna*, it was Kell who personally escorted Miss Wray through his ship.

However, there was business at hand, and on May 22 Commissioner McLane ordered Captain Franklin to sail the *Susquehanna* up the Yangtze River, repeating the attempt of the previous year. This time the steam tug *Confucius* was sent ahead to sound out the channel. On May 27 they dropped anchor outside the city walls of Nanking, the Taiping capital. The *Susquehanna* received visitors, and was soon swarming with Chinese of all classes. While McLane waited for a reply to his dispatch to the leader of the rebels at Nanking, several of his assistants and officers of the ship went ashore.[41] On May 30, Kell, Dr. Fahs, and Midshipman Charles E. Hawley landed, "armed" only with umbrellas, and accompanied by a Chinese servant as interpreter. Their goal was the Porcelain Tower, an imposing structure just west of the city. Having met with no interference, they approached the Tower and observed its desecrated Buddhist idols and inscriptions. Fahs was saddened at the "wreck and destruction which surround this stupendous and magnificent structure; though it still stands as a silent monument of reproof to the evils of civil discord."[42] Finishing their inspection of the Tower, they attempted to retrace their steps but were soon surrounded by an excited and angry crowd. A company of spearmen appeared, closed the street, and ordered the Americans to accompany them. Surrounded as they were by "soldiery and rabble," they had no choice but to obey. Along the way they were being led, they were horrified to see the bloody heads of several Chinese hung up in cages. At this sight their Chinese servant became completely demoralized: "His hair seemed to stand up on his head, his eyes became suddenly bloodshot, and he presented a most pitiable object of fright and despair."[43]

The mandarin before whom they were brought seemed so "grotesque" to Kell that he almost laughed outright. A secretary wrote descriptions of each of the Americans in a book. The officers tried to act dignified and unafraid, while their servant-interpreter, "trembling like an aspen," attempted to communicate between them and the haughty Chinese aristocrat. The mandarin, unimpressed with their request for horses or their insistence that they must return to their ship before sunset, gave orders that they were to go into the city to appear before a higher mandarin—the "Eastern King." Outside again, surrounded by inquisitive and noisy Chinese, the three Americans were determined not to show fear. Two miles inside Nanking, they came to a large house, where their guide began to give instructions on how to conduct themselves before the mighty "Eastern King." Dr. Fahs later wrote an official report which included details of the episode:

> Our anger was at once excited, and we faced [the guide] in a manner that showed him we were not the submissive and servile creatures that he had supposed, telling him at the same

> time that we would kneel to God alone. We also told him we would not appear in the presence of the great man after his demand.

The result was that they were brought to the residence of still another mandarin. After a long wait, during which they were treated with "civility and kindness," they were allowed to return to their ship "after a long and weary day's absence." The following day the Chinese authorities sent a message to the *Susquehanna* that if "any more of the outside barbarians attempted to enter the city they would have their heads chopped off." Thus ended Kell's greatest adventure in China and, as he later recalled, a " 'hair breadth' escape from execution."[44] Commissioner McLane, incensed at the contemptuous messages he was receiving, finally had the *Susquehanna* return to Shanghai. He had, as a result of this trip, developed an intense hostility toward the Taiping movement.

When Kell visited Miss Wray again in Shanghai, she asked him to take several packages to America for her. One was to be delivered personally, if at all possible—the one to Miss Munroe in Vineville. Emma was still the matchmaker, for she later wrote to Bannie:

> I am going to send a young and valuable friend to see you, and tell you as much as he can of me. Who knows but what in the end *he* may be a more agreeable temporary acquisition to your household than *I* could. . . . Let me simply introduce you to my esteemed friend Mr. Kell. . . . I shall request him to deliver it *himself*, to your Father or yourself, in passing through Macon. . . .

Emma was determined that if Kell could not meet Bannie, then he would meet her younger sister, attending school in Savannah. However, all was not as bright as she had earlier supposed; in one respect Kell was not the man she had thought him to be:

> With all my admiration of this pleasant, amiable dignified and fine looking young officer, he is still an unregenerate man (I

do not think he is connected with any Church), and of *such* Darling *always* be careful, ere this running into "temptation," should provoke God's wrath against you, and your bright joyous life be turned into a gloomy, painful shadow. . . . Take care Darling that Satan, with his jealous venom, does not seek to put His one fatal drop into your glowing, clear transparent cup of full life. I send Mr. Kell to you, know and appreciate him, if only as a friend, in that capacity you may have an influence over him, which will one day lead his heart to better things than these of this world.[45]

During his last weeks in China, Kell became ill from the "enervating climate" and was invited into the home of Bishop and Mrs. Boone. Here he enjoyed "the nice Southern dishes" and had everything done for his comfort. He later recalled that their "true Southern hospitality" had restored his health.[46] During his stay at the mission, Emma Wray discussed religion with Kell and learned that his leanings were Episcopalian, "only through slight prejudice to the Presbyterian side." She wrote to Bannie, "I think he is a pious young man, at heart, and only awaits good influences."[47]

The vessels of the Japan Expedition rendezvoused at Hong Kong prior to their departure for America. It was here that Kell was transferred to the *Mississippi* as acting master; years of experience and demonstrated competence were finally bringing their rewards. From Hong Kong he wrote Miss Wray of his transfer and promotion:

It was with many regrets I parted with my old associates, having been with them for forty-four months. The two steamers are ordered home by the same route, touching at Simoda (Japan), then by the Sandwich Islands, across to San Francisco, and around Cape Horn, touching at several ports on the coast of South America, the *Susquehanna* to the port of Philadelphia, and this ship to New York. [The *Susquehanna*] sailed on [September 4, 1854], amidst the peal of cannon, cheering and music, which was truly exciting to myself especially, when they passed us, and our fine Band gave them the parting salute of "Home sweet home." The Commodore takes passage in the mail steamer (tomorrow) and so also to sail at the same time, when there

> will be another round of salutes, etc. He, on his way through Europe, while we steer across the broad Pacific, circumnavigating the Globe. I mentioned . . . my intention of sending your Boxes by one of the Store Ships on account of the uncertainty of the *Susquehanna's* returning to the Atlantic Coast. Since joining the ship, however, I have taken them with me, and hope to deliver them in person.[48]

With Kell's letter was sent a token of his "very high regard"—a lacquered and gilded writing desk. Emma had important news of her own. She was returning to the United States because of "wretched and so precarious" health: "The Doctor has advised me to leave; my friends have, also." She expected to arrive in Georgia at about the same time as Kell.

When the *Susquehanna* sailed from Hong Kong, she had on board Commander Cadwalader Ringgold, who had been declared insane and ordered by Commodore Perry to return to the United States.[49] Ringgold, commander of the North Pacific surveying and exploring expedition, had reached China in May of 1854 and soon afterward been stricken with fever. One of the ships of the Ringgold Expedition, the brig *Porpoise,* had aboard a young midshipman from Macon, Georgia—G. F. Burleigh Baber. Kell and Baber met before their ships sailed, and Baber, believing that Kell would reach Georgia first, gave him a package to deliver to his widowed mother in Macon. Sailing from Hong Kong soon afterward, the *Porpoise* was lost at sea with all on board. Months later, on his return to Georgia, Kell visited the Baber home in Macon to deliver the package, which contained gifts, letters, and a daguerreotype of Midshipman Baber. It was an unhappy mission for Kell, although Mrs. Baber had not yet given up hope of her son's survival.

As the *Mississippi* left the coast of China behind, Kell reflected on his experiences in the Far East and contemplated the future. Many years later Kell would tell his children and grandchildren that at Shanghai he had seen a photograph of the "beautiful and feted Miss Munroe" and that "he determined to win her for his wife."[50]

7

COURTSHIP AND MARRIAGE

In 1855 young and pretty Julia Blanche Munroe was one of Macon's most charming and eligible belles. Born January 31, 1836, Bannie was the fifth child of Nathan C. and Tabitha (Napier) Munroe. Eight children were born to the Munroes, of whom four were living in 1855: Harriet ("Hattie"), Bannie, Sarah Lois ("Tadie"), and Nathan, Jr. ("Nattie"). Since Hattie had married the previous year, and Tadie and Nattie were only thirteen and nine, Bannie was especially close to her parents. Her father idolized her.

Nathan C. Munroe (formerly Munro) was one of Macon's pioneers. Originally from Fort Edward in upstate New York, he had come to Georgia when fourteen years of age with letters of introduction to Major Thomas Napier, a wealthy planter. Nathan became a clerk in Napier's store and eventually (in 1828) married his benefactor's daughter.[1] While still a young man, he established a banking business in Macon. Nathan also planned Macon's first cotton mill and became a director of the Macon and Western Railroad. By 1840 he had purchased property at Vineville, a settlement just outside the city. It was here at Sylvan Lodge that Bannie and her sisters and brother spent a "happy childhood and happy youth."

Nathan was determined to provide his children with the best advantages his money could provide. Hattie was sent to France for three years of schooling and, later, to Bishop Elliott's[2] Montpelier Institute, of which her father was a trustee.

Bannie also attended Montpelier, from 1849 to 1855, receiving religious instruction from the Bishop himself and, after 1852, from the Reverend Seneca G. Bragg. Montpelier was the most exclusive boarding school for girls to be found in central Georgia at that time, and Bannie was fortunate to graduate before its closing—for financial reasons—in 1855. The school offered instruction in ancient and modern languages, the "English branches," "Music, Drawing, Painting in Water Colors and Oil, and Embroidery."[3] Located on secluded and beautifully landscaped grounds, Montpelier provided a perfect environment for learning.

Nathan Munroe indulged his children. For their amusement he had a wooded park on his property fenced in for rabbits and deer. Bannie's numerous pets included canaries, Java sparrows, and a St. Bernard Dog, all to reconcile her—Bannie's father teased—to being an "old maid." He had, after all, married her mother when she was only sixteen. But Bannie did not lack suitors. She knew that she would be choosing among them soon, but meanwhile life was filled with fun and gaiety. And there were occasional thoughts of a handsome naval officer in her daydreams, as she tried to visualize the man described in Emma Wray's letters from China.

On June 22, 1855, while visiting her Aunt Martha and Uncle Hendley (Varner) at Sunnyside, near Griffin, Blanche received a telegram from her pastor, the Reverend Henry K. Reese.[4] It read:

> A Chinese umbrella per steamer Susquehannah
> United States Navy
> Bearer in Macon.[5]

The *Mississippi*, with Kell aboard, had arrived in New York in late April, and—with a three-month leave in hand—Kell had left immediately for Darien. The Kells, already settled at their summer home three miles from the Grove, were delighted to have Donny with them again. They found him much thinner and not in the best of health. While at home he suffered from two attacks of chills and fever, which, they believed, were caused by the debilitating effects of his long sojourn in the Far East. However, Kell was not so ill as to be deprived of the company of his friends. Aboard George Dent's home-built steamboat, Kell served as helmsman, and the two companions visited other friends at their sea-island summer homes. Finally, in June, Kell left for Macon, bringing with him the parcels to be delivered to Mrs. Baber and Miss Blanche Munroe. He looked every bit the traveled officer.[6]

Not long after her return to Vineville from Sunnyside, Blanche returned from a drive and found the Reverend Reese and his naval officer cousin seated on the veranda chatting with her parents. She was finally to meet the man about whom Emma Wray had written so much. Excited, but trying not to show it, Blanche was introduced to Mr. Kell, the friend of Miss Wray and the bearer of a parcel from China. In later years Kell confessed to Blanche that "the supreme moment of his life had come—that he had met his destiny." As he watched her, he was thinking: "How lovely this girl would be to my dear old mother, and in my home." The visit was brief, and Kell remarked on leaving that he would be on the Savannah train that night.

At Sunday church service, however, Blanche was surprised to see the "handsome naval officer" sitting in the Rector's pew. At the completion of the service, Kell left church with the Munroes, assisted Blanche into their carriage, and once again bade good-bye. During the ride home, Mr. Munroe remarked, "For a young man who has been all over the world a time or two, as they say he has, he certainly has very little to say. I tried in vain to draw him out about Japan and the East, but he would not talk!"[7]

The next day Blanche received a note from the parsonage informing her that Kell had been persuaded to remain in Macon another day and asking her to call. With her mother's permission, she spent the afternoon in the company of Kell and other guests of the Reeses. Evening came, and as Kell assisted Blanche into her carriage he remarked that the day had been one of the happiest of his life. He mentioned his intention of returning to Macon in October for the marriage of Matilda Reese and another of his cousins, the Reverend Francis R. Goulding. Disappointed in Blanche's response to this, Kell added: "Miss Munroe, you might have said you would be glad to see me." But, for an answer, Blanche merely laughed.

After returning to Darien Kell requested an extension of his leave on the plea that he had returned from a "long and arduous cruise" and that his presence at home was "most desirable at this time."[8]

Emma Wray, having returned from China, spent part of the summer in Vineville with the Munroes. During her visit she tried unsuccessfully to persuade Blanche to send a message through her to Kell. Emma apparently believed in marriage for others, but not for herself; she was content to live "*single*, with the privileges of being devoted and faithful" to Blanche's "welfare, interest, and happiness." She was delighted that Kell had left a favorable impression on Mrs. Munroe. When asked whether Kell was handsome, Tabitha replied that his "pleasant" face showed he had a soul. Emma felt enough confidence in Mrs. Munroe to advise Blanche to make a confidante of her mother "if anything should occur between you and Johnnie."[9]

When Kell returned to Vineville in October, he spent three pleasant days with Blanche. They walked through the deer park, fed the pets, rode horseback together, and sat and talked on the rustic benches. After the Goulding-Reese wedding at Roswell, Kell returned to Vineville for another day with Blanche. He told her, among other things, that he had been dismissed from the service but had been reinstated through the influence of Senator Berrien. Before returning to Darien, Kell told Blanche he would try to see her again before his leave expired.

While awaiting his orders, Kell received letters from the Navy Department which were indeed welcome; they contained a warrant as master (dated September 14, 1855) and a commission as lieutenant (dated September 15, 1855).[10] After fourteen years in the navy he was now *Lieutenant* Kell, entitled to wear the epaulettes with the single anchor and the single strip of gold lace around the upper edge of his cuffs.

On November 24 his orders arrived: he was to report to Lieutenant Edwin J. DeHaven at Pensacola for duty on the Coast Survey Schooner *Arago*.[11] Several days later Kell, now wearing the insignia of a lieutenant, again headed for Macon. He could not have known of the interest taken in his movements by Miss Wray, who spotted his name in a Savannah newspaper among the list of passengers in one of the boats from Darien. Believing that he was on his way to Vineville, Emma wrote to Blanche: "*Has* my *prayer* been answered Darling—*any*, or *all* or that long cherished prayer for you and him. Oh—may God, in love, grant it, if consistent with his divine wisdom and will!"[12]

On the day that Kell arrived at Sylvan Lodge (December 9), Blanche was entertaining several of her friends, including some male admirers. In the middle of their merriment, Kell arrived—a stranger to all but Blanche. In the awkwardness which followed, Kell retired behind a "cloud of reserve." Finally he asked Blanche to sing "Kathleen Mavourneen," which she did. When she had finished Kell bowed himself out, and Blanche accompanied him to the door. Out of hearing of her guests, he blurted out: "I was never so disappointed in my life! I came to have a quiet evening with you; and this company! I am ordered to Galveston to join the Coast Survey of the Coast of Texas, a work of at least six months or a year. I had so much to say to you. May I write to you?" However she may have felt, Blanche knew her father well, and she replied: "Oh, no! My father does not allow me to correspond with gentlemen." Kell then said that he would write to Mr. Munroe to ask for the correspondence, and Blanche replied, smiling: "I suppose you can do that."

Soon after Kell had left, Blanche confided her news to Emma Wray, and her friend replied triumphantly:

> That Mr. Kell's affection is yours now, you cannot have any doubt, let me congratulate you, my Darling Blanche, with that fervency and truthfulness of feeling, for your *mutual* happiness and welfare. . . . Blanche Kell will sound . . . sweetly in my ears.[13]

Three weeks later a letter from Kell, dated December 31, 1855, arrived for Mr. Munroe; it enclosed another for Blanche. For a day or two Nathan and Tabitha deliberated until one evening, after tea, Blanche went as usual into her father's library to read the newspapers to him. The devoted father drew his daughter to him and said:

> Sweetheart, that Sailor has written me a letter about you. He wants me to give him my sweetheart. Now you must consider all the hardships of a sailor's life, the constant separation while he is at sea serving his country, though it will always be my blessing to have you in his absence. He seems so much older than you do. Did you see the bald spot on his head?

Bannie kissed her father's bald head, saying: "Yes, but the dearest head on earth to me is bald." Pressing her to him, he replied: "The argument is sufficient! But oh, my child, why could you not have chosen, from all that have loved you, some one nearer home—not a stranger." Blanche received her note from Kell and replied the next day. During the following weeks and months, their correspondence developed into an "ardent love, a love that was to crown our days and lighten our path to Heaven."[14]

Kell's new commanding officer, Lieutenant DeHaven, was a veteran of twenty-six years in the service; during 1850 and 1851 he had commanded the Grinnell Expedition in search of the British explorer, Sir John Franklin, lost in the Arctic. The only other lieutenant aboard the *Arago* was James H. Gillis, like DeHaven a Pennsylvanian. The *Arago* sailed to Galveston to continue the survey of the coast south of that port. It was hard and exacting work, with Kell and Gillis on shore (nine miles apart) angling with a theodolite, while those aboard the *Arago* ran lines of soundings. Kell's station was "Castle Jupiter," a small shack containing a table, cot, stove, trunk, instruments for observations, and provisions for three weeks. His sailor-valet had similar quarters. "Castle Jupiter" was about three miles from the village of Quintana, Texas, and Kell made a friend of the postman and principal citizen there, a Mr.

Brown. Brown, like Kell, enjoyed hunting, and with his prize greyhounds provided the naval officer with a new and exciting variation of the sport. Other outdoor pleasures were fishing and an occasional picnic at Cedar Lake. During rain and storms, when work on the survey was delayed, Kell read Macaulay's *The History of England* and Agnes Strickland's *Life of Queen Elizabeth*. Margery Kell recommended that her son also read a recent book of Amelia M. Murray,[15] an English visitor to Darien during an 1855 American tour. Kell was surprised that she "could have found anything complimentary of dear old Darien or its vicinity, arriving in the night and no welcoming hotel, only a lodging place. . . .[16] In Miss Murray Southerners found one who sympathized with their institutions and way of life.

Kell was gratified to learn that his family approved of his engagement. Actually, Margery Kell was deeply relieved, having feared her son's becoming "that unfortunate being—an old bachelor." She, along with her daughters, wrote to Blanche expressing their delight in the match. Kell was hurt and angry to learn that Blanche was making "public property" of his letters to her, and he frankly told her so. Still, letters from Vineville were the greatest source of happiness for the lovesick officer, and an embroidered smoking cap, sent as a valentine, was received with joy.

In March Kell, suffering from "severe chill and very high fever," accompanied the *Arago* to Galveston, where it would pick up supplies. The change did him good, and he recovered sufficiently to attend a masquerade ball given by a Miss Menard of Galveston and Macon. At the ball both Kell and Dr. Charles Martin of the *Arago* dressed as monks and had a "merry time" confusing their dance partners by occasionally changing places.[17]

Returning to the survey, now at Cedar Lake, Kell took up quarters in the unoccupied summer home of Alabama Governor John Anthony Winston.[18] Its contrast with "Castle Jupiter" was so great that Kell could imagine himself "one of the princes of the land in comfort." On April 24 Governor Winston arrived to find Kell in possession of his house and graciously extended his courtesy. For two weeks Kell enjoyed the companionship of the Governor and his brother.

Long periods of bad weather were responsible for the slow progress of the survey and Kell's increasing impatience. He yearned for his "Enchantress," the "little siren" in Vineville, and she in turn wrote him that his "constancy" would be the talisman to keep her heart true.[19]

In late May the survey was discontinued. DeHaven's and Kell's eyes had become so affected by the sun's reflection that they had to be bandaged to protect them from the light.[20] On June 2 the *Arago* sailed for Philadelphia, where DeHaven would work on his report. Kell, who believed that he had secured his senior officer's "good will and friendship," hoped to be assigned the same duty. He feared being sent to the northern survey or to sea ("Imagine such a catastrophe!"), which would further delay his wedding. He was allowed to work with DeHaven, and the reports took them three months. While at Philadelphia Kell was visited by friends and relatives, including cousin James McQueen McIntosh.[21] McIntosh insisted on helping select his cousin's wedding outfit. When the purchase was complete he said: "John, you are a handsome man, and you will simply be stunning, and take that little Georgia girl's breath away in a white silk hat."[22]

In July Charles and Evelyn Spalding made a point of passing through Macon to visit their future sister-in-law. The Spaldings, who lived at the Ashantilly estate left to Charles by his father, traveled frequently, as Charles was active in politics.[23] All three took an instant liking to each other, and Blanche, especially, was surprised and pleased to find a resemblance between Evelyn and her betrothed.

During his dreary weeks in Philadelphia, Kell, surrounded by "piles of formidable rows of books," realized why he had never cared to pursue a business profession:

> Indeed my education has either been sadly neglected or Nature in disposing of her Gifts, withheld from me the boon so much to be desired in this driving age of "young America." If there is anything that would reduce me to the shadow of a walking

> skeleton it would be to play the part of scribe, or to keep accounts in an office! There is that freedom from care and turmoil in our life on the broad expanse of Ocean that admits but one rival to my mind, the quiet retirement of a happy country home, surrounded by loved ones and friends. I find myself in my almost daily correspondence with the little Lady of my heart, in Vineville, putting all these dreams on paper for her benefit, telling her of my long and arduous sea-service, and how some happy day we will seek retirement or "be retired" and "live and love together," through all life's changing years.[24]

The wedding was to be in October. Blanche had wanted Bishop Stephen Elliott to perform the ceremony, but—because he would not be available—they decided upon the Reverend Reese. Learning of Kell's difficulties in securing leave, the Bishop jokingly suggested that the marriage be performed by telegraph.[25]

Finally Kell's request to be detached from the Coast Survey was approved, and on October 2 he left Philadelphia. The wedding would not be held on a Tuesday. Blanche had been advised that Margery Kell was determined to have grandchildren and believed that marriages held on that day would be childless.[26]

The wedding took place on Wednesday, October 15, 1856, at Christ Church in Macon. Over a thousand invitations had been sent out, and several hundred more later added. The sixteen attendants were the closest friends of the bride and groom; Kell and his naval friends made a striking appearance in their colorful dress uniforms. After a week in Macon, during which a grand reception, a ball, and other functions were held, the newlyweds left for Darien.

As Margery Kell had not attended the wedding, this was Blanche's first meeting with her new mother-in-law. To her surprise she found a "very feeble, dear old lady," a "very hearty whole-souled person."[27] Although the whole family treated Blanche with loving affection, Margery Kell outdid herself. As she escorted Blanche through her home, she pointed out her most valuable possessions, saying: "Here, my child, look at *your* china and *your* silver, and this is *your* house. My children know this is their brother John's place, but I hope his sisters will always find a home with him." Blanche asked her how she managed while her son was at sea, and Margery answered: "Oh, my dear, I don't live. I drag through life, thinking of *when* he will come back." The Grove—"beautiful . . . but old and dilapidated from want of means"—provided a sharp contrast with well-kept and immaculate Sylvan Lodge. Blanche could not help thinking how her father, with his "love for improvements," would have transformed it into a "lovely spot."[28]

The following weeks were filled with continuous activities in honor of the newlyweds: "elegant dinner parties, dances in the evenings, a regatta given in our honor by Hon. Thomas Forman, of Broughton Island, and a ten day's entertainment of seventy guests at the estate of Randolph Spalding on Sapelo Island." The spacious rooms in the old Spalding mansion were occupied by the ladies, while the gentlemen were quartered in tents under the live oak trees. A band had been brought out from Savannah to supply music for the evening dances. In addition to a "perpetual feast"—set "at any and all hours" —there were amusements of all kinds, including deer hunting for the gentlemen.[29] Kell came in for a share of good-natured joshing; a toast was offered "for the remainder of the hair off the top of his head that he might with decency get a wig."[30]

But there were moments of loneliness, too, for Blanche frequently yearned for her family and her animals in Vineville. She began to use the endearing names she had for her pets ("Petty," "Pet one") on her husband. On the occasions when Hettie Kell found Blanche closed up alone in her room, she felt offended, considering it "an outward sign of the heart being closed against sympathy;" only a tender kiss from her new sister could console Hettie.[31] One day when Kell found his bride looking sadly out of the window, he insisted that Blanche tell him what was troubling her. Finally she answered: "I wish I knew what time it is!" Relieved and laughing, Kell called to his mother: "Will you do me the favor to bring out a clock? This banker's daughter, accustomed to know the time, can not do without it." After a few days with the new clock, even the Kells had become regulated by it.[32]

After the Christmas holiday, the couple returned to the Grove, and Kell began to be disturbed at not receiving orders, believing that he had been "long enough doing nothing, now four months."[33] When March had come and gone, he wrote to the Department requesting assignment to Brunswick, Georgia, selected as the site for a new navy yard.

In early April Kell brought Blanche back to Vineville and journeyed to Washington to see about his orders. He was relieved to learn that he was ordered to the Receiving Ship *Pennsylvania* at the Norfolk Navy Yard. It meant that Blanche could be with him.

Arriving at Norfolk with his wife on April 20, 1857, Kell made temporary arrangements to stay at a boarding house in Portsmouth. John Hutton had seen the couple off at Savannah, and as their steamer passed his counting house, Blanche felt as though she was leaving her "last link" with home; she had hardly been able to hold back the tears. During her first night in Portsmouth, she dreamed of her beloved old Negro mammy back in Sylvan Lodge.[34]

Kell had left behind a new problem. At the Grove, Margery was being troubled by her neighbor, Robert Barnwell Rhett (retired from politics since his resignation as South Carolina Senator in 1852), and she looked to Donny for help. While having his boundaries surveyed, Rhett had discovered that his line ran straight through fields under cultivation by the Kells. Fortunately, the Kells had a relative who was a match for the politically powerful Rhett. Lawyer-cousin John E. Ward[35] advised the Kells to continue holding the land in question on the basis of its having been cultivated by them for the legal seven years. Rhett, however, continued to press his claim. When he wrote an offensive letter to Kell, Margery let Rhett know what she thought of his conduct. In defense of her action, she wrote to Donny: "I thought if I was silent, he is vain enough to suppose I approved of his letter & now he knows to the contrary."[36]

Kell's new duties—two days and nights out of four aboard

the receiving ship *Pennsylvania*—were not arduous and gave him opportunity to be with Blanche. In Norfolk they found more agreeable quarters at a boarding house kept by a retired navy man. Also boarding here were Lieutenant Charles F. M. Spotswood of Virginia and his beautiful Spanish wife from Minorca.

The five months together at the Navy Yard were happy ones for Blanche and Kell. In later years, when reminiscing, they spoke of Norfolk as the "garden spot of the world" and the "land of Goshen" because of the variety of its foodstuffs. The naval families were very attentive to the Kells. A grand reception was held in their honor, and on another occasion Kell's friends—Dr. Fahs, and Lieutenants Bob Minor and Bayard E. Hand—arranged a shipboard ball for them.

In August, accompanied by her sister Hattie, Blanche went to Philadelphia to purchase the "pretty little things" needed to make a baby's wardrobe.[37] Kell could only have been overjoyed at the prospect of becoming a father. On October 14, the day before their first wedding anniversary, Blanche left for Vineville with the Huttons. Kell intended to apply later for a leave of absence and be with his wife at the time of her delivery. To his disappointment, however, shortly after she had left he was detached from the receiving ship and ordered to the Booklyn Navy Yard for assignment as second lieutenant aboard the store ship *Supply*.[38] Arriving in New York on October 23, Kell was amazed to learn that it would be weeks before the *Supply* would sail. He submitted a request for a two-week leave of absence, stating that "this sudden summons to Sea obliged me to part with my family at a most anxious period, which would in a measure be allayed could my request be granted."[39]

On the first Sunday after his arrival in New York, Kell, accompanied by another lieutenant, attended divine services at the Plymouth Church of Brooklyn (Congregational). Without knowing the identity of the minister, he listened in amazement to a style of preaching hitherto unknown to him:

> I at once saw that he was a remarkable man and orator of his

> peculiar fashion, but certainly not a divine in expounding the gospel, for his debate was more of a stock trade, in which he seemed well posted, and his sermon made up almost entirely of similies [*sic*] and some of them very good, but not suited to the pulpit. One for instance was likening God and the Bible to an Insurance Company; his gestures and actions on the platform from which he preached was more like acting upon a stage, and I could not refrain from smiling several times. . . . I soon made enquiries as to whom the man was and to my astonishment was informed that I had been listening to "Henry Ward Beecher," by accident it so happened and I am gratified that I have heard him but I do not think I will give him another chance.[40]

An unhappy duty for Kell while in New York was his visit to the deathbed of a friend and former shipmate, Lieutenant Reuben Harris. Harris, dying of consumption, weakly clasped Kell's hands a few days before he died. To Kell, Harris was "one of the noblest brother officers and friends I have ever had the good fortune to sail with."[41]

Kell was granted a ten-day leave of absence, but he declined it, fearing that such a short visit would make Blanche "quite sick." He was consoled by the knowledge that the cruise would be a relatively short one to the Cape Verde Islands and Rio de Janeiro with provisions for the Africa and Brazil Squadrons. Lieutenant Gillis, his companion of the Coast Survey, would be sailing on the *Supply*, along with a new friend, Assistant Surgeon Phineas J. Horwitz, to whom Kell became "much attached" during the cruise. Their commander, Lieutenant Andrew F. V. Gray, Kell found to be a "nice little man . . . whose greatest fault perhaps is his being such an inveterate talker. . . ." Still hoping for eventual assignment to the Brunswick (Georgia) Navy Yard, Kell intended to contact Captain James McIntosh, "for he has great influence with the administration, and would no doubt serve me in this with pleasure."[42]

As the days passed and the *Supply* was loaded with provisions, concern for Blanche was foremost in Kell's mind. On November 27 the *Supply* left New York, and her heartsick second lieutenant realized it would be months before he would hear news of Blanche and the baby. Captain McIntosh had given him a letter to the commander of the Brazil Squadron, requesting as a personal favor that Kell be permitted to return to the United States "as speedily as possible... should there be any necessity for any transfer of officers."[43]

Ten days after Kell's departure, on December 6, at Sylvan Lodge, a son Nathan Munroe Kell was born. Soon after, Tabitha Munroe wrote the details to her son-in-law:

> Your little boy is certainly something very uncommon. In the first place he weighed ten and three quarters pounds and his beautiful black silky *profuse* head of hair is the envy and admiration of all beholders. Bannie has discovered numberless charms already and I strongly suspect her fondness as a young Mother will enable her to find her boy the ideal of perfection in a very little while. She has even now begun to trace in his various features a marked resemblance to his Father.[44]

On Christmas day of 1857, far at sea, Kell was hopeful that "God has preserved our beloved child to comfort and even make you happy upon this day.... If our lives are spared, what joy awaits my return to behold in your arms our little one so dear to us both." As he watched the sun rise and set that day while on watch, Kell prayed that if their child had been spared, he might "from this day become more worthy the mercies and blessings that have attended me through life."[45] Blanche had suggested that they begin reading the Bible through, starting on Christmas, so he had read a chapter each from the Old and New Testaments. Marriage had brought a transformation in Kell; in addition to becoming interested in religion, he was abstaining from liquor and trying to limit his smoking.

Blanche was pleased and comforted by the arrival of a letter from Captain McIntosh, revealing the high regard he held for her husband:

> You have in the first place one of the very best men in the world for a husband, in the next place one of the handsomest, and most esteemed among the officers of the Navy, and who if you will only allow him to remain in the service, will eventually make his mark on the pages of the history of his country....

Captain McIntosh advised Blanche to let her baby become accustomed to strangers so that when Kell returned he would instinctively "hold out his little arms to receive his father's embrace and blessing."[46]

On February 20—two and one-half months after the birth of his son—Kell received his first letters from home, including the news he had been waiting for. They had arrived at Rio de Janeiro (after a stopover of almost a month at Porto Praya in the Cape Verde Islands) only to find an epidemic of yellow fever raging. Unable to land their stores, they sailed for Montevideo. (Because of the one night spent in the harbor of Rio, several members of the crew came down with the fever, although none fatally.)

In late July the *Supply* was at the Brooklyn Navy Yard, again being fitted out for a cruise. Kell, however, was determined to "get clear of her, by hook or by crook." Unsuccessful in his request to be placed on waiting orders, he finally set out with a ten-day leave, little realizing that his dream of a happy reunion was to be shattered. Before boarding a steamer for Savannah, Kell stopped at the La Pierre House in Philadelphia to see Tabitha Munroe, who had only recently arrived in that city. He was surprised to find her seriously ill, and before he left her he promised to return with Blanche and the baby.

Tabitha, determined that her son Nattie would receive the same fine Christian education which she herself had been given by Moravian teachers, had decided to enroll him at the Moravian Boarding School at Nazareth Hall, Pennsylvania. Accompanied by John Hutton and the Reverend Seneca G. Bragg, Mrs. Munroe and Nattie boarded a steamer at Savannah. For frail and delicate Tabitha, the trip—which began with their steamer colliding with another—proved to be a nightmare; acute seasickness finally brought on her complete nervous collapse. At the La Pierre House in Philadelphia, Tabitha lingered during a week of "intense misery," before dying on August 4. Summoned by telegram during his wife's illness, Nathan Munroe arrived in Philadelphia too late; he would kiss "the dear lips . . . now cett [*sic*] and icy in death."[47] Blanche and Tadie were given the sad news in Vineville from the Reverend Mr. Reese.[48]

On August 5th, Kell arrived in Macon, only hours after Blanche had learned of her mother's death.

Nathan Munroe, numb with grief, completed the task for which Tabitha had "sacrificed her life." At Nazareth, where he had brought Nattie, he wrote to his daughters of his "agony":

> I will endeavor to arouse my spirit with such strength as God may give me to take care of you my beloved ones. I cannot break up the House where I have seen so much happiness with your angel mother. . . . My poor afflicted Heart is too much stricken to undertake its cares. My dear Bannie, Mr. Kell must lend you back to us while he is gone on his official duties—so that you can keep the house and take care of your poor stricken father and your dear sister.[49]

Days later when he returned to Macon with his wife's body, Nathan, stretching forth his arms to Kell, cried out: "Give me back my child!" With deep feeling, Kell replied: "I will not take her from you."[50]

8

A "SACRED AND HONORABLE DUTY"

Although Kell was granted an extension of his leave, he was determined to gain additional time with Blanche; on August 20 he left for New York to make his request in person. At the Pulaski House in Savannah, a day after leaving Vineville, Kell wrote to Blanche of his hopes for their future:

> You must be convinced my beloved one, not only from often repeated declarations but from the fond love and deep attachment which binds me to you and our precious child, that were I master of my own movements I should be with you always and the constant hope which buoys me up during our separation is that future, which I dream of, when circumstances will permit me to leave a profession so unnatural and blighting to my domestic happiness: by nature I am unfitted for the roving life, home has ever been to me the "dearest spot on earth," but how much more is that home now endeared to me since you have shared it with me and to add yet another link God has blessed me with our dear Boy.[1]

In Philadelphia three days later, Kell revealed to his wife what had been in his heart for many months:

> I hope dear Bannie through God's mercy at the earliest period to unite myself with the church and trust that he will sustain me in so doing. I have long desired it, but have felt myself too prone to sin and now do still so feel, but will trust in him to sustain me, and then should we be separated by broad oceans

> and continents there will be that great comfort to each of us that he watches over us as one and our united prayers will ascend for the guidance of our beloved child.[2]

At the Brooklyn Navy Yard Kell found that Lieutenant Fabius Stanly, a North Carolinian, had replaced Lieutenant Gray as commander of the *Supply*. Months later, when Blanche met Stanly, she considered him "very shrewd":

> [He] is very quick and witty, often cutting and sharp, but still *very* amusing, and tho' I can imagine he would not be either a pleasant Superior officer or sailing Companion, still he can keep a room full of ladies laughing, almost without knowing *at what*—he has a sort of cross and snappish way, that is hard to describe, while with ladies he is very full of flattery and small talk.[3]

Stanly would prove a "disagreeable" commanding officer, and relations between him and Kell were to become strained at sea. Kell learned from him that the *Supply* would sail directly to the La Plata River in South America—a cruise which was expected to be brief.

Unable to secure a detachment from the *Supply*, but successful in having his leave lengthened, Kell returned to Vineville for the time remaining before his ship sailed. He saw his son baptized, with Hettie, Tadie, Baillie, and Charles Spalding as godparents.[4] While in Darien Kell learned that Baillie was interested in buying the "Calder place" not far from the Grove, since he wanted to plant cotton and corn rather than rice, which in the past had proven unprofitable; Baillie had told his mother that he was willing to work for her "with good land but not to toil for naught at the old Grove." After careful deliberation Margery agreed to the purchase, and the sale was negotiated.[5]

By late September Kell was again at the Brooklyn Navy Yard and the *Supply* ready to sail. His cruise (the last Kell would make in the service of the United States) would not be another routine delivery of stores to the Brazil Squadron. They were to be included in a naval expedition sent to back up American claims against Paraguay, whose forces four years earlier had fired upon the steamer *Water Witch.*[6] The expedition was prepared to use force if necessary.

At sea, Kell wrote of experiences which he had had many times, but which he felt would be interesting to Blanche. He tried to convey a picture of his ship riding out a gale, by comparing her to a stallion:

> Picture to yourself a wild horse of the prairie, with nostrils distended and mane flying to the breeze and eyes flashing madness. . . . So madly did the waves dash forward upon us, and then would our good ship as it were, strain every cord to escape the fast following sea, as towering high above it would break close upon our heels, then it was that the ship reminded me of the wild steed of the Prairie. Indeed the Sea was not like itself, but resembled a desert of floating sand driven by the tempest. The sun shone bright in the clear sky above and the wind howled as it lashed the combing sea, driving the spoon drift, like mist through the air, and covering the ocean with a sheet of foam. The scene was grand and magnificent to behold. How constantly are we who travel on the waters of the deep reminded of the wonderful works and goodness of the Creator.[7]

Apparently no one aboard the *Supply* really believed that there would be war. Kell felt that Paraguayan dictator Carlos Antonio Lopez[8] would "act the wiser part" and "early negotiate for an honorable peace." On December 5, when the *Supply* arrived at Montevideo, there was still no anxiety, although Lopez had announced his refusal to pay any indemnity. Once the entire American force arrived, Kell believed, Lopez would be cowed into making a peaceful settlement. Although optimistic about peace, Kell was continually obliged to allay the fears of his wife and mother raised by newspaper accounts of the expedition. He was able to report that the reparations demand had been reduced to a "pitiful amount, which Lopez will no doubt gladly pay for peace." Kell located a caricature sketch of President Lopez, which showed him with "fat jowels [*sic*] and a sharp head." None of the Americans had any respect for the man said to be the "greatest tyrant . . . in this part of South America."[9]

On December 22 Kell was delighted to see his friend Dr. Fahs, now Passed Assistant Surgeon on the *Water Witch*. Fahs wrote in his diary for that day:

> I got a boat and went aboard to see my much esteemed Mr. Kell, who was as much delighted as I was. . . . We spent several hours together talking over past happy days. He showed me a Daguere of his wife and child—the former looked as natural as life. I was much struck with her supremely happy expression of countenance as she gazed upon the innocent babe that rested upon her knees.[10]

The arrival of the sloop *Preble* gave Kell opportunity to see other old friends—Lieutenants Bob Minor, K. Randolph Breese, and Riegart B. Lowry. Unwilling to miss any action, Kell submitted a request to accompany the *Preble* upriver to Corrientes, the rendezvous of the squadron, at the confluence of the La Plata and Parana Rivers. He was not "spoiling for a fight," he wrote, but only longed to "break the monotony" by seeing the interior of the country.[11]

Aboard the *Preble* Kell shared Bob Minor's cabin and delighted in his friend's "dear Society." Far from being a guest, however, he shared in the watches and other lieutenants' duties. The Americans hoped to awe the enemy with their superior force but if necessary were prepared to batter down his forts "at such distances that his show can not reach us, for he has no guns to compare with ours."[12] At Rosario on January 28, they learned that General José Justo de Urquiza of the Argentine Confederation was advising Lopez to negotiate. Fellow-dictator Urquiza was afraid that an American-Paraguayan collision would upset the *status quo* in his own country. Not long afterward the men of the *Preble* learned that Commissioner Bowlin and Commodore W. B. Shubrick had been "graciously received" by Lopez and negotiations completed.[13] At Parana a reception was given to General Urquiza, and Kell found him to be an "agreeable and accomplished gentleman." With the shift in events, Americans were no longer viewed with suspicion and hatred; according to Fahs, the local people "have learned to love us and therefore our nation." In his view, the "moral effect" of the expedition had done "more good for the United States than all the conquests she could have made."[14]

As the *Preble* returned downriver, Kell wrote once more of his resolve never again to be separated from his family. So great was his anxiety about Blanche and the baby that he was determined to resign rather than be sent to sea again: "Before it is too late and I am too old to change I must seek some other work whereby to make my living."[15]

On February 22 at Rosario they found the other vessels of the expedition all gaily decorated in honor of Washington's birthday. Kell was "joyfully welcomed" by his fellow officers on the *Supply*, who demanded the hat and epaulettes of Lopez which he had earlier promised to capture and distribute as trophies of war.[16] At Montevideo soon afterward, all waited eagerly for orders to sail homeward. Kell had a special reason to be impatient. Blanche was again pregnant, and he hoped to be with her before the birth of their second child. He could imagine Munroe, now fifteen months old, in "his little carriage, followed by a troop of Negro children made perfectly happy at being allowed to add to his amusement, at which he is equally joyful."[17]

On May 8, 1859, the *Supply* came to anchor at Brooklyn Navy Yard, and Kell immediately sent a wire to Vineville. He was more confident than ever of securing a shore station. Captain McIntosh had been given the command of the Warrington Navy Yard near Pensacola and had advised his cousin to apply for assignment there.

On the first Sunday after his return to his wife, Kell, true to his promise, was confirmed by Bishop Elliott at Christ Church, much to the gratification of his family and father-in-law. He had returned in time. On June 2, a second son, named after his father, was born at Sylvan Lodge.

Kell's request for assignment to Warrington Navy Yard was approved, and his orders reached him while with his family on the coast. Relieved by this news, Kell spent the next weeks riding about the Grove, absorbed in the old place. He had shaved off his heavy beard and was once again as Blanche remembered him, "a handsome young man."[18]

On July 25, 1859, Kell reported to Captain McIntosh at the Warrington Navy Yard. It had been over seventeen years since he had sailed as a "green" reefer under his cousin's command aboard the *Falmouth*. Now he was sorry to find Captain McIntosh looking "very badly" and troubled with a "distressing cough." Of the Yard itself, Kell wrote glowing accounts, comparing the climate, with its pleasant sea breezes, to that of the Ridge. He was soon at work on a vegetable garden in anticipation of the arrival of his family.

Kell's duties at Warrington began at 7 a.m. with the mustering of the laborers and mechanics, but after dinner (3 p.m.) he was usually free for the remainder of the day. Soon, moreover, he was relieved of the early morning duties by the arrival of another lieutenant, his senior in grade. As second, or junior, lieutenant, Kell's duty hours were reduced to five hours on ordinary days. Lieutenant Charles W. Hays, a "pleasant gentleman from Alabama," was the new officer, and he and Kell kept house together until the arrival of Hays' family. Captain McIntosh, too, looked forward to the arrival of his wife, Lydia, and three daughters in the fall. Lachlan H. McIntosh was already at Warrington to serve as his uncle's secretary.[19]

In early September Lieutenant Hays' family arrived, and Kell moved into the house designated for the junior lieutenant to "commence housekeeping alone, a dreary prospect for the next six weeks."[20] A hurricane and the grounding of the steamer *Fulton* in September brought added duties. Nothing, however, could take Kell's mind off Blanche and their two boys. Writing to her, he confessed that her "sweet company and endearing love" alone could make him happy: "Oh Bannie, would that I could look forward to the time when we were never again to be separated on earth!"[21]

From September 29 to October 5, Kell sat on the court of inquiry investigating the grounding of the *Fulton*, a duty which he feared might delay his request for a thirty-day leave of absence. The request was approved, however, and in mid-October he was at Vineville to make the preparations for moving his family to the Yard.

During a visit to "Rushland," the new McIntosh County

property, Kell found Baillie optimistic over his first cotton yield; the sea-island variety had twice the value of ordinary short-staple cotton.[22] To Margery Kell's relief, Kell agreed to assume responsibility for the notes due on Rushland, with a $1,000 loan from Nathan Munroe and $250 from a Savannah banker. However, Margery had other matters to worry her. Kate Rhett, once a "good neighbor and loving friend," was now forbidden by her husband to have anything to do with the Kells. Margery wished that he would "sell out." Then, too, she was having trouble with her son-in-law, Charles Spalding. Charles was criticizing Margery for not having divided up her property years ago, since he feared that Evelyn might be deprived of what was legally due her. In a letter meant for Kell to read, Charles wrote his mother-in-law:

> There has been a want of compliance with the law in this case which makes some unnecessary difficulty. When you became a widow, the law required that you or some one for you, should administer upon your husband's estate—as he died intestate—and also that, upon the coming of age of the children, a legal distribution of the property should take place.
>
> So far as I am personally concerned I am willing that the present arrangement should go on for awhile, provided nothing is done which will have a tendency in any way to impair Evelyn's rights.[23]

Kell had earlier wanted the Grove property kept intact because of "so small a force and poor lands," but—with Rushland paid for and returning a "moderate income"—he now approved of a division. Margery hoped that after the division Donny would buy out Charles' and Hettie's share of the Negroes so that he and Baillie would own "a nice little property" together.[24]

Margery Kell became increasingly provoked with Charles for criticizing her handling of her estate. Finally, in exasperation, she made known to Donny that she considered Charles a failure:

> I told [Charles] I never had a voice in the matter but acted by

> his Father's advice in everything and I certainly think the old Gentleman showed himself a better businessman than his Son. They both began life with the same amount of property—one hundred Negroes and a plantation and clear of debt—one left a large family and provided well for all—he gave both Charles and Randolph a hundred Negroes and Plantation and each of his daughters on their marriage 50 Negroes and a plantation and left a handsome property besides, clear of debt—and see what Charles has done with his—no family and now a poor man—so I think I followed the advice of the wisest man. Had I divided the Negroes and given poor Baillie his without any land to plant where would they have been now—my only mistake was in continuing to plant here. Our Negroes have increased by being taken good care of and had they not been sold to buy corn we would have had a handsome property.

Margery assured Donny that he would benefit from any division of the property: "I have it in my power to give my share to whom I please—and you shall have the Lion's share."[25]

Kell, his wife and sons, with two of Mr. Munroe's Negroes, arrived at Warrington on November 7 to find a "hot cup of coffee and a comfortable room at Cousin James'. . . ." They moved into their own house that same day to begin what Blanche would later recall as "*one* brief blissful year."

Blanche was soon made aware of the social responsibilities of a naval officer's wife; receptions, parties, and visits became routine obligations at the Navy Yard and nearby Fort Barrancas. Lydia McIntosh, who knew all about these activities, became advisor and substitute mother to Blanche. Blanche in turn helped the ailing Captain McIntosh by her frequent visits and games of backgammon.

At Christmas the Kells had dinner with the McIntoshes and ate roast turkey, plum pudding, and a Creole specialty, gumbo soup. Cousin James, however, was too ill to leave his bed. Meanwhile, at the Grove, Margery Kell was distributing beef and tobacco to her adult Negroes, while Hettie gave out cakes and apples to the children.[26]

When a live sea turtle arrived as a present from Lieutenant Stanly (now on the *Wyandot*) soon after his arrival at the Yard,

Blanche considered it a peace offering, knowing that he and her husband were "not very good friends." She prevailed upon Kell to call on Stanly and invite him for dinner, which he did, and apparently their past differences aboard the *Supply* were forgotten.

Blanche was soon ready to meet her new social responsibilities. On her twenty-fourth birthday she arranged a dinner-party for the McIntoshes. Along with Lieutenant Stanly's turtle, made into a stew, she served oyster soup, boiled red snapper, wild turkey, baked ham, roast beef, assorted vegetables, apple pudding, and peach and whortleberry pie. It was far from the usual Navy Yard fare, however, as often only fish and oysters were available. The navy families usually depended upon their gardens for vegetables, as it was difficult to obtain them from Pensacola.[27] Sometimes, though, there was the unexpected meal, as when terrapin soup, made from what Blanche considered "shocking looking creatures," became the chief article of diet at the Yard.

Among the guests invited to the Kell home were Captain David G. Farragut[28] and Major John H. Winder,[29] both of whom would gain national attention within a few years. A frequent visitor to the Yard, with his daughter Maggie, was U.S. Senator Stephen R. Mallory of Florida,[30] with whom the Kells became acquainted. Kell's more intimate friends among the naval officers were Bob Minor, Willie Whittle, Jack Cooper, James Gillis, and Lewis Warrington. The Kell home became a rendezvous, and Blanche became accustomed to seeing her husband's friends on the porch or stretched out on the rug, romping with Munroe ("Boysie") and Johnny. Munroe delighted in the attention given him by Bob Minor, the big friend who bought him such presents as a miniature sailor suit. When war and separation came, Minor would reminisce about the "happy days" at Warrington Navy Yard with his good friends, the Kells. He never failed to get a hearty laugh from "old John" when he told Blanche that the two of them were headed to town on a "Champaigne frolic" while she stayed at home to take care of the boys.[31]

One afternoon when the nurses had the children on the

Avenue, a stranger, a lieutenant, walked by. Seeing Munroe, he asked: "Girl, whose child is this?" and exclaimed, "The Devil!" on learning that he was Kell's. He asked the same question of the nurse holding the baby, after which he exploded with, "The devil! Hell! Kell is raising a navy for himself; here's the Commodore, and here's the first lieutenant!" When Blanche later heard of her nurses' encounter, she told her husband and asked what ship had arrived. Laughing heartily, he replied, "That's John Maffitt and the *Crusader*. Tomorrow dress yourself in your prettiest morning dress for he will call on you about 11 o'clock. Maffitt loves ladies and children, and I know he will want to see my wife." The next morning, while hurrying to answer the door, Blanche tore her dress but, nevertheless, greeted Maffitt, telling him of her distress over the accident. He replied, "Oh, Madam, you're lovelier in a torn dress than most people are in a whole one." When Blanche commented that he must have kissed the blarney stone, Maffitt admitted that his parents were Irish, but that he was a "son of the ocean—born at sea."[32] Blanche then told him she had heard that he had condemned her boys to a navy life, of which she heartily disapproved. Learning that she meant to persuade Kell to leave the service, Maffitt exclaimed in mock horror: "Why, your husband is the Apollo of the Navy! Would you deprive us of him? How cruel!" Blanche replied, "Yes, indeed; tomorrow if I could."[33]

Early in 1860 Blanche's brother-in-law, John S. Hutton, received the appointment as U.S. Consul to Hanover. Hattie, who had spent three years in France before her marriage, was ecstatic, and her doctors believed that the "Sea air of the voyage and bracing European climate" would improve her health. On reflection, Blanche decided to approve a final cruise for her husband if it was in the Mediterranean, so that she, her children, and father could spend a "delightful quiet year, or two, in the South of Europe."[34]

With the coming of summer, the Navy Yard and its environs became unhealthy, and Kell was bedridden with "chills and fever." Mosquitoes and fleas became troublesome as never before.

Along with summer came an intense interest in national politics and the presidential candidates. There was no question as to whom the Kells supported. Little Munroe delighted the neighbors by showing off the medallion his grandfather had given him. It showed presidential candidate John C. Breckinridge and his running mate, Joseph Lane. Unable to pronounce the name of the Vice President, Munroe had to be content to name Lane as he proudly displayed his "politics."[35]

Captain McIntosh died on September 1. Kell could be thankful that he had been able to bring some comfort to his Cousin James during his final months. Not long afterward, Blanche, again pregnant, returned to Vineville. Kell accompanied her and the children and then returned alone to Florida.

With the election of Lincoln came an increase in disunion sentiment and talk of state conventions to decide the question of secession. Lachlan McIntosh was one of those who stood "on the fence between North and South," claiming to "see the wrong on both sides." He confided to Blanche: "Of course I am *mum* during all conversations on the subject." The talk of secession did not disturb Kell enough to make him abandon the idea of buying a house in Macon. By late November, however, he had changed his mind, convinced that Georgia would secede and he and his family would face "harder times." Nevertheless, he felt he would be "doubly compensated" by the "honorable action" of his state and by a permanent union with his wife and children, "no more to be invaded by yellow documents." Randolph Spalding assured his friend that Georgia would not "overlook the welfare of her sons in the public service."[36]

Margery Kell was pleased to learn that her son had become a "strong" secessionist, believing that the secession of Georgia would result in Donny's getting a "long leave." She wrote him: "I look forward to having you and your family with us as the greatest blessing that can befall me." Surprisingly, Randolph Spalding, who in the past had always been "a Union man" like his father, was now "strong for secession," while his brother Charles was opposed to disunion.[37]

By December secessionist sentiment had so intensified that

Lachlan McIntosh, who a few weeks before had been neutral, would write Kell from Savannah:

> I am clearly of the opinion, that Georgia will secede, and of *seven states* we may well be assured. We are all of one opinion here, unless perhaps the northern class of merchants, of whom there may be some, who still cherish the idea of Union, it being inseparable when viewed in the light of dollars and cents. The test is at hand for all such however, and we will weed them out as with a hoe. . . . We had better have open and bitter enemies to fight to the death than lukewarm friends to foster to our own detriment. . . . I think were I you I would not resign until the inauguration of Lincoln, . . . while your willingness to serve under the present administration will have its effect. In any event, you will I know "face the music" and will ponder my . . . suggestion.[38]

Kell now shared the view of the secessionists that "the South has borne with the aggressions and insults of the North until it has reached beyond the point of compromise." He had decided to "abide the will of the state and trust that whatever course is taken, will result for her good, as well as for our interest as individuals." However, Kell feared that the more radical politicians, "inflamed by a misdirected patriotism of speech," might bring Georgia into "an undignified and perilous position."[39]

Despite his decision to follow his state in whatever direction she chose, Kell would demonstrate no disloyalty to the United States while still in her service. When a United States court of inquiry later investigated the circumstances behind the surrender of Warrington Navy Yard to the Florida secessionists, the civil engineer of the Yard testified: "Lieutenant Kell always said that when Georgia seceded he would resign. This he did, but as long as he remained in the service he acted in good faith. . . ."[40]

On December 19 at Sylvan Lodge, a daughter, Blanche, was born, and on the following day Kell arrived. South Carolina seceded the same day.

When a convention met a Milledgeville on January 16 to

decide on secession for Georgia, Kell was present as an observer. On January 18 (in secret session) the ordinance for secession was adopted.[41] Within an hour after the vote was announced, Kell had returned to his hotel room and written his letter of resignation:

> Georgia having this day resolved to withdraw from the Confederacy of which she has hitherto been a member; It becomes my first duty to the State to which I owe allegiance, to resign my commission as a Lieutenant in the Navy of the United States, which I herewith tender.[42]

It is probable that he was the first Georgian to resign from the service of the United States after that state had seceded. To Kell, this was a "sacred and honorable duty." His decision to resign influenced at least one of his naval friends—fellow Georgian Charles M. Morris, who resigned January 29, 1861.[43] Thirty years later, Kell would have no regrets regarding his course of action:

> I have no apologies to make. While I loved my country, I loved honor more, and stood by my native State and Southland with all the ardor of my nature. Here were my Highland ancestors buried—the brave men who came with Oglethorpe to plant freedom on a Southern soil and leave to their descendants an honorable record of truth, loyalty and courage.[44]

9

THE GEORGIA NAVY

With the secession of his state and his own resignation from the United States Navy, the thirty-eight-year-old Kell had reached the most critical period of his life. As a mature and experienced senior officer, much would be expected of him by Georgia and the Southern Confederacy. Years later Kell recalled that in 1861 he felt his youth was far behind him: "Life began anew for me, stern and sacred duties, to which I gave myself with the best ability at my command."[1]

Mary Kell, like her mother, had the mistaken view that Donny would now be home "for a long time." And yet, Mary was aware that unless the seceding states were "sufficiently numerous and united" there was a strong likelihood of war. Realizing the "frightful" odds against the South, she anticipated the organization of an "efficient and strong coast guard."[2] Baillie had already joined a militia unit.

The week after his resignation, Kell returned to Warrington Navy Yard to put his affairs in order. During his absence the Yard had been surrendered and was now controlled by troops and naval personnel representing the seceded state of Florida. The officers with Union sympathies had left, but Commander Ebenezer Farrand, a New Yorker, and Lieutenant Francis B. Renshaw, a Pennsylvanian, had remained to serve the Southern cause. Another Pennsylvanian, Passed Assistant Surgeon William S. Bishop, to whom the Kells had become much attached, had left for the North with "almost a broken heart." Kell learned that in the course of three days Bishop had "so changed that he could scarcely be recognized as the same man."[3]

Kell was surprised to find that the new commandant of the Yard was Captain Victor Randolph, now in the service of Florida, whom he had not seen since his court-martial. Seeing him again brought back a flood of unpleasant memories for Kell, although neither man referred to their association of twelve years before.[4] After being received "with great cordiality" by Randolph, Kell was offered "the conveniences of the Yard."[5]

Kell's house was being used as official headquarters by the new authorities, but Mrs. Farrand had moved the pictures, silver, and other valuables into her own home for safekeeping. Missing, however, were Blanche's preserves, jams, jellies, and pickles. Although he had permission to remove or dispose of whatever he could, Kell was unable to find many buyers, and he lacked transportation for the larger items. However, he considered his loss of two or three hundred dollars as a "trifling" amount compared to that of others. After spending less than twenty-four hours at the Yard, he returned to Vineville.

On January 30 Kell received from the Adjutant General of Georgia, Henry C. Wayne, an offer from Governor Joseph E. Brown of an appointment in the Naval Service of Georgia, with the same pay and allowances as provided by the United States. Kell accepted without hesitation.

On February 13, at Milledgeville, he was commissioned a commander in the state service. On that day he also took the oath of allegiance before Judge Eugenius A. Nisbet. Nisbet was the man who had earlier drafted the ordinance of secession. The oath read:

> I *John McIntosh Kell,* do solemnly swear . . . that I will bear true allegiance to the State of Georgia, and that I will serve her honestly and faithfully against all her enemies or opposers whatsoever, and observe and obey the orders of the Governor of the State of Georgia, and the orders of the officers appointed over me according to the rules and articles for the government of the Navies of Georgia, so long as I remain under the control

> of Georgia, and should I be transferred by said State to the Confederacy of States, which have seceded or may secede from the government of the United States, and may adopt a confederated Government, I will thenceforth bear like allegiance, and render like services to said confederacy, by whatever name it may be known.[6]

Also in February, Captain Josiah Tattnall, one of the navy's veteran officers,[7] resigned to serve his native state; he became Flag Officer of the Georgia Navy. If during his life Kell had heroes, Josiah Tattnall was among them. From their brief association he considered him to be the most "perfect gentleman and sailor" he ever knew.[8]

Although Georgia had competent senior officers in Tattnall, Kell, James D. Bulloch, and Lieutenants Aeneas Armstrong[9] and Charles M. Morris, she still had no navy. Adjutant General Wayne was desperately trying to secure vessels, even resorting to sending agents North. By mid-February he had located a vessel, the *Everglade*,[10] which had formerly carried passengers in the inland passage between Savannah and Jacksonville. It was believed that the steamer, a paddle wheeler with engine and boiler on deck, could be converted into a gunboat for coast defense. Renamed the *Savannah*, she would become the flagship of the Georgia Navy, which by May of 1861 would include three other vessels; none of these, however, was equal to the task of defending the coast from invasion.

On February 20 Kell left Blanche and the children at Darien and proceeded to Savannah. During his one day at Rushland, Kell had "walked all over the plantation, examined all the ditches,... planted his Grape-roots and cuttings," and appeared to Baillie "the most eager, interested man" he had ever seen.[11] At the "Georgia Naval Rendezvous" in Savannah, Kell joined Charles Morris, Lachlan McIntosh (appointed Purser in the Georgia Navy), and Assistant Surgeon Thomas J. Charlton in their effort to enlist a crew for the *Savannah*, which had not yet arrived. They hoped to recruit at least fifty men.

There is no record of Kell's reaction to the *Savannah* when he first boarded her on February 24. It was probably much like that of his friend John Maffitt, who, as her commander three months later, damned her an "absurd abortion of a man-of-war."[12] According to another naval authority, Captain James D. Bulloch, "a rocket exploding among the flimsy joiner work of her deck cabins would have set her on fire, and a single shell . . . would have blown her up."[13]

Kell's official orders were to provide "such protection to the persons and property of the sea islands and of the coast as his vessel [could] afford." As the only vessel in state service, the *Savannah* was to cruise from the Savannah to the St. Mary's river, "with a view of giving confidence to the planters along the coast and assurance of security in their property." Kell and Morris were instructed to "make the Savannah do as much duty as can be had out of her."[14]

While the purchase of the *Savannah* was being completed, Kell and his newly arrived midshipmen—James A. Meriwether, Isaac C. Holcomb, and Richard F. Armstrong (all formerly midshipmen in United States service)—lived aboard the brig *Bonita* in Savannah harbor. Over fifty men had been shipped, but only five or six of these were experienced sailors. Not a single Negro could be persuaded or bribed to ship aboard the *Savannah* as a servant, apparently because of fear.

After an inspection of the ship, the chief engineer reported that unless repaired her boiler would not last a month.[15] Kell was working almost constantly, organizing and ordering the many items needed for a vessel of war. To his disgust, he found that it required a search of most of the shops in the city to locate even minor items. Finally, on February 28 he took formal command of the *Savannah*. Work—especially the repairing of the ship's boiler—was "all engrossing."[16]

Meanwhile, Blanche was becoming increasingly worried over the reports of "war, war, war," although her father had resigned himself to the prospect. He wrote:

> It is the price we pay for liberty. . . . I trust, hope and pray that a returning sense of right and justice in [*sic*] the part of the North may avert War, and that God will interpose to prevent anarchy and bloodshed. But He knows best and We must trust Him.[17]

The unrest of the times was also affecting the Negroes on the coast. Sixty slaves from a plantation near Rushland ran off, and, on returning, announced that on March 4 they expected to be free. Reading Lincoln's inaugural address of that date, Kell observed: "I do not think it is calculated much to intimidate the President of our Southern Confederacy."[18] In Vineville, Nathan Munroe took a different view:

> The stubborn madness and obstinate imbecility of the new administration as foreshadowed in Lincoln's inaugural looks very much like they will never learn wisdom without a trial of Southern mettle. Still we hope that omniscient wisdom may overrule their folly.[19]

On March 8 the *Savannah* steamed to Fernandina, Florida, to collect two cannon from Fort Clinch on Amelia Island to be delivered to Fort Pulaski. Now manned by sixty-one men, she had aboard another senior officer—Lieutenant Aeneas Armstrong, brother of Midshipman Armstrong. At midnight on the 8th, Kell brought his ship to anchor a mile below Darien and went ashore to surprise his family. He found his "poor little wife worn out with anxiety."[20] As for Kell himself, Blanche observed that he was "almost run off his feet and out of his wits attending to the Steamer." During the several hours he was with his wife he seemed "very anxious and uneasy." Kell was afraid that some of his men, having a month's advance pay and being "very new to military discipline," might "get on a frolic," or even desert. In spite of such fears, however, he praised the men as "very good and orderly."[21]

With a "heavy heart, and under severe trial," Kell left his family at noon the next day, and the *Savannah* steamed southward to Fernandina. Kell was optimistic that his crew could become a "formidable body" when properly drilled; their arms consisted of revolvers, cutlasses, and pikes. There was as yet no heavy armament aboard the *Savannah*, but two twelve-pound howitzers back in Savannah would be brought aboard as soon as carriages could be provided.

At Fernandina, learning that the governor of Florida refused to part with the guns, Kell telegraphed Governor Brown and was told to return to Savannah without them. On his return Kell found that the Governor and Flag Officer Tattnall had arrived to inspect the *Savannah* and the *Huntress*, a vessel which had been purchased in New York. Tattnall would find no cause for optimism even later when the *Resolute* and the *Lady Davis* were added to his "squadron." He would admit to an English journalist: "I have no fleet. Long before the Southern Confederacy has a fleet that can cope with the Stars and Stripes, my bones will be white in the grave.[22] His own brief experience with the *Savannah* convinced Kell that that vessel could never be used for ocean cruising. The best he could say of her was that with her upper saloon removed she might be "adopted to island navigation to run along the coast in moderate weather."[23]

Kell's next "cruise" allowed him three days at Darien, during which the division of the Grove property was finally settled. He brought Blanche a spyglass, as he knew that she spent much of her time on the housetop watching for his ship. The three midshipmen were invited to dine at the Grove, and Blanche found them "a pleasant set of young men, all from the up country, and all much put out with the sandflies."[24] She already knew the family of young Dick Armstrong[25] from Macon; his mother had been like a second mother to her during her girlhood.

Toward the middle of April, Kell brought the *Savannah* to anchor off old Sunbury, the town of his boyhood memories. It had now been over twenty years since a ship had appeared at what had long been a dying town. Kell wanted to study the navigation at Sunbury in preparation for a duty he expected soon—bringing the body of Captain James McIntosh to its final resting place. To Kell's surprise, the sight—and noise—of the steamer caused the "terror stricken inhabitants" to believe that the Yankees had arrived. One man was seen fleeing into the woods.[26]

Soon afterward Kell was ordered to pick up the Jackson Artillery Company (a Macon unit) at St. Simon's Island and convey them to Savannah. While at Brunswick he learned of the bombardment and surrender of Fort Sumter. At the Grove, "a great excitement prevailed" when the news came. Neighbor Rhett, at his Altamaha plantation for "rest and recreation," became like a "wild beast in a cage," fearing for his three sons who had participated in the engagement. To Blanche the news was disastrous: "How terrible the future seems, if we are indeed to have a civil war! May God have Mercy upon us, for only His Almighty arm can now prevail."[27] Later, Nathan Munroe would regard Lincoln's call for troops as "bluster and bravado," believing that it would bring the remaining slave states into the Confederacy.[28]

Within several days of his conveying the body of Captain McIntosh to Sunbury,[29] Kell's service with the Georgia Navy came to an abrupt end. At Savannah confidential orders reached him, dated April 17, from Montgomery:

> Proceed to New Orleans and report to Commander Raphael Semmes C.S. Navy for duty.
>
> S. R. Mallory
> Sec. of Navy[30]

On May 1 Kell and his family arrived at Vineville, and that afternoon the new baby was baptized at Christ Church. Late that night, while the children were asleep, Kell took his departure. Months later, during her husband's absence, Blanche confided to her private journal:

> Never shall I forget the agony of this parting. I wrote him that it was to me like the rending of body and soul. His grief was equal to mine. He hung over each little sleeping treasure—went from trundle bed to cradle—then from cradle back to bed, gently kissing each one many times. . . . I told him that I could not give him up, that I felt as if some great calamity would befall me, but he said, "My sweet wife, have more faith; you feel so, perhaps, because in our separation you lost your Mother." Then we knelt down together and committed each other and our little ones to God's holy care and keeping. I felt this parting so keenly that I made myself sick with weeping. I was unable to be up the next morning. When my bright boy awoke he asked

> for his Father and I told him he had gone far away, but that he kissed him many times for "Goodbye" the night before. He then said, "My poor papa. I'll never see him anymore." I said, "Oh, my son, don't talk so. We will ask God to bring dear papa back."[31]

A week before her husband's departure, Blanche had written to her father: "I have no courage where my own are so nearly concerned. . . . I would never have been among the 'heroic women of the Revolution.' " Three years and four months were to elapse before she would see her husband again, and by that time two of their children would be dead. For both Kell and his wife, a time of great trial had come.

ILLUSTRATIONS

First taste of war: the Battle of Santa Clara January 2, 1847.

"Ghost Ship" at anchor in New Harbour, Singapore, December, 1863.

PHOTO TAKEN IN 1861—
COLLECTION OF MUNROE D 'ANTIGNAC

Blanche, Boysie, Dot (on her mother's lap), and Johnny as Kell remembered them.

Peabody Museum, Salem, Mass.
The Luff aboard his ship off South Africa in 1863.

Museum of the Confederacy
The *Alabama*, most successful of the Confederate raiders.

Philadelphia Museum of Art

The end of the *Alabama,* as seen by Edouard Manet.

Adjutant General Kell

COLLECTION OF MUNROE D' ANTIGNAC
Kell's Birthplace: Laurel Grove, as sketched by Hetty Kell

10

C.S.S. SUMTER

The duties of a ship's executive officer require that officer to have a thorough knowledge of his ship and the way she handles in all situations; he must also be familiar with the duties of every officer and sailor aboard. It has correctly been said of the naval executive officer: "All the drudgery of the ship is his. . . . The demand upon his temper and his abilities is enormous." Kell admitted that "all devolves upon me." The duties of a ship's executive officer in the old navy have been described by Francis A. Roe, Kell's fellow shipmate aboard the *Albany*. According to Roe:

> There is no position so wearying, none so trying, none so much needing wisdom and good judgment, good temper and professional skill. In his general deportment he is supposed to represent the captain's wishes, and yet avoid any blunder the captain himself may make. He is the great *conservative* element in a ship-of-war. He stands between officers and themselves, between officers and men, and, as need be, between the captain and all the rest.[1]

However, Kell thought hard work had its advantages: "It may be all the better for me since my mind has not had time to dwell upon the home that is so dear to me."[2] He assured his wife that under no circumstances other than the present emergency would he have left her and the children:

> Were it not for this unjust and unholy war made upon our beloved country, when our homes, our honor, and all that is dear to us on earth is assailed by a fanatic and wretched people who would even enslave us if they could I feel assured that under no other circumstances could I have left you for this length of time.[3]

Yet Kell had cause to be gratified by his new position. His orders to New Orleans had been personally approved by Commander Semmes, who had remembered the young passed midshipman of twelve years before. Semmes later wrote: "When it was decided, at Montgomery, that I was to have the *Sumter*, I at once thought of Kell, and, at my request, he was ordered to the ship."[4] The ship in question, the *Havana* (a former mail steamer on the New Orleans to Havana line), was to be refitted and commissioned as the *Sumter*, the first of the Confederate commerce raiders. Semmes was anxious for the chance to cripple Northern resources through this means. Kell, as his "luff," could perform more valuable service for his country on the high seas than on the pitifully inadequate *Savannah*.

The *Sumter*, however, would not be ready for several weeks; then, she must be gotten past the blockade. Throughout May and into June they worked, until the ship could hardly be recognized at the former *Havana*.[5]

As the *Sumter* stood downriver awaiting an opportunity to elude the U.S.S. *Brooklyn*, Kell made arrangements for his family's welfare. The Confederate Navy Agent was to provide his wife with an allotment of $100 per month for the next two years. Nathan Munroe was to be Kell's attorney during his absence. Among the last tokens of love sent to Vineville was a package containing toys for the children and a recent daguerreotype for Blanche. He wrote that the *Sumter* would have no announced cruising schedule as her movements were secret. With a "pleasant set of officers, a good crew, and a fine ship," he was optimistic about success.

On June 30 the *Sumter* made a hairbreadth escape to the open sea, after which her officers and crew drank a toast to their present and future success. That evening one of the *Sumter's* officers wrote in his journal:

> The Sumter has run the blockade at last! She is now bounding over the blue waters of the Gulf of Mexico; and if she does not soon slacken speed she will ere many days be in the Caribbean Sea. Everything was managed admirably.[6]

Blanche learned of the escape of the *Sumter* through the newspapers. It would be months before she would receive firsthand news from her husband, but meanwhile the picture taken of him at New Orleans would be some comfort. It showed a resolute, determined-looking man of erect bearing. However, the closely trimmed beard and shaven upper lip would not remain so; at the time he left New Orleans, Kell vowed that no razor or scissors would touch his face until he was once again with his family. After several months at sea, the most outstanding feature of Semmes' "luff" would be "a magnificent beard, inclining to red."[7] Along with Kell's impressive height and bearing, the beard made him appear even more the dedicated, veteran sea dog. In contrast, Semmes' carefully waxed moustaches and imperial-style chin whiskers (earning him the nicknames "Old Beeswax," "Old Bim," and "Marshall Pomp" by his sailors) made him appear more of a scholar than a naval officer. Semmes, although a highly competent officer, possessed certain traits that had made him a controversial figure even before his present assignment. He was not one whom most men could get to know well, and he had long been known as a maverick and a loner. Semmes took his causes seriously, and he was now utterly devoted to serving the new Confederacy in the best way he could. Fortunately for both Semmes and Kell, they could work together effectively. Semmes had made an ideal choise of a "luff." However, this was no partnership; Semmes was number *one* on his ship and expected the complete loyalty of his officers and men. In later years Kell admitted to his wife: "I could not remonstrate with Captain Semmes; he was my superior officer and fifteen years my senior."[8]

After the war Kell would publicly reveal little of his relationship with Semmes, nor would he write of his commander except in the most complimentary terms. In Kell, Semmes had a man who met the most rigid requirements of his position. As naval authority Roe has observed: "The relations of the captain and the executive officer must be intimate and to a great degree confidential. There must be mutual confidence, or there will be mutual distrust."[9] Dr. Francis L. Galt, the officer who was closest to both Semmes and Kell, bears this out: "[Kell's] cordial co-operation with his commander led to very pleasant intimate relations."[10] Another glimpse of the relationship between the two is revealed in the recollections of a Confederate midshipman who served aboard C.S.S. *Georgia:*

> Captain Semmes was an austere and formal man, and with the exeception of Dr. Galt, the surgeon, and Mr. Kell, his first lieutenant, he rarely held any intercourse with his officers except officially. He waxed the ends of his mustache (which the sailors called his "st'unsail booms") and he would pace the quarter-deck alone, twisting and retwisting those long ends.[11]

As Semmes saw it, his position necessitated his being reserved and solitary most of the time. Thus his communications with his officers were usually restricted to affairs concerning the ship. It would be a mistake, though, to assume that Semmes was different from most other commanders in his official behavior. His officers and sailors apparently felt a great deal of respect for him, and Semmes was wise enough to know the pitfalls of overexposure or familiarity for one in high command. As Roe observed:

> There is a natural feeling among the crew of every ship, of aversion to see the captain too frequently prowling about, as if seeking to find fault with someone. An instinctive feeling betrays itself, that the captain had better be in his cabin, or taking a quiet walk upon his quarter-deck.[12]

However, Semmes was not always happy with this situation; he wrote, "I felt exceedingly its irksomeness, and was always glad of an opportunity to escape from it."[13]

While the *Sumter* cruised the Caribbean in search of American merchantmen, Kell's family was increasingly exposed to the trials of war. Baillie was now a lieutenant in the McIntosh Regiment of Light Dragoons (Cavalry), while Charles Spalding was lieutenant colonel of the same regiment. They were assigned to the defense of the county, so both were near enough for frequent visits home. In September of 1861 Randolph Spalding became aide-de-camp to General Alexander R. Lawton, with the rank of colonel, and—soon afterward —colonel of the Twenty-ninth Georgia Infantry Regiment.

Although the Kells were often worried over Donny's safety, there was also cause for rejoicing. Hettie sent congratulations to Blanche after reading of the sixth prize taken by the *Sumter*. In September "glorious" news was received that the Queen of Spain had opened up all her ports to ships of the Confederacy. Blanche now felt that her husband would be "quite safe."[14] Unfortunately, however, there would be a continuous flow of false reports that the *Sumter* had been destroyed or captured. Bob Minor (now at the Bureau of Ordnance and Hydrography in Richmond) realized Blanche's concern and tried to comfort her with what official information he received. He hoped Kell would be returned to the Confederacy: "There is duty enough to be done here, and we need clear heads and strong wills to work out the problem of our independence."[15]

With both sons serving the Confederacy, Margery Kell now had to assume all responsibility for property and servants. At sixty-eight years of age she was still better able than her daughters to manage affairs. Mary and Hettie could paint and sew but lacked their mother's drive. So, evidently, did Evelyn, who remained with her mother and sisters while her husband helped in the defense of the coast. By early 1862 Federal incursions along the coast were causing near panic among civilians. Port Royal had fallen the previous fall, leaving Savannah and other points exposed; Fort Pulaski itself was under heavy siege. Leaving the Grove in the care of her trusted servant, Belinda, Margery warned her: "When the Yankees come, you must be *very* civil; say 'do, Massa, don't trouble my old Missis' house'; and be sure and not say a word about your having a *young* master." Belinda was also instructed how to use wet blankets to put out fire in the event of a shell falling on the house. Despite her apparent ability to take the war in stride, Margery was not without fears. As she packed her belongings at her old home, she said: "I could not have courage to do all this if I really thought they would burn our dear old place."[16] At least keeping busy helped her to forget the war, or so she said. Since both Rushland and the Grove were in danger of Yankee raids, Margery rented a house in Liberty County in case they had to leave in a hurry.

By the middle of March, Darien was practically deserted; at Rushland, Margery observed refugees with their loaded wagons passing by almost constantly. Hettie had left by train for Macon, and Mary was already at the house in Liberty County. Margery, with only Evelyn as companion, felt her responsibility "very great... but there appears to be no one to take my place and I look to my God for strength to bear and suffer his will." She had already made plans for leaving Rushland at a moment's notice, with two ox carts to carry her baggage and the Negro children. The Negroes were not to be completely trusted, however. Although they told their mistress they were "satisfied" and "nothing could induce them to go," she found that when "thrown with the enemy... they change their mind." Her experience with a runaway had convinced Margery that it was best not to try to force any change on them.[17]

At Vineville, Blanche, although far from danger, was very much aware of the war. On April 7, 1862, she heard a rumor—supposedly originating from Captain Maffitt—which claimed that Semmes was a "political prisoner" and Kell was now commander of the *Sumter*. Nathan Munroe had heard a different version of the account—that it was *Kell* who was the "political prisoner." However, they later learned the truth: Purser Henry Myers of the *Sumter* was the man in question, having been arrested at Tangier with the former consul to Cadiz. To Nathan, the "pusillamity [*sic*] of the British Government" in not interfering on behalf of the two men was a "stench in his nostrils."[18]

In April Baillie's enlistment expired, and he returned to Rushland to care for his mother and sisters. His mother insisted that if he were drafted he must try to purchase a substitute, as she could not give him up again. Baillie, however, was either unable or unwilling to buy a substitute; at any rate, he was soon back in the army as a private in the Fifth Georgia Cavalry. Margery had decided to remain at Rushland rather than become a refugee. Therefore, before leaving his mother, Baillie hired a man for $100 a year to take charge of the Negroes.

After the fall of Fort Pulaski (April 10, 1862), Charles Spalding resigned his commission to take care of his slaves and those of his deceased brother, Randolph.[19] Charles purchased a 480-acre estate near Quitman in Brooks County, far from the coast, where he could safely keep his Negroes. Although he offered to bring the Kell Negroes with him, Margery declined his offer.

Unknown to his loved ones in Georgia, Kell had arrived at Nassau on June 8, 1862, believing he would soon be reunited with his family. The cruise of the *Sumter* had ended five months before, at the Bay of Gibraltar.

On the morning of January 18, 1862, a group of the British officers stationed at Gibraltar had accompanied Sir William J. Codington, Governor General of the Crown Colony, to the highest elevation of the Rock. There (at 1450 feet above sea level) they could clearly see a vessel aflame several miles away, off the Spanish coast. They could also see another vessel, soon identified as the *Sumter*. One of the Canadian officers—Lieutenant Brown Wallis of the 100th Regiment—years later recalled: "No one had any idea that the *terrible pirate* 'Sumter' was on our side of the Atlantic much less *in* the Mediterranean Sea."[20] At 7 p.m. the *Sumter* rounded Europa Point, entered the Bay of Gibraltar, and came to anchor off the "Old Mole." She had had one of her more successful days, having captured the bark *Neapolitan* (which was burned) and *Investigator* (which, because of her neutral cargo, was released on bond). During a six-month cruise of the Caribbean, off the coast of Brazil, and now near Spain, the *Sumter* had captured eighteen American merchantmen, and of these seven had been burned. Kell, who could take credit with Semmes for her successes, was full of praise for the little ship: "Frail and unseaworthy at best, her career was a marvel. . . . No ship of her size, her frailness, and her armament ever played such havoc on a powerful foe!"[21] One of the British observers on Gibraltar who visited the *Sumter* after her arrival could hardly believe that this was the dreaded "pirate" ship they had heard so much about:

> I could scarcely believe that so poor a vessel could have escaped so many dangers. She is a screw-steamer, with three masts, a funnel strangely out of proportion to her size, and a tall, black hull, so high out of water that she gives you the idea of being insufficiently ballasted. Four 32-pounders peeped from her sides, and a large 8-inch pivot-gun was on her main-deck forward. . . . Her unsightly appearance arises from the alterations that have been made in her decks. In order to afford more accommodation, and to give more cover for the engines and guns, a light temporary flush-deck has been built over what was originally the only deck of the ship. This raises her an additional ten feet out of water, and at the same time dwarfs her masts and funnel. She is crank and leaky. Her engines are partially above the lower-deck, and, with the object of preserving them from the effects of gunshot, they are surrounded by a cylindrical casing of 6-inch wood covered with half-inch bars —a very poor protection against an 8-inch shot. Her officers and crew number ninety in all. The latter are a hardy set of fellows, ready for any work—men who would stick at nothing. They are of all nations—even the Irish brogue was among them. The commander, Captain Semmes, is a reserved, determined-looking man, whose left hand knows not what his right doeth.[22]

A number of other Britishers, including Lieutenant Brown Wallis, soon rowed out to the famous "pirate" ship. The young Confederate officer on deck escorted the men to the wardroom, where wine and conversation were enjoyed. As Wallis sat near the partly opened hatchway, he was startled to hear the booming "clarion" voice of an officer in the process of dressing down a junior officer for having allowed the visitors aboard. When Wallis met the officer of the "clarion" voice, he was thoroughly impressed. As he later recalled, the lieutenant—

Kell—was the "embodiment and realization" of his ideal of a naval officer.[23] During the weeks that followed, Confederate and Canadian became friends, and the latter did all he could to help Kell enjoy his visits to the Rock, even arranging for him to participate in a fox hunt in the adjacent cork forests. On a clear day later that spring, Wallis and Kell, with Lieutenant Robert T. Chapman of the *Sumter*, rode on horseback along the upper ramparts of the Rock. At anchor far below them were ships of all nations, the most striking being the *Warrior*, 380 feet long, the first ironclad vessel in the British navy. She was anchored off the Mole, within half a dozen cable lengths of the *Sumter*, and the latter vessel—less than half her size—looked pitifully "diminutive by contrast." Greatly impressed, Chapman said: "Oh, if we only owned that one ship we could lay waste every seaport city in the Northern states." Kell replied humorously: "Chapman, you are an impetuous fire-eater, and as your senior officer I must inform you that we wouldn't do anything of the kind, because it would not be necessary; for, like Davy Crockett's coon, they would 'crawl down.' "[24]

In port there was no letup in Kell's duties, and he had great difficulty keeping a tight rein on the crew. At every port a certain amount of drunkenness, misconduct, and desertion was anticipated, but now a sizeable number of sailors saw no reason to remain any longer on the *Sumter*. Several of the deserters asked the American consul for protection, including George A. Whipple, a seaman who had been with the ship since New Orleans. Whipple was no Confederate; a native of Massachusetts who happened to be in New Orleans when war broke out, he had shipped on the *Sumter* to avoid being drafted into the army. His true feelings had been revealed when, returning drunk from shore leave, he shouted curses at Captain Semmes and the Confederate flag. Whipple's punishment was extreme; Semmes had him put in irons and a straitjacket and later tied up by his thumbs.[25] Now at Gibraltar, Whipple was able to desert, swearing vengeance against the man who had ordered his punishment. He sought out the American consul and signed a deposition that the *Sumter* had received coal in a neutral port, a fact vehemently denied by Semmes. Later, Whipple shipped aboard the *Kearsarge*, one of the Federal vessels which had arrived to prevent the *Sumter* from escaping to sea. During the next two years aboard the *Kearsarge*, he would dream of revenge.

On the night of March 8, after the *Kearsarge* came to anchor "within a stone's throw" of the *Sumter*, the stillness of the night was broken by exuberant strains of "Dixie," countered by "The Star Spangled Banner." Some of the crew of the *Kearsarge* actually spoke of swimming over to the *Sumter* during the night to sink her.

Earlier, Kell and other officers had made a thorough inspection of their ship. Their report was not encouraging. Boilers, a condenser, important machinery, and the upper works required a complete overhaul; some of the planking was badly worm-eaten.[26] For more than two and a half months, Semmes and his officers remained with the *Sumter*, until on April 7 a telegram arrived from James M. Mason, Special Confederate Commissioner to England. That evening Semmes summoned the wardroom officers to his cabin and asked each his opinion on whether or not to give up the *Sumter*. The decision was unanimous that it would be impossible to get her into proper condition. That night an officer wrote in his journal:

> This news is received on all hands with great joy. We are heartily sick of the life of inactivity we have been leading for the past three months, though much regret will be felt at leaving the old ship which has carried us over so many miles of ocean and through so many perils.[27]

Kell felt the same way: "As we passed out of the harbor of Gibraltar we cast a lingering look at the little vessel that had been our 'home on the rolling deep' during those last exciting months."[28] Kell's orders were to make his way back to the Confederacy and report by letter to Secretary Mallory.[29]

Arriving in England, Kell visited the Huttons at Southhampton, their home since John had resigned his United States consulship to Hanover. In London the Confederate officers met Commissioner Mason, and Kell was "delighted" with the "true Southern hospitality," which included clay pipes and Virginia tobacco.[30] But even more satisfying to Kell was his finding a letter from Blanche, the first and only one to reach him since he had left New Orleans almost a year before. It was dated March 18, 1862. Eagerly Kell devoured every word: Blanche's heartsickness at his long absence and concern for his safety; the state of affairs on the coast affecting his mother and their property; and the death of the friend who had been closer than a brother ("My heart is made sick and sad . . . when I think of the end of poor Randolph, he who I had loved so much").[31] Kell learned too of the false reports and rumors that had been tormenting Blanche. He tried to console her:

> A long long weary time indeed has it been to me my beloved wife, although happy in the knowledge that you and our precious children are with those whose tender care will make home all that it can be in my absence; not so however has been your hard fate, far better would it have been could you have heard nothing of our cruise, rather than to be distressed by the false reports of the Northern papers, whose fiendish fabrications caused me much anxiety for the pain they would give you.[32]

A rendezvous for Confederates and sympathizers near Hampstead, London, was the church (St. Peter's) and parsonage of the Reverend Francis W. Tremlett at Belsize Square. Here, with Tremlett's mother and maiden sister, Louisa, serving as hostesses, Semmes, Kell, and other officers received every attention. Louisa Tremlett accompanied Kell on a shopping expedition and helped him select dresses, shoes, and other articles for Blanche.

Kell was soon aboard the English passenger steamer bound for Nassau. With him was his Cousin John E. Ward, who had long since resigned his appointment as United States Minister to China and was returning to Georgia. Arriving at Nassau on June 8, they found that port bustling with activity. Captain Maffitt was preparing to launch the Confederate raider *Oreto (Florida)* on what would be a highly successful cruise.

Only days from home and family, Kell received news that could only have caused deep anguish: he and Semmes were to return immediately to England. A new ship was being fitted out, and he was again to be Semmes' executive officer. Unlike the *Sumter*, however, this was to be a new and "superior" vessel.

Kell wrote several times to his family from Nassau, repeating his news in case letters were captured. He also sent the box he had intended to deliver personally. His advice regarding the Negroes was that they should be moved into the interior, "far away from the influence of the seaboard." He hoped that Blanche's Uncle Hendley Varner, in Sunnyside, would take charge of them until the end of the war. Kell feared that if the Negroes were left in the charge of anyone else, it could "prove very explosive as well as demoralizing to them, leading an idle life."[33]

On July 13 Semmes and Kell left Nassau and arrived back in England three weeks later. Their months aboard the *Sumter* would prove invaluable experience for them on their new ship, C.S.S. *Alabama*.

11

C.S.S. *ALABAMA*

Arriving at Liverpool, the Confederate officers were surprised to find that "the bird had flown." The *290*[1] (christened *Enrica* at her launching) had left port ten days earlier. However, Commander James Bulloch assured them that he had matters well in hand. Bulloch had ordered the *290* to sea to prevent her from being seized by British authorities. American agents in Britain had learned the purpose of the vessel recently launched at the Laird Shipyard and had demanded immediate seizure. Knowing he must act promptly, Bulloch had staged a mock trial run of the *Enrica* on July 29, complete with a party of guests to allay suspicion. That afternoon Bulloch explained to his guests that he wished to keep the ship out overnight, and they returned to Liverpool by tender. The escape of the *290* had been possible only because of luck and superb timing. Her temporary captain—Matthew J. Butcher, a confidant of Bulloch[2]—had prepared the ship for sea, engaged a crew, and transacted the necessary business. Most of the crew knew the truth about the ship on which they had signed, but Bulloch had no intention of violating international law by enlisting a British crew for a Confederate vessel while within the United Kingdom.[3] However, he had instructed his paymaster—Clarence R. Yonge—to "mix freely with the warrant and petty officers, show interest in their comfort and welfare, and endeavor to excite their interest in the approaching cruise." Yonge was directed to win friends for the cause of the Confederacy by stressing its fight for "liberty." He was instructed further:

> [Captain Semmes] will be a stranger to the ship and crew, and will be in a position of great responsibility and embarrassment. You have it in your power to smooth away some of his difficulties in advance.[4]

Semmes, Kell, and Dr. Galt spent the next several days making preparations for their rendezvous with the *290*. Other officers joined them, including Richard F. Armstrong of the *Sumter*. Recognizing the competence of this officer, Semmes had promoted him from midshipman to second lieutenant of the *290*. Despite his youth (Armstrong had just turned twenty), the young Georgian had more experience and proven ability than the other available Southern officers except Kell. Of Armstrong, Kell would say, "he had all the requisities of a fine and daring officer."[5] Semmes' other senior officers (all young men) included Joseph D. Wilson, a Floridian, as third lieutenant; John Low, an Englishman, as fourth lieutenant; and Arthur Sinclair, of an old naval family, as fifth lieutenant. Then there were Becket K. Howell, a brother of Mrs. Jefferson Davis, as marine officer (despite the fact that there would be no marines aboard the *290)*, and an Englishman, David H. Llewellyn, as assistant surgeon under Dr. Galt. J. S. Bulloch, brother of Commander Bulloch, served as acting master, while Edward Anderson and Eugene Maffitt served as midshipmen. Kell took a special interest in the careers of these young men. The complement of officers was sufficient even before Semmes left Liverpool.

On August 11 Kell received a visit from John Hutton, who brought him letters from Blanche dated April 4 and May 27. Kell wrote to reassure his wife that if he were captured he would not be treated as a "pirate": "They dare not treat us with more harshness than others as they know well some of their high officials will suffer for it."[6] Blanche was to continue sending her letters in care of her sister Hattie or to Frazer, Trenholm and Company in Liverpool. Kell assured her that he would write from each port at which they stopped.

On August 13 the Confederate officers, including Commander Bulloch, were aboard the steamship *Bahama*. Seven days later they reached their point of rendezvous: Praya Bay at the Island of Terceira in the Azores. They gazed eagerly at the vessel for which the Confederates held such high hopes. For Kell it was love at first sight. As he recalled many years later: "I think she was the most beautiful ship that ever touched the sea."[7] Soon they were aboard her. After the fragile *Sumter*, the *290* was close to luxury. She was built of the best available materials, copper-fastened, with condensing apparatus and a cooling tank to supply fresh water at sea. Under steam and sail (she was bark-rigged) the *290* was capable of speeds up to 13 knots.[8] However, she would ordinarily be under sail—her hatches closed and chimney stack lowered—disguised as a merchant ship. No Confederate ensign would fly from her rigging until she had thus deceived her prey.

Bulloch already had a deep attachment to the ship to which he had "given so much care." He confessed: "Every aspiration of my heart is bound up in her."[9] Originally, Bulloch was to have commanded the *290*, but the pressing need for his services as agent in England had prevented this. The Confederacy had to have ships built abroad for her infant navy.

The crew of the *290* was already busily engaged in transferring stores, coal, and heavy guns from the bark *Agrippina* (consort to the *290*) and would now transfer more guns, powder, and shell from the *Bahama*. The work continued over the next three days, after the vessels were moved outside Portuguese territorial waters to avoid any incident with the authorities. All went well, despite the difficulties created by the ocean swells.

Semmes was still left with the problem of enlisting a crew. He had been sizing up the sailors, including those who had arrived with him on the *Bahama*. By now few were ignorant of the identity and mission of the *290*. Shrewdly, a number of sailors refused to commit themselves. Semmes noted: "The sharp fellows, thinking I am dependent upon them for a crew, are holding back and trying to drive a hard bargain with me."[10] On August 24 the vessels headed for open sea; several miles off the harbor, Semmes made his move. Aboard the *Bahama* a starboard bow gun was fired, and on the *290* the English flag was hauled down and the Confederate ensign—a "splendid white flag" with cross and stars in the upper quarter—was raised. The band broke into "Dixie," followed by cheers from the officers and sailors on both vessels. The *290* was now the Confederate States Steamer *Alabama*. Semmes, admittedly "nervous about the success of this operation," had all hands piped aft to the quarter-deck of the *Bahama*. His secretary, Breedlove Smith, read Semmes' commission and orders from the Confederate government. Then Semmes addressed the men:

> Now, my lads, there is the ship; she is as fine a vessel as ever floated. There is a chance which seldom offers itself to a British seaman—that is, to make a little money. I am not going to put you alongside of a frigate at first, but after I have got you drilled a little, I will give you a nice little fight. There are only six ships that I am afraid of in the U.S. Navy. We are going to burn, sink, and destroy the commerce of the United States. Your prize-money will be divided proportionately, according to each man's rank, something similar to the English Navy. . . . There is Mr. Kell on the deck, and all who are desirous of going with me, let them go aft, and give Mr. Kell their names.[11]

Semmes addressed those he saw holding back: "Any of you that thinks he cannot stand to his gun, I don't want."

The men who signed were motivated primarily by Semmes' promise of generous pay and prize money—in gold—good food, kind treatment, and grog served twice a day. Kell would admit: "A sailor is a sailor. He has few attachments, and as a general thing doesn't care what flag he is under."[12] Semmes had been obliged to accept the men's terms. His seamen were promised a monthly *L* 4 10s., petty officers *L* 5 and *L* 6, and firemen *L* 7. But Semmes was glad to get the men on even these generous terms: "I was afraid a large bounty in addition would be demanded of me."[13] With a crew of eighty-two sailors, he needed forty more men to make up a full complement. That evening was spent in preparing allotments for the wives of some of the men and paying two months advance wages. Except for occasional small allowances, the men would not receive the rest of their pay until the end of the cruise. Prize money was to be paid after the war had ended. One of the English sailors who signed on that day penned in his journal: "I became a naval sailor in this fine ship. I shall be happy and perhaps become rich." The man was favorably impressed with his new captain: "He is always kind and polite to everyone and he speaks like a Devon man. I think that he is a fine and good man."[14]

Late at night Commander Bulloch, accompanied by Captain Butcher and the sailors who refused to sign on the *Alabama*, steamed away on the *Bahama* back to Liverpool. Semmes lost no time in setting his own course for open sea. The next morning the *Alabama* rolled and tumbled in the North Atlantic as Kell began the job of getting things organized. Semmes, retiring below "to quiet worn nerves," knew that his "luff" had no easy job ahead. He noted in his journal: "The first lieutenant is trying to bring order out of chaos, in getting his crew into shape."[15] It would take a week to put the ship in order. The most urgent work was getting the eight guns (six 32-pounders and two pivot guns—an 8-inch solid shot and a 100-pound Blakely rifled gun) ready for firing and the men assigned to battle stations. Kell, the office responsible for disciplining and drilling the crew, found them to be a "mixture." Thirty or so were "very fine, adventurous seamen," but the remaining fifty, from the slums of Liverpool, "looked as if they would need some man-of-war discipline to make anything of them."[16] Semmes was quite frank in his evaluation: "One has all sorts of characters to deal with in a ship's crew, and a vigorous arm is necessary. The boys . . . are most incorrigible young rascals."[17] It would take three months before Semmes considered his crew to be in "fair fighting trim." He took satisfaction in maintaining the discipline he considered appropriate for a ship-of-war:

> My code was like that of the Medes and Persians—it was never relaxed. The moment a man offended, he was seized and confined in irons, and, if the offense was a grave one, a court-martial

> was sitting on his case in less than twenty-four hours. The willing and obedient were treated with humanity and kindness; the turbulent were jerked down, with a strong hand, and made submissive to discipline. I was as rigid with the officers as with the crew, though, of course, in a different way. . . . My crew were never so happy as when they had plenty to do, and but little to think about. Indeed, as to the thinking, I allowed them to do very little of that.[18]

In spite of this, the depositions of sea captains and mates from vessels captured by the *Alabama* indicate something of the difficulties being faced by Semmes and his officers. One observed: "The officers are Southerners, and with the exception of the captain and first lieutenant seem ignorant of their sea duties. The discipline on board was not very good, though the men seemed to be good seamen. They were over an hour setting the two top-gallant sails." And another: "I observed that there was no discipline on board the steamer excepting when Capt. Semmes or Lieut. Kell was on deck."[19] Semmes himself—in entries in his journal—gives ample evidence of dissatisfaction on the part of the crew. As he believed, many of his sailors "thought they were shipping in a sort of privateer, where they would have a jolly good time and plenty of license." He observed:

> Constant cruising, vigilance against being surprised by the enemy, salt provisions, and a deprivation of the pleasures of port . . . are probably what most of them did not expect. A tight rein and plenty of work will cure the evil.[20]

The sailors were not the only ones who needed disciplining. Chief Engineer Miles J. Freeman, who had served in the same capacity aboard the *Sumter*, was suspended for disobeying orders and using "improper language" to Kell. As Semmes saw the incident: "Engineers in general seem to think that they have a sort of separate command, and that they are, to some extent, independent of the first lieutenant."[21] It was not long, however, before Freeman was reinstated as chief engineer.

The *Alabama* had been at sea ten days when—on September 5th—the whaling ship *Ocmulgee* was sighted. She was to be the first of sixty-five prizes of the Confederate raider during the twenty-two months of her cruise. Semmes' orders were to destroy the commerce of the North, but to avoid engagements with the enemy's vessels of war. In the case of the *Ocmulgee*, capture was easy, as her crew were at work on a whale lashed alongside the ship. The officers were allowed to bring off a trunk of clothes each and the sailors a bag apiece. Stores from the prize were brought aboard the *Alabama*, and the next morning she was burned. Aboard the *Alabama* the officers of the *Ocmulgee* were put in irons in retaliation for the treatment of Paymaster Myers of the *Sumter*. The use of irons would continue with the prisoners (officers and sailors alike) taken from the first several captures, but it ended after Semmes felt that he had made his point. Kell described the usual method of taking a prize:

> As soon as we sighted a ship we would hail her. If she didn't stop we would fire a blank cartridge across her bow. If she still refused to respond we would send a shot in front of her, and that would bring her to. Our long-range guns were of invaluable service in this business. When we hailed a ship we generally had the U.S. flag flying and kept it up until we were alongside. Then we would lower a boat and send an officer on board; but just before he boarded her the U.S. flag would come down and up would go the Confederate flag. Our officer would go to the captain of the ship we had caught, demand his papers, order him into the boat and bring him on board. Admiral Semmes always remained in his cabin when a capture was made and the captains of our prizes were taken before him there. He examined their papers and questioned them closely. If the ship was found to belong to a citizen of a neutral country, a fact which the captain's papers would always reveal, she was at once released. When we discovered that we had the property of a citizen of the United States we took her officers, crew and passengers (if she had any) on board. We then went through her cargo and appropriated what we needed—for . . . we lived almost entirely on our prizes. When we had all we wanted, we set fire to the captured ship and sailed away to look for another.[22]

Either Kell or Armstrong would estimate the value of the prize, because in cases of an American-owned vessel carrying neutral-owned cargo, the vessel would be released on bond. This meant that the value of the vessel was to be paid to the Confederate government by her owners at the conclusion of hostilities. When a ship was so released, she was obliged to relieve Semmes of all his prisoners.

Kell, who supervised the distribution of every prize, made it a hard and fast rule that no boat's crew could board the vessel until after all the liquor found aboard was thrown overboard or placed in a safe place. This policy caused a great deal of dissatisfaction among those sailors looking for opportunities to loot. For these men, the daily ration of grog—served morning and noon by an officer aboard the *Alabama*—was inadequate.[23] In spite of all the precautions taken, however, liquor was frequently smuggled aboard the *Alabama* from the prizes. Semmes and Kell were continually troubled by the results of these violations of discipline. Even their best sailors, they found, could not be trusted with whisky.[24]

After supplies had been transferred to the *Alabama*—along with charts and chronometers—the boarding officer would direct the men in breaking up furniture or gathering mattresses. Lard or other inflammable liquid would be poured on this, and a fire set. Watching a burning ship had a certain exhilarating effect upon Kell. He wrote:

> To watch the leaping flames on a burning ship gives an indescribable mental excitement that did not decrease with the frequency of the light, but it was always a relief to know the ships were tenantless as they disappeared in lonely grandeur, specks of vanishing light in the "cradle of the deep."[25]

Within five weeks after the burning of the *Ocmulgee*, the Confederates had consigned a dozen more vessels, mostly whalers, to the flames, and this was only the beginning. However, one vessel, the *Tonawanda*—carrying a cargo of grain—was spared because of the women and children aboard for whom the *Alabama* lacked proper accommodations. The ship was used as "bait" to lure another ship for an easy capture and to carry off the prisoners taken since leaving the Azores. Aboard another ship—the brigantine *Dunkirk*—was a deserter from the *Sumter*, seaman George Forrest. Semmes ordered a court-martial to decide Forrest's punishment, and it was decided that he should serve without pay on the *Alabama* for the remainder of the cruise. However, he would be eligible to share in prize money.[26]

Far more important than the deserter Forrest were the new volunteers coming from captured vessels. Semmes soon had thirty additional sailors and was only ten short of his full complement of one hundred and twenty. By the end of the cruise he would have an assortment of sailors representing most of the seafaring nations. Kell admitted to his own favorite class of seamen: "The thoroughbred downeaster is the best seaman that sails the ocean. He is handy and trusty and has little dread of storms or shells. Next to him, and in special directions superior to him, is the British tar."[27]

After cruising the vicinity of the Azores for as long as he felt it wise, the *Alabama* was headed toward Newfoundland, while Semmes planned a move that—if successful—might prove a turning point in the war. Because his plan had to be scrapped, Semmes never mentioned it in his writings. However, Kell did. The plan called for the *Alabama* to be brought into New York City's outer harbor at night. There, the merchant ships were to be boarded and their crews transferred to the lightship, after which the ships were to be set afire. The *Alabama* would make her escape before dawn.[28]

A hundred miles off George's Bank—on October 16—the *Alabama* ran into a cyclone, one of the worst ever experienced by Kell. The hatches were battened down and life lines passed along the decks to keep the men from being washed overboard. As the barometer continued to fall, the sea became "one sheet of foam and spray from the violence of the wind." The ship rolled and plunged, head and stern, taking tons of water on her decks. The winds tore away the main brace, the main yard snapped in two, and the maintopsail was torn into shreds. Working under great difficulty, the men succeeded in securing the main yard and lowering the spars to the deck. Suddenly all was calm. Anticipating what would happen next, Semmes said to his "luff": "Mr. Kell, in a few minutes we will get the wind with renewed violence in the opposite direction." Kell gave the necessary orders to the men, and the yards were braced and storm staysail secured. Minutes later, the storm came with even greater violence than before.[29] As Kell recalled of those terrible four hours: "It would be impossible to convey an adequate idea of the fury of the terrible typhoon."[30] That night, a sailor noted in his journal: "Only the skill of our Captain and Mr. Low, the Fourth Lieutenant, saved us from a watery grave."[31]

Although within two hundred and fifty miles of New York City, Semmes decided to give up his plan of attack and attend to repairs. He also had to rendezvous with his coal ship, the *Agrippina*. As the *Alabama* sailed for Martinique in the Carribbean, she added six more vessels to her growing list of captures. From one of these—the *T.B. Wales*—the Confederates secured a main yard to replace their loss. With it in place they were "complete again in . . . sailing capacity."[32] The capture of this ship brought an unexpected but not unpleasant surprise for the Confederates. As passengers were the U.S. Consul to Mauritius, his wife, and three young daughters: The latter soon became "very much at home" aboard the *Alabama*—where the best wardroom cabins were put at the disposal of the family. Kell would later write: "I feel sure they never denounced us as pirates."[33]

Arriving at Fort de France on November 18, the Confederates found the *Agrippina* at anchor. Kell was sent to call on the French Admiral to report the arrival of the *Alabama*. He was "received . . . pleasantly" and given a warning. Captain Robert McQueen of the *Agrippina* had—under the influence of whisky—indiscreetly made known the identity of the vessel for which he was waiting. The Admiral advised that the *Alabama* be brought under the guns of the fort for protection before any American warships arrived. When Semmes learned of this, he ordered McQueen to proceed immediately to Blanquilla Island off the coast of Venezuela. He could not risk remaining at Martinique for his coaling.

Throughout the afternoon native "bumboats" brought their wares—fruits, tobacco, and pipes—to the *Alabama*. Not all the articles being brought on board were so innocent. Seaman George Forrest managed to get rum on board the ship and distributed to the roughest element in the crew. Forrest had had enough of the *Alabama* and was determined to take advantage of the opportunity to incite mutiny while in port. Late in the afternoon, after visitors had left the ship, Kell heard an uproar on the forecastle. Going forward to investigate, he was greeted by the curses and threats of at least a score of men. A belaying pin missed its mark as Kell stood his ground. He ordered those men who appeared to be sober to seize their drunken comrades, but not a hand was raised. When Semmes appeared, he saw a surly, defiant crowd of drunken sailors gathered together near the foremast. Most of the other sailors seemed hesitant. Semmes, realizing that the men had only sheath-knives and belaying pins, while his officers were well armed, turned to his "luff" and said: "Mr. Kell, give the order to beat to quarters." As drum and fife were heard, the men automatically fell in at their stations. Semmes and Kell then passed along the men as they stood at the guns. Semmes eyed each man, and whenever he observed one drunk, he ordered him seized by his comrades at station. Twenty sailors were taken and put in irons, and Semmes ordered them to the gangway, where buckets of sea water were to be dashed over them by the most rugged of the quartermasters. At first, the men laughed and swore: "Come on with your water; we're not afraid of it!" However, as bucket after bucket was emptied over them, they began to gasp and choke. Soon they were begging for mercy. An occasional snicker could be heard from the sober men still at their stations during the two-hour-long treatment. When Semmes thought the men had had enough, he gave the order to "beat the retreat." The irons were removed and the mutineers allowed to go below to their hammocks. Only Forrest, the ringleader, would be punished further. Semmes ordered him "spread eagled" in the rigging for stretches of four hours at a time.[34] A court-martial would decide his ultimate fate. According to Semmes, the incident at Fort de France was the only case of mutinous conduct aboard the *Alabama*.[35] As the ship left the French island the morning following the disturbance, one of the crew wrote in his journal: "Some of our fellows are very down-hearted. They say that the rats have all left our good ship and that we will soon be dead men."[36] This time, however, the *Alabama* had gotten away in time. The U.S.S. *San Jacinto*, steaming outside the maritime limit in expectation of waylaying the *Alabama*, was successfully evaded in a night escape.

On November 26, at the barren island of Blanquilla, the sentence of the court-martial was executed. Forrest was to be discharged in disgrace, having forfeited the right to any prize money. He was landed on the island with only the clothes he wore.[37] The man was no loss to the *Alabama*. Years later Kell recalled Forrest as "a short, thickset fellow with dingy yellowish hair. . . . He was positively ugly and one of the most vicious fellows I ever knew."[38]

The crew was allowed liberty on the island and issued rifles for hunting and sport. There was nothing else to do, as Blanquilla was inhabited only by four Spaniards who raised goats and jackasses. Midshipman E. Maffit Anderson, in charge of the liberty party, allowed the sailors to disregard Semmes' implicit orders. In a private letter, Anderson wrote of the men:

> They forgot themselves, and commenced killing goats, jackasses and everything else that they could come across. We all thought that it was very good fun, but it was good for all hands that Captain Semmes knew nothing of it.[39]

After coaling at Blanquilla, Semmes set his course for the eastern end of Cuba. He was anxious to capture a New York-bound steamer carrying California gold for the United States Mint. On December 7 they captured the steamer *Ariel*, headed for Aspinwall on the Isthmus of Panama. Although she carried no gold, her safe contained $8,000 in U.S. Treasury notes and $1,500 in silver. Aboard were one hundred and forty marines, seven officers, and five hundred passengers, in addition to the regular crew. The passengers included a large number of terrified women and children. Among the naval officers was Commander Lewis C. Sartori, whom Kell remembered from the Pensacola Navy Yard. No word was exchanged between the two men who now found themselves on opposite sides of civil war.

Semmes had a special reason for wanting the *Ariel* burned: she was owned by Commodore Cornelius Vanderbilt, a bitter enemy of the Southern Confederacy. With Lieutenant Low in charge of the *Ariel*, she was escorted to Kingston, Jamaica. However, before he reached that port Semmes received a report of a fever epidemic there. The *Ariel* was then released on ransom bond. The Confederates took some little consolation in the loss of their prize. Commander Sartori had assured Low that he would correct "the erroneous rumors in circulation about the *Alabama*." As Sartori admitted, everyone aboard the *Ariel* had received "the most courteous treatment." Kell hoped that Sartori's word would help discredit the tales of "lawless piracy" circulating in the Northern press; on reflection, Kell decided that it did not really matter so long as the Southern cause was being strengthened by their efforts.[40]

Semmes set his course for the desolate Las Arcas Islands, off Yucatan. Here during the last days of 1862, he put his ship in order: calking, painting, tarring, and taking on more coal. Since the small islands were devoid of all life except birds and sea turtles, the men were deprived of the "pleasures of port." They had to satisfy themselves with killing a few turtles and raiding the nests for eggs. Semmes felt that his discipline had finally brought results:

> It has taken me three or four months to accomplish this, but when it is considered that my little kingdom consisted of 110 of the most reckless sailors from the groggeries and brothels of Liverpool, that is not much.[41]

As he concluded a letter to Blanche on the first day of the new year, Kell tried to be cheerful. There was at least one reason to be thankful: "We are still able to defend our homes and firesides from the wicked invasion of the Northern horde." Kell expressed the hope that in 1863 peace and independence would become a reality.

Kell's family had had a year of many trials. The war was

coming ever closer. Early in November Blanche, with her three children and two nurses, had left Macon by train for the coast to spend some time with Margery Kell. Blanche spent the night of her arrival in Savannah but missed the carriage the next morning. Walking with her children, she met her friend and former teacher Bishop Elliott near Christ Church. When he learned her plans, the Bishop exclaimed: "The Yankees have cut the road; you must go straight back to your father's house and be taken care of till this dreadful war is over."[42]

Margery Kell, expecting Blanche at Rushland, had in desperation tried to get word to her to stay away. Federal soldiers (mostly armed Negroes) had come to within a mile of Rushland and were taking away many of the slaves. Margery learned that one of the white officers had called her neighbor, Mrs. King, "an old sinner, going to the grave with her soul stained with the guilt of slavery." Perhaps Margery had her own private misgivings about slavery, for she confided to Blanche that the words of the abolitionist were ones she could "exactly understand."[43]

Blanche, after reluctantly giving up the idea of going to Rushland, remained in Savannah another day. She met her husband's cousin John Ward, who told her of his earlier meeting with Kell. Blanche was escorted about the city by Captain Frederick W. Sims, the betrothed of her sister Tadie. Sims, captured at Fort Pulaski and imprisoned at Governor's Island, had only recently been exchanged.[44]

On the return trip to Macon, Blanche was pleased when an old family friend—Colonel Lucius Lamar—sat next to her. Lamar, after speaking enthusiastically of the *Alabama* and her captures, asked Blanche how she was bearing up. Blanche could not hold back. She answered:

> Colonel Lamar, I wish I could say bravely, but I cannot. My father is too old and too feeble to go. My little brother only fifteen and a half has gone to the war,[45] and I do want a cup of good coffee, real coffee, so much.[46]

Kell's optimism for the year 1863 would have been shattered had he known what lay ahead for his family.

12

THE TRIALS OF WAR

It was four months since Semmes had taken command of the *Alabama*, and he believed he now had the "well disciplined ship of war" necessary for a bold strike at the enemy. Documents and newspapers taken from the *Ariel* had revealed that the Federals were preparing to launch an expedition of thirty thousand men under General Nathaniel P. Banks for an invasion of Texas. About a hundred vessels were to arrive off Galveston—already in Federal hands—about January 10 and land the troops. Semmes intended a surprise night attack, blasting away at the vessels of the fleet while running at full steam before making his escape. Nearing Galveston on the morning of January 11, a confident Semmes noted in his journal: "My crew are a fine looking body of men, have been well drilled, and are not adverse, I think, to a trial of skill and force with the enemy."[1]

As the *Alabama* approached Galveston, the lookout was not alert, and they appeared in plain view of several vessels anchored off the bar. Observing that a gunboat was firing on the city, Semmes exclaimed: "Well, they would not be firing on their own people. Galveston is recaptured and Banks' great expedition a failure!"[2] Shortly, one of the vessels was seen to be getting up steam. The *Alabama* stood under topsails while the stranger approached stern on. Semmes intended to draw her away from the rest of the fleet, knowing that distance and darkness would be his best allies in the event of a fight. It was already 4 p.m.

The approaching vessel was—unknown to the Confederates—the U.S.S. *Hatteras*, commanded by Homer C. Blake. The *Hatteras* was an iron side-wheel steamer (a former river excursion boat) with her engines exposed and unprotected. A Confederate naval authority later made the observation: "There is no doubt that the *Alabama* was the superior ship, and barring an accident . . . she ought to have won."[3] Commander Blake was not naively sailing into Semmes' trap. After having signalled "Suspicious Sail," he had been ordered by the flagship *Brooklyn* to investigate. In his report, Blake admitted that, "from the general character of the vessel and her maneuvering," he expected to encounter "the rebel steamer *Alabama*."[4] Blake planned to close with the raider, since his guns were most effective at close range. At a distance of about 100 yards, he hailed: "What steamer is that?" The answer came back: "Her Britannic Majesty's Ship *Petrel*. Who are You?" Blake answered: "United States Ship - - - -" The name was lost in the wind. Finally Blake called out: "If you please, I will send a boat on board of you." During the exchange, both vessels had been maneuvering for better combat positions. They were twenty miles from the Federal fleet, and, at 6:30 p.m., it was dark. A boat from the *Hatteras* shoved off toward the *Alabama*.

To Semmes' question "Are you ready for action?" Kell replied, "The men are only waiting for the word." All were at their stations on the starboard battery; guns were set and loaded with 5-second shell. Semmes instructed Kell: "Don't strike them in disguise; tell them who we are, and give the broadside at the name." Raising his trumpet, Kell sang out: "This is the Confederate States Steamer *Alabama*!—Fire!" Flashes of flame spat out, and the Confederates' broadside struck iron. As she was struck repeatedly, the side of the Federal steamer lit up, showing long rents. The wind was now blowing in the direction of Galveston and the Union fleet. With no moon to guide them, the men had to judge the distance for sighting by the flash of enemy guns. Blake steamed directly for the *Alabama*, hoping to board her, but (he later complained) his speed was diminished by "foulness of bottom." The range between the vessels was so close that musket and pistol shots were exchanged.[5] The action became a running fight in parallel lines, with the vessels nearing then separating from each other. Semmes stood on the horse-block above the rail of his ship, observing the action as best he could. Unable to suppress his excitement, he called out to his gunners: "Give it to the rascals! Aim low, men! Don't be all night sinking that fellow!" The men were also caught up in the excitement as they sighted their guns. Whenever a shell struck home, a boatswain's mate exclaimed: "That's from 'the scum of England'!" "That's a British pill for you to swallow!" Shells entering the hold of the *Hatteras* were setting fires and causing explosions. One entered the cylinder and—with his engine room filling with steam—Blake could no longer maneuver his ship. The *Hatteras* was sinking rapidly. Blake ordered his magazine flooded to prevent the ship from blowing up and a lee gun to be fired in surrender. Only thirteen minutes had elapsed since the beginning of the action, during which the *Alabama* had fired eight broadsides. From his position on the horse block, Semmes called out: "Mr. Kell, the enemy have fired a gun to leeward; cease firing." As the order was given, over a hundred voices were raised in cheers. The raider steamed closer to the *Hatteras*, and Kell inquired whether they had surrendered. Hearing answering cries for assistance, Kell gave the order, "All hands out boats to save life!"

Within an hour, the Federal officers and sailors—a total of one hundred and twenty-six—were picked up and taken to the *Alabama*.[6] When Commander Blake came on deck and delivered up his sword, Semmes finally learned the name of the ship he had sunk.[7] Smacking his lips with pleasure, he gave up his stateroom to Blake, while the other officers were accommodated according to rank and the crew placed on the berth deck. The latter were placed in single irons. After rewarding his own crew with grog, Semmes made haste to get clear of possible pursuers; with her lights extinguished, the *Alabama* was soon far from the coast. The raider had not been seriously damaged, although one shell had narrowly missed the middle starboard gun crew. A second shell had gone through the

Alabama's side, under the main chains, and lodged in the opposite timbers, while another had ripped into and through the funnel.[8] But Semmes and his men considered themselves fortunate to have come out of the contest so well. In a longer engagement the Blakely gun would certainly have caused difficulty, for—as Kell later stated—"It became easily heated, from deficiency in metal, and the powder charge would have to be reduced on account of the recoil."[9]

The morning after the fight, while Kell was on deck supervising repairs, Commander Blake appeared. He recognized Kell and saluted him: "How do you do, Mr. Kell? Fortune favors the brave, sir." Kell thanked him and added, "We take advantage of all fortune's favors."[10]

Nine days after her victory, the *Alabama* arrived at Kingston, Jamaica, to land the prisoners, take on coal, and make additional repairs. Soon after their arrival, Semmes gladly accepted the opportunity for a few days respite in the hills, leaving Kell in charge of the ship. As Semmes would one day write:

> Kell was of wonderful assistance to me, in this respect. I always left the ship in his hands, with the utmost confidence, and my confidence was never misplaced. He was . . . an excellent disciplinarian, and being, besides, a thorough master of his profession, I had in him all that I could desire.[11]

After three days of rest and seclusion, Semmes learned that the *Alabama* was ready for sea. However, all was not well; Paymaster Clarence Yonge had been "disgracing himself," and the liberty men had not returned to the ship. Yonge had gone ashore with *L* 400, supposedly to settle accounts, but had, instead, become thoroughly intoxicated. Learning of this, Kell had him carried aboard the ship under arrest. When Semmes returned he lost no time in ordering Yonge to pack up and leave the ship at once.[12] Yonge was the only one of his officers whom Semmes was forced to discharge. The case was especially galling to Kell, who had recommended his own ardently Confederate brother-in-law, John Hutton, as paymaster. There still remained the problem of getting the liberty men back on board.

Kell would admit: "Carried away with victory, many of [the men] got gloriously drunk, and gave me a good deal of trouble to get them back and properly sobered."[13] Only with the aid of the local police were most of the missing sailors returned. Writing in his journal, Semmes was bitter as he observed: "It will take me at least a week to get the rum out of them, and to try the more vicious by court-martial."[14] On January 25 the *Alabama* proceeded to sea and headed toward the coast of South America.

Kell had time for occasional diversions. Lieutenant Sinclair would later describe Kell and Dr. Galt playing checkers and the "luff" entertaining the wardroom officers with stories of the old navy.[15] Kell's beard had become somewhat of a vanity by this time. Not only did it make Kell look older, but it tended to accentuate his important position aboard the ship. With it, he was easily mistaken for a British sea captain. Kell's beard had a devoted admirer in Bartelli, Semmes' steward. Bartelli "took pride and pleasure in brushing and platting [the] luxurious beard."[16] Kell himself wrote of evenings spent on the bridge, watching the light of burning ships, while he reflected on "man in his sinful nature warring with his brother man." During these moments, the officers would "seek the refreshing influences of past social enjoyments" by talking of "home and absent friends."[17] There were rare moments, too, when Semmes would join his officers in relaxed smoking and talking. A favorite topic of conversation was the South and the progress of the war. News of Confederate victories on land and sea never failed to lift the men's morale, while news of defeats was received with gloom. However, since most of what was read was found in Northern newspapers from captured prizes, they found reason to be skeptical of news that indicated Southern failures and defeats. References to the *Alabama* as an "infamous pirate" were infuriating; yet these gave satisfying evidence of how badly Northern commerce was being hurt. Semmes had a special admiration for a fellow "pirate"—John Maffitt—whose midshipman son was one of his own young officers. Kell would one day tell Maffitt of the "great admiration" Semmes felt toward him: "I can picture now his smile—he never laughed—which lit up every feature when narrating your deeds, especially your entrance and exit from Mobile Bay in the *Florida*."[18]

One of Kell's social functions was presiding over the wardroom mess, where, because of Semmes' personal disdain for liquor, nothing stronger than claret was ever served, despite the fact that Semmes ate alone in his own cabin. Nor would Semmes allow card playing among his officers. It is doubtful whether Kell himself ever unbent with the officers (aside from Dr. Galt), who were so much younger than he. But as an observer, he naturally would have enjoyed the singing, music-making, dancing, and improvised plays of the sailors during the evening hours. At these times, "the discipline of the ship was wont to be purposely relaxed," and roars of laughter would resound from the forecastle. The entertainment invariably concluded with a rousing chorus of "Dixie," and a hundred or more voices were raised in "an uproar of enthusiasm."[19] At 8 p.m. all merriment came to an end as the night watches were set.

The man who knew Kell better than any other officer during the *Sumter* and *Alabama* cruises was Dr. Francis Galt. Years after the war, Galt recalled those years and his friend. According to Galt, Kell's "steadiness of temper" had been under the "firmest control." Concerning Kell's competence as an officer, he wrote: "The modesty of his nature . . . was guarded by an undeviating adherence to a line of action in his duties which made it very easy for those associated with him to know exactly what was to be expected of him." Galt added:

> He had a very keen sense of injustice, and was always ready to remedy any act which showed a want of this elementary trait of human nature. Intent always in carrying out the details of his duties, perfectly content to see that his ship was the most important thing to attend to, and the natural curiosity of men to visit foreign places, to look at, or engage in any social functions had no power to prevent his first seeing that his duties as an officer were the first work in hand.[20]

There was at least one other officer who felt differently. He was Second Lieutenant Armstrong, a competent officer whose capabilities were recognized by both Semmes and Kell. Armstrong was too good an officer to let the first lieutenant know his personal feelings toward him or let them interfere with his duties. It was only many years after the war that he confessed: "How I used to hate him. He used to make us youngsters stand around, and after we were made lieutenants we thought ourselves as important as he." Following the war, a more mature Armstrong came to appreciate the qualities of his former superior officer. He would say: "Captain Semmes may well give him the credit of the discipline and much of the success of the ship. It was duty, first, last, and always, with our first officer, and no boyish nonsense either, except in our frolics ashore on off duty days."[21] During the twenty-two-month cruise of the *Alabama*, Kell was off the ship for only a total of twenty-two hours, less than any other man aboard her.

The crew were of different opinions regarding their "luff." According to one alleged *Alabama* sailor, Kell was referred to as "Kill-or-cure" by the crew.[22] Another sailor wrote Kell years after the war that he was "the only man we fellows on the berth deck would fight or go to hell for. You were liked and respected by all the crew."[23] Still another seaman, a gunner's mate, reminisced in later years: "Mr. Kell, you were kind and good to us all, but we sure had to mind you and I'm glad of it."[24] An interesting observation is that made by Captain Evan P. Jones of the yacht *Deerhound* shortly after the sinking of the *Alabama*. Jones had the opportunity to observe a number of officers and sailors from the raider after they had been plucked from the water, and—aboard the yacht—were being taken to Southampton. He noted: "Semmes seemed to be greatly reverenced by his crew, but I think Kell had their deepest regard. According to their idea, Kell was Semmes' mainstay and chief counsellor, and the commander owed much of his success and reputation to his first officer's sagacity and promptness of resource."[25]

But the opinion of an English sailor given just after the sinking of the *Alabama* was far different. He told a reporter: "As a rule the crew liked and respected Semmes, but detested the first lieutenant, who was a low lived bully, and a man without any principle."[26] Kell, responsible as he was for maintaining discipline, could hardly have been popular with many of the sailors punished on his or on Semmes' orders, and this sailor could well have been among these men. Semmes himself said of his "luff": "You will scarcely recognize him . . . when you see him . . . on deck, arraigning some culprit 'at the mast' for a breach of discipline."[27]

Regardless of how the crew may have felt toward him, Kell would later be loud in his praise of them. After the war, the stories of the *Alabama* and her crew that were critical of either would arouse Kell to a fury. He stated: "With our peculiar service, and with our ports locked against us, we were compelled to observe the strictest discipline, both with officers and crew. As the executive officer who enforced this discipline I may say that a nobler set of young men filling the position of officers, and a braver and more willing crew, never floated."[28] Kell recalled: "Every day, whether it brought us a prize or not, had its duties. We were employed all the time. I was constantly putting the men through drills with small arms and with guns. . . . It was my duty to see that the crew and ship were in order at all times and I believe I did so."[29] If the accounts of captured Yankee mariners can be believed—and certainly these men had no love for Semmes or the Southern Confederacy—conditions on the *Alabama* were far from ideal. According to one such source:

> The sailors appeared like a lot of thieves, taking everything they could stow about their persons, and not appearing to take any notice of their officer, the officer himself not seeming to know much about a ship, except as regards the burning of her. . . . So little discipline was there that the Alabama's men were smoking segars [*sic*] in the boat that took the Captain on board the Alabama's decks. The men were lying about aft, as well as forward, smoking pipes and segars. . . . The ship was very dirty, and everything looking in disorder.[30]

Without question there were skulkers and troublemakers among the crew, and discontent increased as the cruise lengthened. According to the English sailor who detested Kell, "There is no principle among the men, and very little enthusiasm in the cause." Later in Cherbourg, he would provide a news reporter with a "sour grapes" account of sailor life aboard the *Alabama*:

> Many of the men have been heavily fined by sentence of court martial. It has been a custom to punish the men sometimes for the most trivial offences by taking away their pay. On one occasion a man was fined five pounds for cutting a duck's throat taken out of a prize. Whenever we took a prize the officers always made a rush for all good eatables and drinkables, while the men were not allowed a single article, and severely punished if they touched anything. When the bread was full of maggots and the provisions in the *Alabama* of the very worst description, tons of the very best provisions, taken from prizes, have been sunk rather than give them to the men. Semmes' idea was this:—If he allowed men to take anything from a prize he supposed that the man who actually went to the prize would get it and keep it, without sharing with the others.[31]

After a coaling stop at Fernando de Noronha in April,[32] the *Alabama* arrived at Bahia on May 11. Two days later the C.S.S. *Georgia* arrived, commanded by William L. Maury. It was a "joyous experience" for Kell to meet old shipmates of the *Sumter*—Lieutenants William Evans and Robert Chapman. There was much news to exchange, and the *Alabama's* officers took particular delight in relating the details of their sinking of the *Hatteras*.

After ten days at Bahia, the *Alabama* was again at sea, and in the following weeks added to her growing list of captures.[33] Forty miles from Cape Town, South Africa, Kell again began a letter to Blanche. It was now over a year since he had heard from her, and he did not know whether she was receiving his letters through the blockade. Kell no longer believed in a quick end to the war. As he saw it, if the South was unable to achieve a military victory during 1863, then the North, exhausted and war-weary, would repudiate President Lincoln in the 1864 election. A new President, he believed, would "come in upon the popular cry of pious measures."[34]

On July 30 the *Alabama* arrived at Saldanha Bay, northwest of Cape Town, to undertake repairs and take on supplies. Again, the misconduct of the liberty men increased Kell's overload of work. One of the men went so far as to draw a revolver on one of the master's mates. After stopping all further liberty, Semmes admitted his low opinion of the "sailor class of the present day," of which he thought his men typical: "I have a precious set of rascals on board—faithless in the matter of abiding by their contracts, liars, thieves, and drunkards."[35] His only consolation lay in the fact they were not Southern men.

For Kell, after the tedious work of supervising and disciplining, came welcome relief from duty in an invitation from an admiring Boer to accompany him on an ostrich hunt in the interior. Armed with shotguns, Kell and his companions from the *Alabama* succeeded in shooting one of the birds, but their buckshot had no effect.[36] Nevertheless, they enjoyed the day's diversion from ship duty. At Saldanha and the other stopovers near Cape Town, the officers and men of the *Alabama* were amazed and delighted at the admiration and praise they received. They were treated as heroes. Daily, throngs of friendly Boers came aboard the ship. Semmes, wearing an "old grey, stained uniform" with "battered shoulder straps", received the visitors in his cabin, where he was beseiged with requests for his autograph. He dismissed praise of his sinking of the *Hatteras* with the admission that "both in tonnage and in armament" that ship was "rather inferior to his own."[37] Kell, proudly pointing out the Blakely gun for the special attention of visitors, remarked: "When we fought the *Hatteras* these conical shells struck her one after the other in capital style; they exploded with magnificent effect and lit up her whole broadside."[38] One visitor expressed amazement at finding "so small a vessel carrying such large metal."[39] A photographer from Cape Town, taking pictures of Semmes and his officers, included one of Kell with the impressive-looking gun.[40] Kell would always remember the pro-Southern Boers who had provided the most cordial welcome ever accorded the *Alabama* and her officers. Both he and Semmes were given valuable ostrich feathers by admirers.[41]

The *Alabama* next rounded the Cape of Good Hope and stopped at Simon's Bay for additional repairs. Semmes had become thoroughly disgusted by the conduct of his sailors. In spite of precautions, liquor was smuggled on board, and there was much insubordination. Worse still, as Semmes complained, "With one or two exceptions the whole crew have broken their liberty—petty officers and all. [My sailor] is as big a drunkard and as great a villain as ever." The captain knew better than to pay the bills presented against his men. When it came time to leave Simon's Bay, fourteen of the crew were missing (some, reportedly, at "Black Sophie's" bordello in Cape Town) and Semmes was compelled to impress "11 vagabonds, hungry and nearly shirtless" to replace them. It would take weeks to make sailors out of them, as well as to "work the grog" out of the rest of the crew before they settled down into "good habits and cheerfulness."[42]

The *Alabama* next cruised between Africa and Brazil before returning to Simon's Bay. By this time, Semmes was feeling the pressing demands of duty. "Disgusted" with the sea, he felt it time to quit a life of "hardships and discomforts" suited only to "the youthful, or, at most, the middle-aged."[43]

Had Kell known of events in Georgia, he would have thought of little else but his family. The war had so affected his loved ones that neither their lives—nor his—would ever be the same. On June 11, 1863, two newly formed black Union regiments had landed from gunboats on the coast of McIntosh County, Georgia. Although Darien had been deserted for at least three months (Confederate militia at the Ridge taking little action), the town was put to the torch on orders of Colonel James Montgomery. Montgomery justified the burning—contrary to orders he had received—by saying, "We are outlawed and therefore not bound by the rules of regular warfare."[44] The Grove, a mile from town, was spared, but Margery and her daughters—now at the Retreat—were convinced they could never return. In a letter to Blanche, Hettie wrote despairingly of her mother:

> She has given up. She is sick at heart. She is grieving so over old Darien. She says she has no heart to write Donny for she

> has nothing good to tell him. She thinks we shall never live at the Grove again and is really miserable about it.[45]

When Margery was well enough to write to Blanche, she referred to the town as her "oldest friend": "It is linked with my earliest recollections and I feel that we would be so isolated at the Grove without Darien."[46] Unknown to Margery, the worst was yet to come.

Earlier, in April of 1863, at Sylvan Lodge, the Kell children contracted the whooping cough from their Negro playmates. Munroe and little Dot suffered more than Johnny and lost weight rapidly. A trip to Sunnyside in June seemed to do them good, and Blanche believed that they had fully recovered. In her despair for her husband's safety, the children were her only consolation. Munroe asked continually: "When is papa coming? I hate Yankees; they keep my papa away." And Dot, finding her mother despondent, would pat her cheek, kiss her, and say, "Poor papa, so far away from his little girl and mama and bubbers."[47]

On September 9 Dot suddenly became feverish and complained of a sore throat. A few days later, Johnny and Munroe also showed the same symptoms. After diagnosing their ailment as diphtheria, the doctor plied them with potash, iron, whisky, and quinine in a desperate attempt to save their lives. Dot was the sickest of the three, although "restless and capricious." She allowed only Blanche to nurse her and loved being rocked to sleep in her arms. The baby girl would kiss her mother's picture of Kell, worn as a shawl pin. She continued to fail, until—on September 24—death came. Johnny cried bitterly, but Munroe "seemed awed into silence." After his sister was buried, the older boy began to speak of wanting to go to heaven to be with "little Sissy." Horrified at the thought of losing her firstborn, Blanche finally asked him: "Son, if God should take you home to Heaven, that happy land you love to sing about, what must I tell papa for you?" The boy, lying on his mother's lap, answered, "Mama, you will know what to tell him," but when Blanche asked again he said, "Tell him I kiss him."

Four days after Dot's death, Blanche—sewing by the trundle bed—heard Munroe speaking to his brother: "Johnny, you may have my marbles. I don't want them anymore!" Later that evening his condition worsened, and he died at daybreak the next morning.[48] His mother had him laid in a grave beside his sister at Rosehill Cemetery. In the weeks that followed, Blanche would throw herself, sobbing "in frantic agony," across the graves. Her old servant Ned tried to comfort her, saying, "Don't cry so my little missis. Your mother got them children. She'll love 'em and keep 'em till you come."[49]

In desperation Blanche wrote to Secretary Mallory requesting that her husband be returned to her. It was her wish that Bob Minor be her husband's replacement, since she believed that he would be Kell's own choice. Mallory assured Blanche that he would try to communicate with Kell; however, the *Alabama* was beyond his reach.[50] Early in November Blanche left for the Retreat, where she remained with her sympathetic in-laws for the next month. It was at the Retreat that Blanche began keeping a private journal, intended "for her husband only." In it she laid bare her emotions, recalling everything she remembered of her dead children for her husband to read if ever he returned. Daily, she poured forth her grief:

> Oh God have mercy on my desolate broken heart! Give me resignation and submission to thy holy will, whatever it may be! I have been sick and feeble all this week—sometimes I fancy my time is not very far distant, and that I could better give up life now, than after my husband's return—he has been gone *so long, so long*! three long sad years!! I tried to bear it stoically, for poor erring creature I thought this separation was to be my earthly cross! God willed that it should be more bitter—more heavy to be borne![51]

Blanche's continuing despondency finally caused her mother-in-law to scold her. Margery wrote that if she were near a hospital—as Blanche was—she would be volunteering to help the wounded soldiers. She assured Blanche that she could offer comfort to the men without having to become a nurse. Eventually, in the summer of 1864, Blanche made her first visit to one of the Macon military hospitals and was soon making regular visitations. Accompanying her was her friend Mary Day.[52] As Blanche later recalled: "I fanned the fevered sufferers, and bathed poor stumps of arms and legs, finding solace for an aching heart in trying to alleviate the physical pain of those heroes of the lost cause."[53]

As Blanche faced her grief in late 1863, her husband was on the other side of the globe, in the Indian Ocean. The *Alabama* was now encountering fewer American vessels, and Semmes believed that the trade "is nearly broken up. Their ships find it impossible to get freights." Semmes was tired and ill after over three years at sea. He admitted in his journal that he was "quite knocked up with cold and fever" and "supremely disgusted with the sea and all its belongings." Semmes longed for a chance to just "lie by and be quiet."[54] His sailors were still causing trouble. After cigars, taken from the *Winged Racer*, were divided among the officers and crew, a number of the sailors threw theirs overboard "in a contemptuous manner." Semmes immediately had the "ringleaders" arrested, and, soon afterward, court-martialed. But this was only part of Semmes' discipline problem. The testimony of an officer of the clipper ship *Contest*—burned on November 11, 1863—gives an indication of how serious conditions aboard the *Alabama* may have been:

> Crew much dissatisfied, no prize money, no liberty, and see no prospect of getting any. Discipline very slack, steamer dirty, rigging slovenly. Semmes sometimes punishes, but is afraid to push too hard. Men excited, officers do not report to captain, crew do things for which they would be shot on board American man-of-war; for instance, saw one of crew strike a master's mate; crew insolent to petty officers; was told by at least two-thirds of them that [they] will desert on first opportunity. Crew all scum of Liverpool, French, Dutch, etc. *Alabama* is very weak; in any heavy sea her upper works leak badly; she has a list to port that she may fight her starboard guns. Fires kept banked; can get steam in 20 minutes. Except at muster no uniforms worn. Crew rugged; keep a lookout at foretop-gallant yard daytime; at night, two waist lookouts. Officers on duty have cutlass and

> revolver; never saw Semmes in uniform; puts on sword at muster. Have given up small-arm drill, afraid to trust crew with arms. While on board saw drill only once, and that at pivot guns, very badly done; men ill disposed and were forced to it; lots of cursing.[55]

On December 21 the *Alabama* arrived at New Harbour, a short distance from the British colony of Singapore. They would spend two days here taking on coal and provisions. The *Alabama*'s reputation was well known. When news of her arrival began to circulate among the natives, there were excited exclamations of "Kappal Hantu!" ("Ghost Ship!")[56] On the 23rd visitors were allowed on board, and the Confederate officers, in dress uniform, proudly gave tours of their ship. Europeans and natives alike crowded aboard. It was a friendly crowd, and the Confederates were delighted with the goodwill and support they received. The narrative of a British resident of Singapore sharply contrasts with Northern accounts of the deterioration of discipline. After a tour of the ship, he noted:

> I could remark no sign of impatience, much less of insubordination. Nor could I attribute this contented behaviour to fear of the officers, who were far from rough or domineering in their manners; so that I conclude whatever may be their hardships or the precarious nature of their pay and emoluments, the crew of the *Alabama* would stand by her in case of danger.

The same British gentleman was also filled with praise for the officers with whom he conversed. The latter admitted quite frankly that capturing and destroying merchantmen was losing its excitement for them, and the Britisher was left with the feeling that they would eventually risk an encounter with an armed enemy ship. However, he concluded that Semmes was "a man slow to move on a rash enterprise."

When the *Alabama* arrived at New Harbour, eighteen American merchantmen were in port. However, within a few days of their arrival, about one-half had changed owners and were flying the flags of other nations. It was little wonder that one of the Confederates remarked: "We don't care much whether or not we succeed in destroying any more of the enemy's merchantmen; we have done enough already; our presence alone in these waters will now suffice to ruin the eastern commerce of the Federal States."

Proud of their record of accomplishments, the *Alabama* officers continued to be annoyed at denunciations in the Northern press of their alleged "piratical" activities. On this sensitive issue, they were especially anxious to present their own rebuttal. While at New Harbour, an officer explained:

> You must remember, sir, that we but retaliate on our enemy that destruction of property which he has been the first to inaugurate in this war. His power at sea was by a simple chance too much for us to cope with from the first, or we should by this time have had a small navy of our own, built in our own dockyards; and as we have been content to fight him in the field with a disparity of numbers, so we should have attacked him at sea with a weaker force. Such has not been our fortune; but it has been our fortune to obtain this and some few other ships, and to bring them to bear on our enemies' most salient point. General Gilmore himself, when he uses the advantage which the Federal ships have placed in his hands to destroy from his batteries the warehouses and mansions of Charleston, endorses our course as legitimate. It is true, Charleston has its forts and batteries which do their best to protect these defenceless buildings, but does this alter the parallel? Is it confessed that the merchant shipping of the Federal Government can find no protection in the Federal navy? and if it is so confessed, is it urged that we should therefore hold back from the advantage which our enemies' defencelessness gives us in one particular, while he advantages to the full by our insufficiently protected state in another? No! When the Northern hordes pause on their onward raid by the consideration of the inability of the Confederate Government to afford protection to its cities, then may we too pause on our course, for the reason that the Federal Government cannot or will not spare ships from the blockade of Southern ports to protect her foreign shipping.[57]

On the night of December 24, thirty miles out of New Harbour, the *Alabama* hailed the barque *Martaban*, flying the English flag. Despite the flag, she was believed to be American. As Kell would say, "We could tell them as infallibly by the 'cut of their jib' as we could detect by their sharp brogue the nationality of their captains."[58] The captain, after producing British papers, insisted that his was an English ship. Claiming the protection of his flag, he refused to accompany the boarding party to the *Alabama*. For the first time, Semmes was forced to personally board a captured vessel. Declaring the ship's papers a forgery, he ordered that the barque be burned. Later, the skipper, aboard the *Alabama* and under oath, admitted that he had "tried a game of bluff." Two days later Semmes had destroyed two more ships—these undeniably American—but he was troubled at the possibility of adverse reaction to his burning of the *Martaban*. His prisoners were put adrift in longboats to make their way to New Harbour as best they could. With them Semmes sent a report which attempted to justify the destruction of the *Martaban*.

Early in 1864 the *Alabama* left the Indian Ocean and headed for European waters. Semmes noted in his journal on May 21: "Our bottom is in such a state that everything passes us. We are like a crippled hunter limping home from a long chase." During almost two years at sea, the *Alabama* had never been long enough in any port for a thorough overhaul of her hull, rigging, and engines. Since her fires had never been allowed to go out, flues and pipes had never been properly cleaned. On April 23 Semmes made a target of the prize *Rockingham*. Shot and shell were used—according to Semmes—"with reasonable success."[59] Others thought differently. Of twenty-four rounds fired, only seven were seen to have any effect.[60] The prisoners from the *Rockingham* attributed this to bad shooting, but there were other possibilities, of which Kell gradually became aware. Upon investigation, he found that many of the shell fuses were faulty. It would later be found that a large quantity of powder had become damp because of the magazine's proximity to the condensing apparatus. Powder had so deteriorated that several barrels would have to be thrown overboard only a day before the action with the *Kearsarge*. Even the supply of powder put up in cartridges and stowed in copper tanks, which Semmes assumed was still in good condition, had—he would later admit—deteriorated, "perhaps to the extent of one-third of its strength."[61] The size of the problem would not be known until weeks later. But there was no question that the *Alabama* needed to be put up in dry dock for repairs that would take at least a month. As Kell observed, the ship was "loose at every joint, her seams were open, and the copper on her bottom was in rolls."[62]

At midday on June 11, 1864, the *Alabama* dropped anchor at Cherbourg, France. During her twenty-two months at sea, she had overhauled 294 vessels. Of this number, fifty-five American merchant ships (valued at over $4,500,000) had been burned and ten others (valued at $562,000) bonded. It was a record that would not be equalled by any other Confederate raider. The presence of the *Alabama* at Cherbourg was an embarrassment for the French authorities there. Since the docks were naval property, only Emperor Napoleon III—away on a vacation—could give the necessary permission for her to be docked. However, Semmes was allowed to land his prisoners and take on coal.

On June 14 the U.S.S. *Kearsarge*, commanded by John A. Winslow, appeared off the breakwater. Semmes had learned the day before of her coming and faced three alternatives: he could continue waiting for permission to dry-dock, he could leave Cherbourg at once without taking on coal, or he could fight. If he made the first choice, he would lose most of his crew, and the Federals would be waiting in greater strength for him to leave. And Semmes—who was actually spoiling for a fight—had no intention of making a getaway. His knowledge of the *Kearsarge* convinced him that his own ship was a match for her.[63] When the *Kearsarge* steamed into view, Kell, glass in hand, stood on the quarter-deck trying to make out hull, rigging, and battery. He saw a "smooth black hull," but—since her principal guns were pivoted—he could learn little of her battery.[64] However, Semmes believed he had adequate knowledge of the *Kearsarge*, since he had seen her at close range two years earlier at Gibraltar.

Soon after the arrival of the *Kearsarge*, Semmes summoned Kell to his cabin. He said:

> I have sent for you to discuss the advisability of fighting the *Kearsarge*. As you know, the arrival of the *Alabama* at this port has been telegraphed to all parts of Europe. Within a few days, Cherbourg will be effectively blockaded by Yankee cruisers. It is uncertain whether or not we shall be permitted to repair the *Alabama* here, and in the meantime, the delay is to our advantage. I think we may whip the *Kearsarge*, the two vessels being of wood and carrying about the same number of men and guns. Besides, Mr. Kell, although the Confederate States government has ordered me to avoid engagements with the enemy's cruisers, I am tired of running from that flaunting rag![65]

Kell was not really convinced that the decision to fight was a wise one, but—as he later admitted—he "could not remonstrate with Captain Semmes." Instead, he reminded him of their defective powder and of the fact that at target practice with the *Rockingham* only one in three fuses had been good. Semmes shrugged off Kell's concern, saying: "I will take the chances of one in three." There was nothing left for Kell to say except, "I'll fit the ship for action, sir."[66] As he later wrote: "I saw his mind was fully made up, so I simply stated these facts for myself."[67] Kell began ordering preparation of shell rooms, guns, and other equipment. Cutlasses and axes were sharpened for hand-to-hand combat, should a boarding take place. From the 15th to the 18th they took on coal, filling bunkers with a full load of three hundred and fifty tons. As for morale, Semmes noted in his journal:

> My crew seen to be in the right spirit, a quiet spirit of determination pervading both officers and men. The combat will no doubt be contested and obstinate, but the two ships are so equally matched that I do not feel at liberty to decline it. God defend the right, and have mercy upon the souls of those who fall, as many of us must.[68]

Soon after the *Kearsarge* had arrived, Semmes had sent a message to Winslow (through the American consul at Cherbourg) of his intention to fight. He received no reply from Winslow, who had earlier been advised by Secretary of the Navy Gideon Welles: "To accept or send a challenge would be to recognize the pirates on terms of equality, elevating them and degrading our own."[69] But Winslow had no intention of allowing the *Alabama* to escape. It was arranged with the American consul that men be stationed on the bluff overlooking the harbor. They were to fire signal rockets in the event that Semmes tried to leave port under cover of darkness.

By June 18 Semmes felt that his ship and crew were ready. He refused to be influenced by the "unanimous feeling" of the French port authorities, who advised that he should avoid combat with a "superior force." Semmes would write in his official report after the battle: "Mr. Kell, my first lieutenant, deserves great credit for the fine condition in which the ship went into action, with regard to her battery, magazine, and shell rooms."[70] But when Captain George Terry Sinclair, Confederate naval agent in Europe, arrived at Cherbourg from Paris only hours before the battle, he found the *Alabama*'s officers looking "rough, jaded, and worn out." He observed of Semmes: "He seemed to have weighed the matter well in his own mind, and determination was marked in every line of his faded and worn countenance."[71] Before disembarking, Sinclair advised Semmes to keep his ship at a respectful distance from Winslow's powerful 11-inch pivot guns.

The evening before the fight Kell wrote letters to Blanche and his mother, knowing that they might be his last. He had good reason for gloom. He had finally learned that, should he survive the battle, his beloved Boysie and Dot would never welcome his return.

13

FIGHT OFF CHERBOURG*

Sunday, June 19, 1864. The day was bright and cloudless, with only a slight haze. On the *Alabama* the fires had been started shortly after 6 a.m. As Semmes inspected his men, dressed in clean white frocks and blue trousers, he commented on their smart looks. He also remarked to Lieutenant Sinclair, "If the bright, beautiful, day is shining for our benefit, we should be happy at the omen." The officers, in their best uniforms, were tense with excitement as they paced the decks. Decks and brass work were immaculate from recent holystoning and polishing, and overhead flew the Confederate ensign. Musing over his prospects, Semmes surprised his fifth lieutenant by asking, "How do you think it will turn out today, Mr. Sinclair?" Sinclair, unaccustomed to being consulted by his captain, replied: "I cannot answer the question, sir, but can assure you the crew will do their full duty, and follow you to the death." Semmes replied, "Yes, that's true," and began his pacing of the quarter-deck.[1]

Kell continued to be the busiest officer aboard, as he supervised the final preparations for battle. The decks were sanded and tubs of water were placed along the spar deck as a precaution against fire. Then the men were sent to their stations, apparently convinced that the *Kearsarge* would be as easy to defeat as the *Hatteras* had been.

At about 9:45 a.m.[2] the *Alabama* got under way. She passed in front of the French ironclad frigate *Couronne*, which had

*My account of the *Alabama-Kearsarge* fight appeared in *American Heritage* (April, 1972) as "The Last of the Alabama" (N.C.D.)

started her own fires hours earlier. The *Couronne* would escort the Confederate raider to the three-mile limit to make certain that there was no violation of French territory. As the *Alabama* passed the liner *Napoleon*, the crew of the French vessel manned the rigging and gave three rousing cheers, then their band broke out with "Dixie." Thousands of spectators—Confederate and Union sympathizers alike—were arrayed upon the hillsides, on the breakwater, atop buildings, and aboard vessels. Among those situated to watch the fight were Englishman John Lancaster and his family, vacationing aboard their private yacht *Deerhound*. That morning at breakfast the family had held a vote to determine whether to attend church services or watch the fight from their yacht. The children all elected to see the action. In addition to the *Couronne* and the *Deerhound*, a few pilot and fishing boats trailed along. Aboard one pilot boat was the artist Edouard Manet, equipped with pencils, colors, and sketchbook. Manet would produce one of the most accurate representations of the *Alabama-Kearsarge* engagement.[3] The Cherbourg photographer, Rondin, had brought his equipment onto the old church tower overlooking the harbor, and he would take at least one recognizable photograph of the fight.[4]

After the *Alabama* steamed around the breakwater and sighted the *Kearsarge*, three miles away, Semmes headed his ship directly toward the enemy. The starboard battery was prepared for action. Semmes ordered Kell to have all hands piped aft, and, when they had gathered, he had his secretary read them a prepared speech.[5] Semmes had prepared his speech with great care, for he wanted to arouse the men. Breedlove Smith read:

> Officers and Seamen of the Alabama: You have, at length, another opportunity of meeting the enemy—the first that has been presented to you since you sank the *Hatteras!* In the meantime you have been all over the world, and it is not too much to say, that you have destroyed, and driven for protection under neutral flags, one half of the enemy's commerce, which, at the beginning of the war, covered every sea. This is an achievement of which you may well be proud; and a grateful country will not be unmindful of it. The name of your ship has become a household

> word wherever civilization extends! Shall that name be tarnished by defeat? The thing is impossible! Remember that you are in the English Channel, the theatre of so much of the naval glory of our race, and that the eyes of all Europe are at this moment, upon you. The flag that floats over you is that of a young Republic, who bids defiance to her enemies, whenever and wherever found! Show the world that you know how to uphold it! Go to your quarters.[6]

The sailors cheered enthusiastically, shouting "Never! Never!" at mention of defeat. One of their number, in a later interview, stated the reason for their optimism:

> The crew fully expected from the beginning that they would be led by Captain Semmes close alongside the Kearsarge so as to commence the action at close quarters and finish by boarding her. It was expected that Semmes would lead the boarders in person, for though we had as fine a crew as any ship afloat, yet we had not a single competent gunner on board, excepting the captain of the forward pivot, a hundred pound rifle gun. He was an old English man of war man, trained in the British navy. The captains of the other guns were not competent gunners, though brave men.[7]

The sailors returned to their quarters, where they stripped to the waist and were allowed to smoke and rest to reserve their strength.

Aboard the *Kearsarge* shortly after 10 a.m., the signal bell had just summoned the men for divine service. Captain Winslow, wearing a rather rusty-looking uniform, was opening his Bible when the lookout gave the cry, "Here she comes! The *Alabama!*" Winslow closed the Bible and told a cabin boy to bring up his side arms. He ordered the drummer to sound quarters. James Wheeler, acting master, ran to the hatchway of the wardroom mess and shouted to the startled officers below, "She's coming! She's coming, and heading straight for us!" Within two minutes all the men were at their stations. It is likely that they recalled Winslow's remark of three days earlier: "My lads, I will give you one hour to take the *Alabama*, and I think you can do it!"[8] He had also warned them, "Semmes is a tricky man and may try another *Hatteras* game on us." Running on a full head of steam, the *Kearsarge* was turned northeastward to open sea. Winslow wanted the battle to be fought well outside the three-mile limit both to avoid any incident with the French authorities and to prevent Semmes from escaping. Aware that he would have a greater advantage at close range, he ordered his guns loaded with five-second shell and sighted for five hundred yards.

After reaching the three-mile limit, the *Couronne* turned and left the *Alabama*, which was still headed toward the *Kearsarge*. Meanwhile, the *Kearsarge* had moved seven miles out to sea before turning around. Then, as the two vessels steamed directly at each other, the decks of the *Kearsarge* were sanded. Winslow's plan was to run down the *Alabama* or, "if circumstances did not warrant it, to close in with her."[9]

Semmes, standing on the horse block, the highest point on deck, had his glasses trained on the *Kearsarge*. His two pivot guns were rotated to starboard, as he intended to engage the enemy on that side. Semmes realized that the two 11-inch Dahlgrens on the *Kearsarge* gave the Federals an advantage at close range, while his own 100-pound Blakely pivot gun was most effective at long range. He had it set for two thousand yards and loaded with solid shot. Lieutenant Armstrong—commanding the gun—was instructed to have his gunners aim low—at the hull of the *Kearsarge*. Better to fire too low than too high, Semmes told his men, as the ricochet of their shot over the smooth water would remedy any defect in their vertical aim.

It was now about 11 a.m.,[10] forty-five minutes since they had rounded the breakwater. When a mile and a quarter's distance from the *Kearsarge*, the *Alabama* sheered, discharging her Blakely. The shot went high. The *Kearsarge*, on full steam, came with such speed that the *Alabama* was able to discharge only two more shot, which were also too high and damaged only the rigging.

Suddenly Winslow sheered off, presenting his starboard battery. The men responded instantly to his order: "All the divisions! Aim low for the waterline! Fire! Load and fire as rapidly as possible!"[11] The thirty-pound rifle gun on the topgallant forecastle, manned by the marine detachment, was the first fired. A shell struck the *Alabama* near her forward port, throwing out splinters and wounding a man at a gun. A sailor later recalled: "He leaped away with a leg smashed, and another man at the next gun fell dead. The shell caught our slide rack, and I think the man was killed by one of our own shot, which was thrown against him by the shell of the *Kearsarge*."[12] The *Alabama* next received a full broadside. Winslow intended to run under the *Alabama's* stern, but Semmes' keeping his broadside exposed prevented this. At five hundred yards, both ships were forced into a circular track under full steam, moving in opposite directions and each fighting her starboard side. The positions of the ships reminded one Yankee sailor of "two flies crawling around on the rim of a saucer."[13] They would make seven complete circles before the end of the action, gradually lessening the distance between them by about a hundred yards.

The action was now continuous on both sides. An assistant engineer on the deck of the *Kearsarge* was able to see shot and shell from the *Alabama* "skip like stones . . . thrown to ricochet until they burst to windward with a hollow roar, sending aloft a shower of glittering spray."[14] The *Alabama* fired at least two shots for every one of the *Kearsarge*. Although Kell believed that his men "handled their guns beautifully,"[15] he would also give due credit to his adversary: "She came into action magnificently."[16] The "luff" was standing near the eight-inch pivot gun commanded by Lieutenant Wilson, when suddenly an 11-inch shell exploded through the gun port and—as Kell later recalled—wiped out "like a sponge from a blackboard one-half of the gun's crew." A second shell killed one man and injured others. Then a third shell from the *Kearsarge* struck the breast of the gun carriage and spun around on deck without exploding. Seaman Mars, compressor man, quickly picked it up and threw it over the side. Lieutenant Wilson, in a state of shock at being struck by blood and limbs, was in no condition to continue his command. Mars signalled to Kell, requesting permission to clear the deck. Kell bowed his head in assent, and the remains were shoveled into the sea.[17] After the deck had been re-sanded, the places of Wilson and the dead and wounded were filled on Kell's order by Midshipman Anderson and eight men from a nearby thirty-two-pound gun. They worked coolly and methodically.

About twenty minutes after the action began, the spanker gaff that flew the *Alabama*'s colors was shot away, and the flag fell to just above the deck. Another flag was immediately raised at the mizzenmast head. At about the same time, a shell from the *Alabama* struck the hull of the *Kearsarge*. The men on the *Alabama* cheered, believing they had "knocked her engines to pieces," before they realized there had been no damage. With a "look of astonishment on his face,"[18] Semmes turned to his chief officer: "Mr. Kell, our shells strike the enemy's side, doing little damage, and fall into the water. Try solid shot."[19] This was done, and later both shot and shell were used alternately.

Positioned on the horse block to best direct the maneuvering of the ship, Semmes left his gunners with "no particular orders" during the action.[20] However, it was later claimed by his sailors that he offered a reward to the men who could silence the two 11-inch guns that were causing such havoc aboard his ship. During the fight Semmes is reported to have said of his opponents: "Confound them, they've been fighting twenty minutes, and they're cool as posts."

Kell distinguished himself throughout, and Semmes later praised his "coolness and judgement."[21] Another officer later recalled Kell's behavior during the fight:

> Nothing could exceed the cool and thorough attention to details of our first lieutenant. . . . From point to point of the spar-deck in his rapid movement he was directing here, or advising there; now seeing to the transfer of shot, shell, or cartridge; giving his orders to this and that man or officer, as though on dress-muster; occasionally in earnest conversation with Semmes, who occupied the horse-block, glasses in hand, and leaning on the hammock-rail; at times watching earnestly the enemy, and then casting his eye about our ship, as though keeping a careful reckoning of the damage given and received. Nothing seemed

to escape his active mind or eye, his commanding figure at all times towering over the heads of those around.[22]

Aboard the *Kearsarge*, Captain Winslow stood atop an arms chest on the starboard side of the quarter-deck, half of his body exposed above the rail, as he overlooked his own deck while scrutinizing the enemy. He repeatedly gave the order, "Faster, sir! Faster! Four bells!" to his third engineer, while holding up four fingers signifying "Full speed ahead!"[23] He gave orders in the same manner to Quartermaster William Poole at the helm. In addition to his other duties, Winslow watched the oncoming shells, directing the men near him when to dodge them. Other officers were also warning their gun crews when to drop to the deck. Men would drop flat, supporting themselves on hands and toes until the shot had struck or gone "howling" by, then spring up to resume action. Seaman John Bickford, working the pivot gun, had a shell pass so close that the air suction caused him to gasp. When his gun captain asked why he had not dodged it, he answered, between gasps, "Haven't time, sir. I'm busy." Cheer after cheer rent the air as shot and shell poured into the *Alabama*. There were exclamations of "That is a good one!" "Down boys—give her another like the last!" "That's for the pirates!" as the men calmly and precisely worked the guns.[24] Drenched in sweat and covered with powder stains, they were alternately laughing, talking, and cheering. The sponger of one gun was so stained with a "thick coating of burnt powder that it was hard to tell where blue undershirt ended and skin began." Kell's counterpart on the *Kearsarge*—Executive Officer James S. Thornton—passed from one gun to another, advising the crews: "Don't fire unless you get good aim; one shot that hits is better than fifty thrown away."[25] There was a brief pause in the action at one of the pivot guns as both vessels became enveloped in smoke. To an officer's anxious inquiry as to the cause of the delay, a gun captain replied, "Nothing is the matter, sir. She is all ready to give him a dose." "Then why in hell don't you fire?" demanded the officer. "I'll fire, sir, as soon as I get sight," came the unruffled reply. The smoke soon disappeared, and a missile from the gun struck the ocean close to the *Alabama*'s water line, sending a shower of spray into the air.[26] There was even comic relief for the Federals. To the amusement of their shipmates, two old sailors used up a box of ammunition firing a 12-pound howitzer boat gun.

Among the many observers on shore was Captain Sinclair. Equipped with "splendid glasses," Sinclair noted that, although the *Alabama* fired three shots for every two of her opponent, she usually fired too high. He also noticed a difference in the powder smoke of the two ships: that from the *Alabama* resembled "puffs of heavy steam," while that of the *Kearsarge* was "much lighter."[27] It was obvious to those taking part in the action that there was a difference. As Kell later recalled, "The report from the *Kearsarge*'s battery was clear and sharp, the powder burning like thin vapor, while our guns gave out a dull report, with thick and heavy vapor."[28] Thus was Kell proved correct in his earlier evaluation of the condition of the *Alabama*'s powder and the extent of its deterioration. The situation was far more serious than Semmes had believed at the time he sent his challenge to Winslow.

There was no question, moreover, as to the superiority of the gunners on the *Kearsarge*. Kell would admit that the Yankee guns were "served beautifully, being aimed with precision, and deliberate in fire."[29] One well qualified to know about the *Alabama* and her crew was Commander Bulloch. He would write that her sailors "had not been trained to judge of distances, and were wholly without the skill, precision and coolness which come only with practice and the habit of firing at a visible object and noting the effect."[30] Captain Winslow noted in his official report: "The firing of the *Alabama* from the first was rapid and wild. Toward the close of the action her firing became better." An *Alabama* sailor admitted: "Our guns were too much elevated, and shot over the *Kearsarge*. The men all fought well, but the gunners did not know how to point and elevate the guns."[31] A marine corporal on the *Kearsarge* noted the effect of this on the morale of the Federals:

> When the battle commenced it made our hair stick right up

> strait but after we had got settled down to work and saw by their rapid and haphazard fire that they were not doing us much damage we took it easy; they would fire when they were in their smoke and when we were enveloped in ours.[32]

The corporal also observed that in their haste and excitement, the *Alabama*'s gunners fired off about six of their ramrods, resembling "black meteors with their long tails."[33] Of the more than three hundred shot and shell fired by the Alabama during the hour-long engagement,[34] only twenty-eight struck the *Kearsarge*, and none of these did any significant damage. On the Federal side, the *Kearsarge* fired 173 shot and shell (mostly shell), a large number finding their mark and accounting for the "fearful work" of destruction. No grape or canister was used, although Winslow had a large quantity on hand.

Although the shells of the *Kearsarge* were taking a heavy toll in killed and wounded, the *Alabama* remained on the offensive, her captain waiting for the lucky shot that would cripple his opponent. At length, his forward pivot gun crew sent a 100-pound shell smashing under the counter of the *Kearsarge*, glancing along until it lodged in the rudderpost. As the *Kearsarge* trembled from the shock, the sailors on the *Alabama* cheered loudly. Here was their lucky shot. However, their cheers died when the anticipated explosion failed to occur. For Semmes and Kell, the failure was bitter; to his dying day each would believe that faulty powder or a defective fuse had prevented the shell from exploding. They were convinced that this shell alone could have sunk the *Kearsarge*. At the very least, they believed, it should have made the rudder inoperable and thus influenced the outcome, since the *Alabama* was still very much in the action.[35] Actually, however, if the shell had exploded at first contact—when it was supposed to—it would have damaged the ship's counter, some twenty feet from the sternpost.

John Bickford, a first loader on the *Kearsarge*, had a different version of the failure of so many shells to explode: "It's true that quite a number failed to explode, but it wasn't the fault of the shells. It was the fault of the excited men who fired them."[36] According to Bickford, almost all of the unexploded shells from the *Alabama* still had on the lead caps which should have been ripped off by the gun loaders, as Bickford himself was doing.[37] As he explained, unless the lead cap was removed to expose the fuse primer—set to explode in so many seconds—it was impossible for a shell to explode. The Yankee from Gloucester, Massachusetts—afterward awarded the Medal of Honor for "marked coolness and good conduct" during the fight—told of his experience with a shell he identified as Semmes' "lucky shot":

> I was standing on the starboard side of the gun, with my foot directly on the planksheer, when all of a sudden I heard the whir of a shell, a Blakely, and instantly my foot got a jar that seemed to fill it with pins and needles. That sixty-eight pound [*sic*] shell had struck the planksheer and gone way through it, at least so far that it exposed its primer, or where it should be, but I saw that the patch was still there on the shell, and I knew that it never could explode, that it was just as harmless as a solid shot would be in a like situation.
>
> Well, of course all the gun crew jumped back, looking for an explosion. I just turns round and says to 'em, "Never mind that, boys, it won't go off, because they forgot to take the patch off." I stayed where I was, loading the gun, and all the fellows jumped right to work again.[38]

A shell from the *Alabama*'s Blakely gun caused the only casualties on the *Kearsarge*. It passed through the starboard bulwarks below the main rigging, exploding on the quarterdeck and injuring three sailors at the after pivot gun. William Gowin, the most seriously injured, refused assistance and dragged himself to the forward hatch, where he was helped below by the surgeon.[39]

The twenty-eight shot and shell which struck the *Kearsarge* did no major damage. Twelve struck the hull, while eight were believed to have damaged the rigging. Two of the boats were put out of commission and one of the sails was badly torn. A shell entered the funnel of the *Kearsarge* and exploded, tearing out a space about three feet in diameter and throwing metal about the deck. A piece of the shell passed through the dipper of a thirsty fireman who had just raised it to his lips. For a moment the funnel appear to be falling as it rocked to and fro. A 100-pound shell ploughed across the roof of the engine room skylight, coming within fourteen inches of Engineer McConnell before passing harmlessly overboard through the port rail.[40]

During the latter part of the fight, the *Alabama* received the full effect of accurate and deadly fire. Seaman James Hart, carrying a shell to his gun, was blown to pieces. The "first serious disaster" to the ship was the destruction of her rudder.[41] For the remainder of the action, steering could be done only by using tackles. At about the same time—forty-five minutes after the battle had commenced—an 11-inch shell passed through the starboard side, emerging and exploding on her port side and tearing great gaps in her timbers and planking. To the exuberant *Kearsarge* sailors, it "raised the very devil."[42] A coal bunker bulkhead caved in, filling the fire room and almost burying the men under coal. With only two boilers left working, the *Alabama*'s steam pressure was greatly reduced.[43]

Filled with smoke and steam and with gaping holes in her hull, the *Alabama*—careening heavily to starboard—was in no condition to continue fighting. It was either escape, surrender, or be destroyed. The men were ordered to lie low, as it was feared that Winslow would now order a raking fire. But Semmes was not ready to surrender. He believed that by shifting the weight of his battery from starboard to port he might raise the shot holes above the water line. The ship was now five miles from the coast and with luck might make the three-mile limit. He gave the order: "Mr. Kell, as soon as our head points to the French coast in our circuit of action, shift your guns to port and make all sail for the coast." The helm was righted, the fore trysail sheets and two jibs hoisted, and the evolution executed successfully. At the same time, the pivot guns—after being cleared of the dead—were shifted to port with only a brief pause in the action. Kell appeared at the skylight above the engine room, and in a "voice of thunder" ordered the men below: "What is the matter in the engine room? Put on steam!"[44] Engineers Brooks and O'Brien, covered with sweat and coal dust, answered that the *Alabama* carried all the steam she could manage without blowing up. Then reconsidering, O'Brien declared, "Let her have the steam; we had better blow her to hell than to let the Yankees whip us!"[45] But it would take more than the extra twenty-five pounds of steam to save the *Alabama.* Winslow had anticipated Semmes' intentions and steamed across his adversary's bow. He was now in a position to rake her.

Aboard the *Alabama,* none could doubt the seriousness of the situation. An officer, looking out a port and seeing the water rushing into the gangway at every roll, was certain that the *Alabama*'s "last moments were close at hand."[46] A sailor later recalled: "Our men were then very fatigued and many disabled and wounded. We still fired as well as possible from the port side, though we knew the day was lost." Seaman John Roberts, who had been ordered by Kell to loose the jib, had executed the order and was returning to the deck when he was struck by a shell in the lower abdomen. With his entrails protruding, he succeeded in reaching the deck and was stumbling toward his gun when he fell dead.[47] O'Brien came on deck to report that the rapidly rising water was almost flush with the furnace fires. He found Semmes on the horse block with a handkerchief tied around his hand to cover a painful although superficial wound. Semmes listened in silence, then replied: "Return to your duty!" The engineers were now certain that they would go down with the ship. Engineer Pundt said bitterly: "Well, I suppose Old Beeswax has made up his mind to drown us like a lot of rats! Here, Matt! Take off my boots!"[48] On deck there was some confusion, "though nothing like a panic, excepting on the part of one or two."[49]

For the second time the Confederate colors were shot away, this time falling to the deck. There was now some confusion aboard the *Alabama*—and a misunderstanding aboard the *Kearsarge*—possibly due to the erroneous belief that Semmes had surrendered. Semmes ordered Kell to find out how long the ship could float. Going below, Kell found the sight "appalling." The holes in the hull were "large enough to admit a wheel barrow."[50] Surgeon Llewellyn was at his post, but the wounded man on his table had been swept away by a shell. Kell returned to the deck and reported that the ship could not remain afloat for more than ten minutes. Semmes gave the order: "Then, sir, cease firing, shorten sail, and haul down the colors; it will never do in this nineteenth century for us to go down, and the decks covered with our gallant wounded."[51] As there was no white flag available, two men on the spanker boom held up a makeshift one—the white portion of the Confederate ensign.[52] The officers and men on the *Kearsarge* would later claim that when they observed the white flag and the firing of a lee gun they ceased firing, but that two more shots were fired from the *Alabama*, one from the forward pivot gun.[53] Unconvinced that his enemy had surrendered, Winslow cried out: "Give it to them again, boys; they are playing us a trick!"[54] Each of his gun captains obeyed the order instantly, firing five volleys into the *Alabama*. Two 11-inch shells struck the coal bunker, throwing up coal dust as high as the yardarm. Aboard the doomed raider, Kell cried out: "Stand to your quarters, men. If we must be sunk after our colors are down, we will go to the bottom with every man at his post!"[55] And among the sailors the word was passed, "There's no quarter for us!"[56] But when the white flag was again raised on the spanker boom, all firing ceased. Semmes then ordered Kell: "Dispatch an officer to the *Kearsarge* and ask that they send boats to save our wounded—ours are disabled."

Finding the dinghy undamaged, Kell put Master's Mate Fullam in charge of her with instructions to surrender the ship and request assistance. Marine officer Howell, a nonswimmer, was allowed to take an oar as one of the crew. When Kell discovered that one boat was only slightly disabled, he directed the removal of the wounded to it. Among these was Seaman James King—"Connemara"— a troublemaker who had caused Kell many a headache since shipping on the *Alabama* at Singapore. As Kell stood briefly over the mortally wounded sailor, King seized his hand and kissed it. Amazed, Kell could not help thinking of the numerous times King had been punished on his orders.[57] Lieutenant Wilson and Dr. Galt were placed in charge of the boat and the wounded taken away, for the ship was settling fast. Winslow—who remembered how the *Hatteras* had been lured to destruction by Semmes—was apparently uncertain whether the *Alabama* was actually sinking. He continued to wait for more evidence. Only after Fullam had come aboard (after first deliberately dropping his sword over the side of the dinghy), was Winslow aware of the situation. Fullam delivered his message, then looking up and down the deck, asked where the dead and wounded were. When told that only three men had been wounded, he exclaimed, "My God, and it's a slaughter house over there!"[58] (He would later be astonished to learn that only nine men had been killed on the *Alabama* during the combat.) When Lieutenant Wilson came on board the *Kearsarge*, his appearance confirmed Fullam's account of the "slaughter" on the *Alabama*. He was covered with blood from the casualties at his gun early in the fight, and he still believed that sixteen of the seventeen men of his gun crew had been killed. Wilson offered Winslow his sword, but Winslow graciously refused it.

Aboard the sinking vessel Kell gave the order to abandon ship and directed the men to find a spar or whatever else might assist them in keeping afloat. As the men stripped to their underwear, Kell urged them over the side. He then returned to the stern, where Semmes, Bartelli, and a few other sailors were preparing to abandon ship. They were almost level with the ocean. Seaman Mars assisted Semmes as he removed his coat and boots, while the sail maker, Henry Alcott, helped Kell to pull off his boots. In the brief moment it took to do this, Kell recalled that on numerous occasions he had had Alcott punished for infractions of discipline.[59] Semmes still wore his cap (turned inside out), trousers, and vest, while Kell had stripped to his shirt and underdrawers. Both men had unceremoniously discarded their swords while undressing. Seaman Mars—one of the best swimmers on the ship—was entrusted with Semmes' papers (dispatches and accounts).[60] Unfortunately, no one knew that Bartelli, who remained at his Captain's side, could not swim. It was now every man for himself. Wearing a life preserver, Semmes slipped into the sea, followed by Kell,[61] who held onto a grating for support. The water "was like ice, and after the excitement of battle it seemed doubly cold."[62] The men swam off as best they could to escape the vortex of the sinking ship. As the *Alabama* "settled stern foremost, launching her bows high in the air," Kell turned for a final look. He later recalled his feelings at the sight:

> As the gallant vessel, the most beautiful I ever beheld, plunged down to her grave, I had it on my tongue to call to the men who were struggling in the water to give three cheers for her, but the dead that were floating around me and the deep sadness I felt at parting with the noble ship that had been my home so long deterred me.[63]

Kell's grating was not adequate, and he found the waves breaking over his head "distressingly uncomfortable." He later recalled: "I felt my strength giving out, but strange to say I never thought of giving up, though the white caps were breaking wildly over my head, and the sea foam from the billows blinding my eyes."[64] Noticing a makeshift float of empty shell boxes, Kell shouted to a sailor, a good swimmer, to examine it. The man called out: "It is the doctor, sir, dead." Llewellyn, like Bartelli, was unable to swim, a fact of which his shipmates were unaware. Eight others also drowned before help came. Even good swimmers like Kell found it difficult to remain afloat. Seeing his senior officer weakening, Midshipman Maffitt began to disengage his life preserver, gasping out, "Mr. Kell, you are so exhausted, take this life preserver." Kell, however, knowing that the boy was prepared to sacrifice himself, refused.[65] After what seemed like hours, but was actually only about thirty minutes, Kell heard a voice cry out, "Here's our Luff!" An *Alabama* sailor in one of the *Deerhound*'s boats had recognized the expansive beard floating on the water.[66] Kell was seized by the back of his neck and lifted into the boat.

Together with several of his crew, Semmes had already been rescued by the boat from Lancaster's yacht. Stretched out in the stern sheets "as pallid as death," he opened his eyes and gave his uninjured hand to Kell, who inquired, "Are you hurt?" "A little," came the answer. The hand injury was indeed slight, but he was suffering from exhaustion.[67] They were brought immediately to the *Deerhound*, where Kell learned the identity of the yacht and its owner. To Kell's surprise, he found Fullam aboard her. Winslow had allowed him to pick up survivors, and by not returning to the *Kearsarge*, the master's mate had cheated the Federals of several prisoners, including Howell, the brother-in-law of the Confederate President. From Fullam came the report that the *Kearsarge* had been protected by "chain armor". He had seen the places where the *Alabama*'s shot had torn the cover planking away, indenting and breaking the chain beneath.[68]

The rescued men were made comfortable. Semmes had the jacket of an English lieutenant loaned him by Lancaster, while Kell wore that gentleman's carpet slippers and a pair of his trousers. Lancaster asked Semmes to what part of France he wished to be taken. He smiled at the reply, "Oh, any part of Great Britain."[69]

As the Confederate raider settled stern first, Lieutenant Thornton aboard the *Kearsarge* passed the word, "Silence, boys."[70] Seaman Bickford told his gun crew that one could yell when licking a man "but not when you had him down." The reaction of one Yankee sailor was recorded in his journal:

> I was glad to see her go down and still I felt sorry for the poor fellows. It was a hard fight to see the poor fellows struggling in the water, some of them badly wounded, but still clinging to everything that they could lay their hands on to support themselves until our boats got near enough to pick them up.[71]

As the Federals began rescuing the men still in the water, some, it was later claimed by *Kearsarge* sailors, would deliberately throw up their hands to avoid rescue. Only by the use of boat hooks were some of these men taken alive.[72] On board the *Kearsarge*, frightened prisoners gazed up in terror at the main yardarm, claiming that Semmes had warned them they would be hanged as pirates if captured. Much to their relief, they learned they were prisoners of war and would be treated humanely.[73] One *Alabama* sailor, mistaking Winslow for the ship's steward, asked him for whiskey. Identifying himself, Winslow gave him some whiskey and added, "My man, I am sorry for you." And pointing to his colors, he said, "That is the flag you should have been under."[74] Not all the men on the *Kearsarge,* however, had good will in their hearts. One sailor had an old score to settle with Semmes. George Whipple, formerly of the *Sumter,* had never forgiven him the punishment he had received aboard that vessel. Whipple crouched on the top gallant forecastle holding a Sharp's rifle, as he waited expectantly for Semmes to be brought on board. Discovered by some of his shipmates, he told them, "Captain Semmes shall never come on board this ship alive." Unsuccessful in persuading Whipple to give up his plan, the men finally reported him to an officer, who had the rifle seized.[75] Among the bodies brought aboard the *Kearsarge* was that of William Robinson, the carpenter, who had been Whipple's shipmate aboard the *Sumter.* Robinson had drowned, apparently because his drawers had slipped down around his ankles, exhausting him in the water.[76] Whipple was "much affected" by the death of the man who had nursed him to health after his ordeal on the *Sumter.*[77]

Suddenly, the *Deerhound* was observed to be "stealing away." Bob Strahan, captain of a thirty-two-pounder, turned his gun directly upon her.[78] However, Winslow sent an officer to order him not to fire. As the *Deerhound* steamed away, the men waited in vain for the order to stop her. Years after the war, Executive Officer Thornton told an interviewer:

> I was waiting impatiently for the order to come to fire on the English yacht which had rescued Semmes from his sinking ship. I never for a moment doubted that such an order would be given. But it was not, and I felt so indignant that I almost lost self-control. I felt for awhile that it was a barren victory and that we had spent our powder all for nothing.[79]

Winslow later claimed he did not know the *Deerhound* was escaping; he refused at first to believe she could be "guilty of so disgraceful an act."[80] Although there is no reason to doubt Winslow's statement, the ship's surgeon declared, "Probably not another person on board the *Kearsarge* was of the same opinion. . . . Captain Winslow alone is responsible for the escape of Semmes."[81]

Winslow was generous in victory. Calling his sailors to muster, he read them a prayer and announced: "We have won the battle without loss of life; God must have been on our side. The *Alabama*'s men have been in the water, and you are requested to give them some of your clothing and report any expense to me. These men have surrendered; I want you to use them as brother shipmates. Your dinner will be served out to you. Share it with them."[82] When the grog tub was brought up, all were allowed to refresh themselves.[83]

Meanwhile, as the *Deerhound* steamed toward Southampton, the Confederates on board felt thankful they had been saved from death or imprisonment. When the officers tried to thank Lancaster, he merely told them, "Gentlemen, you have no need to give me any special thanks; I should have done exactly the same for the other people if they had needed it."[84]

14

RETURN TO GEORGIA

Upon their arrival at Southampton on the evening of the 19th, Semmes and Kell checked into the Kelway Hotel. Received in royal style, they were assigned rooms recently occupied by a prince. They found themselves the center of attention. Throughout the city the *Alabama-Kearsarge* battle was being discussed, and few Englishmen were disparaging the *Alabama*, considered a gallant underdog. Publicly, Semmes said nothing to credit Winslow his victory. He continually stressed the fact that he had been "completely deceived" as to the strength and armament of the *Kearsarge*. Had he known that she was "iron-clad" and more heavily armed than the *Alabama*, he said, he would not have fought; for him to have done so would have been "madness."[1] An English reporter observed that Semmes seemed to "be laboring under mental anguish and to feel most acutely the complete defeat he had experienced and the death and sufferings which that defeat had caused."[2]

A telegram to John Hutton in Liverpool brought Kell an immediate offer of assistance. Hutton was the only person to whom Kell wrote a brief account of the fight.[3] Friends and sympathizers, including Commissioner Mason, Captain Bulloch, and the Reverend Tremlett, soon arrived in Southampton. Mason personally thanked Mr. Lancaster for having saved the lives of Semmes, Kell, and other officers and sailors.

The morning after their arrival in Southampton, Semmes and Kell located a tailor shop to purchase badly needed clothes.

Its proprietor was so delighted with his customers that he invited them to his private apartments in the same building for cake and wine. While they were eating, however, he returned from his shop to tell them: "Gentlemen, I shall have to request you to return to your hotel. Your presence here has completely blocked business on this street." Leaving the shop, the officers found the street filled with thousands of curious admirers who were hoping for a glimpse of Old Beeswax and his "luff." The police had to clear a passage for them.[4]

That same day, at their hotel, Semmes showed Kell two keys he had had in his vest pocket at the time he jumped into the sea. One—the key to the strongbox of the *Alabama*—he gave to Kell, and the other—the key to his cabin—he kept. Later, in London, Kell had his key gilded into a shawl pin for Blanche. Another memento he later acquired was a small piece of ivory etched with the Confederate seal on one side and the *Alabama* on the other. Kell's most precious keepsakes, however, were his watch and a lock of Blanche's hair, the only items he himself had been able to save. He had tied the watch onto the waistband of his underdrawers with the lock of hair.

After Semmes had made out his official reports, he and Kell looked forward to a much needed period of relaxation. Tremlett was anxious that they return with him to London, and his sister wrote Kell promising he would have no speeches to make and would see only a few "old friends and Rebels."[5] But there were still the duties of settling the affairs of the ship and paying off the crew. When, by June 30, these had been attended to, Semmes and Kell went to Millbrook, a few miles from Southampton, for rest. Afterward, the two officers accepted the hospitality of Tremlett at the parsonage. In London sympathizers presented Semmes with an engraved sword and silk Confederate flag, while Kell received an elegant brace of pistols.[6] At the Huttons, Kell received a welcome letter from Blanche—dated April 28, 1864—which contained a picture of his surviving child. He was deeply moved by his wife's suggestion that she join him abroad; to Kell it proved that "a country possessing such women, such mothers, and such daughters, *can not* be conquered."[7] It troubled him that he was unable to let her know of his safety and his plans for returning to the Confederacy. He left *L170* sterling with Hutton to be drawn upon in the event of his capture while running the blockade.

On June 30 orders were issued in Paris by Confederate Commander Samuel Barron for the officers of the *Alabama* to return to the Confederacy. Those taken prisoner by the *Kearsarge* had been paroled (except for Chief Engineer Freeman)[8] along with the crew. Not all would return immediately,[9] but on July 9 at Liverpool, Kell and Dr. Galt boarded the English mail steamer *Europa*, bound for Halifax. On the next day a telegram was delivered to Sylvan Lodge:

Richmond

The Alabama was sunk off Cherbourg but Mr. Kell was saved and was in London on 20th June.

F. W. Sims[10]

Colonel Sims, after learning of the battle, had sent the telegram in the hope it would reach Blanche before she saw the newspaper reports. It was received in time; only hours later the news reached Macon. At the same time, however, there was more critical news for Georgians—their property and very lives were at stake. Blanche wrote: "The Yankees are *almost* on us—the fight will either take place, or Atlanta fall, in 48 hours. Everybody is leaving it that can, panic stricken, and of course Macon will go next."[11] However, although Atlanta was taken by Sherman's army, no attack on Macon followed, and after days of intense anxiety, relative calm returned. Blanche was able to return to her journal and pour forth the grief she would share with her husband.

It had been a sad parting for Kell and the officers and men of the *Alabama*. The great adventure had ended. Semmes would travel with Tremlett to the Continent for his health and would return to the Confederacy later. This late in the war there could be no second *Alabama*. Aboard the steamer *Europa* was an old shipmate of Kell's—Robert T. Chapman, former second officer of the *Sumter*.[12] Chapman had the responsibility of bringing the newly made great seal of the Confederacy from London to Richmond.[13] As the steamer stood off Queenstown, Kell scribbled a final letter to Louisa Tremlett: "You are one whose affection and regard I shall love to cherish through life and whom Mrs. Kell will learn to love as a Sister, for the 'parsonage' will be known to her as my 'English home.' "[14]

Unfortunately, the *Europa*, "the tortoise of the line," was "deficient in the comforts and appliances of more modern vessels."[15] Nor did the Rebels find the other passengers companionable. A Confederate officer noted that "the old paddle wheel tub was crowded with Yanks who scowled at us in a very unfriendly way."[16] Also aboard was Midshipman Edward E. Preble of the *Kearsarge*, bearing official dispatches to Washington. Kell later observed: "I am not sure that he relished my presence on board the ship."[17]

In Halifax ten days later, Kell and Galt, as "representatives of Captain Semmes and the South," were given a "handsome entertainment" by the local vicar-general of the Roman Catholic Church, who was an ardent Confederate sympathizer. They began the next stage of their journey—bound for Bermuda—on the steamer *Alpha*. Aboard her, the Confederates again kept to themselves. Midshipman James M. Morgan of C.S.S. *Georgia* later recalled an incident of the voyage:

> In the early mornings we would gather on the little poop deck and pass away the time until the gong sounded for breakfast, when we would fall in behind Commander Kell, according to rank, and in Indian file walk into the saloon and take our seats. Commander Kell was a most commanding figure. . . . [His beard] reached to his waist and flowed over his breast like a waterfall—it was very red. He allowed only his intimates to see it, however, as he kept it plaited and stuck down his shirt collar. Ordinarily his beard looked to be about three inches long with the ends all turned in under his chin. One morning we were seated as usual on the poop when Commander Kell produced from the inner recesses of his shirt front the wonderful beard and proceeded to comb it out. Before he had finished the intricate operation the gong sounded, and with his habitual consideration for others, he said that he would not keep us from our breakfasts

while he put up his extraordinary hirsute adornment, and he led the way to the saloon with his great beard flowing over his manly chest. As he entered the door the passengers were all seated at the breakfast tables, and to our great consternation some idiot screamed out, "The pirates are going to take us!" Then followed a scene I shall never forget. Men dove under the tables and the women fell on their knees and begged for mercy. As for us—we were simply scared into speechlessness. It was Commander Kell's beard that had caused the fright—the passengers jumping to the conclusion that there were other pirates secreted on the ship, and that the time to take her and make them walk the plank had arrived. The captain of the *Alpha* rushed aft to find out what had happened, and even he did not recognize Commander Kell at first. Of course there was a hearty laugh when the mystery of the beard was explained, and we were all much better friends for the rest of the voyage.[18]

Unknown to Kell, his movements were being carefully watched by Federal agents. A telegram to the Commander of the North Atlantic Blockading Squadron from Secretary of the Navy Welles warned:

Lieutenant Kell and several of the crew of the *Alabama* left [Halifax] on last steamer for Bermuda, with intention to run blockade at Wilmington and procure a vessel in place of the *Alabama*.[19]

At Bermuda on July 27, the day before he was to depart on the blockade runner *Flamingo*, Kell wrote Blanche a letter to be sent on another vessel in case he was captured. It was his first letter to her since the sinking of the *Alabama*.

I know my poor afflicted wife that the suffering you have been forced through has worked terribly upon your nervous system.... God in his wisdom has taken from us our first born and noble son, and our only darling daughter. You and our only son, our Johnny, are all I have left on earth to comfort me, then for our sakes be strong in the trial God sees fit to put upon us, for in running this risk of getting home I but do my duty to my country and to my family.... I must see

> our bleeding country in this desperate struggle and strike a blow for liberty upon our own beloved soil. Although my sufferings have been greater in the service I have been on in being seperated from my wife and children regardless of the hardships encountered, I am proud to think that our country has appreciated these services, and my heart now yearns for home. Oh Bannie! God *will* be merciful to us, and unite us and our precious and only child. My poor heart yearns and longs to take you to it and talk of our angel children, our Munroe and darling daughter.

Kell reassured Blanche that if he were taken prisoner he would not be mistreated, as "we hold at this time too many prisoners of theirs, and my exchange would be made in regular order."[20]

On July 28 the vessels of the blockading squadron off Wilmington, North Carolina, were especially vigilant; all had received instructions to "make every effort" to capture Kell and his party.[21] The *Flamingo* was one of the three sloop rigged steamers which had recently been built in England for special service as blockade runners.[22] She had sailed from Glasgow with a cargo which included ten cases of ale, brandy, and sherry.[23] She would require skillful handling as well as her speed of 16 knots to get her safely into Wilmington.

For excitement this voyage would equal any ever made by Kell. As they approached the Carolina coast at night, they lost their bearings due to the drunken state of the *Flamingo's* officers. Therefore, they stood to sea until daybreak. At the first light of dawn, five blockaders were seen, two ahead of them and three on their quarters. Putting on all her steam, the *Flamingo* surged ahead as the shell fired after them fell short; soon they outdistanced their pursuers. Kell and the other Confederate officers on board took charge of finding their bearings, and that night they "passed in under the very guns of the blockaders, like a flash of lightning." Once safe under the guns of Fort Fisher, a bottle of champagne was brought up and a toast to their success was "heartily quaffed."[24]

Immediately upon landing, Kell sent a wire to Nathan Munroe: "Arrived safely will come immediately hope to arrive friday morning advise Mother."[25] When she learned the happy news, Blanche shared her joy with her journal:

> Oh! God! another thanksgiving. My husband has come safely into port—how can I thank thee sufficiently for the blessing! And will I, can I hope *so soon* (the telegram says friday noon), to rest my sorrowful heart in *his* keeping? My poor beloved who left *four* treasures, and is coming back to *two*![26]

In a freight car to Macon, Kell rode with several Confederate soldiers. One of them, after learning his name, remarked:

> That is a very uncommon name, but I've heard it before. A little lady helped nurse in the hospital in Macon with that name. She used to come in leading a beautiful little curly headed boy by the hand. She dressed in deep black, and we all thought her husband had been killed in the war. We asked Dr. Green, and he told us. She had lost her children with diphtheria, but her husband was an officer in the Navy.[27]

This news came as a shock to Kell; he was dumfounded that Nathan Munroe had allowed Blanche, in her nervous condition, to be involved in such work.

Soon came the reunion Kell and Blanche had so long prayed for. It would be two weeks before Blanche would again turn to her journal:

> I have been very happy—happy in *him*—as much so as I shall ever be on earth again. Our cup of thanksgiving has been mingled with tears, and the undercurrent of anguish has sometimes swelled out—how sweet his pitying sympathy then—he, who in the strength of his godlike perfect manhood can forget his own grief to comfort his poor wife.[28]

The second day after his return, Kell and Blanche visited the hospital. He met her special friend, a one-armed soldier boy, and invited him to return with them to Sylvan Lodge. As Blanche watched the maimed youth trying to balance himself as he gathered grapes in the scuppernong arbor, she "blessed God" that her husband had returned to her alive and uninjured.

Soon after his return, Kell was pleased to receive his long

overdue commission as commander in the Provisional Navy. Secretary Mallory sent a personal letter of congratulations in which he mentioned "the arduous duties which you have so long and ably performed as the Executive officer of the *Sumter* and the *Alabama*." The commission, retroactive to October 4, 1863, was granted *"for gallant and meritorious conduct as first Lieutenant and Executive Officer of the C.S. Steam Sloops Sumter and Alabama under the command of Captain Raphael Semmes."*[29] Kell would say that had he known of his promotion while at sea he would not "willingly have left Captain Semmes and the *Alabama* even to take a command."[30]

Among the many letters of congratulations was one from a fellow classmate of the "date of 1841"—North Carolinian James I. Waddell—written from Paris. Waddell would soon gain a reputation of his own as commander of C.S.S. *Shenandoah*, the last of the Confederate raiders.[31]

It would be a long time before Kell could talk with Blanche about the *Alabama-Kearsarge* fight. He began to speak of it once, and Nathan Munroe noticed a "deadly pallor" come over his daughter's face; he insisted that Kell not mention it again until her health had improved. But the *Alabama* was still very much on Kell's mind. Blanche awoke one night to find her husband moaning and tossing in his sleep; he was reliving the anguish of the *Alabama's* last hour.

One day a tattered Confederate soldier came to Sylvan Lodge begging for shoes and a hat. Blanche gave him a worn military cap, money, and a hot meal. Half an hour after the soldier had left, Kell discovered that his new English hat was missing from the hat rack. A week later, while on a drive with Blanche, he recognized his hat on a passing soldier. Ordering the driver to stop, he seized the boy and began shaking him. Ignoring the protest that the hat had been bought from a Negro, Kell shouted; "You are a disgrace to your Confederate uniform! You took this when my wife gave you an old cap, the money for shoes, and your breakfast! I am ashamed of you! You shall not have my hat!" And so saying, he seized the hat and tossed it up to his driver.[32]

In August Kell visited his mother, sister Mary, and Charles

and Evelyn Spalding in Brooks County. The women were grateful for the "many comforts" he had brought them from England: boots, shoes, gloves, slippers, stockings, towels, scissors, tea, chocolate, toothbrushes ("a treasure"), and a thimble. From the Retreat Kell left for Richmond, where he obtained an extension of his leave.

With Sherman's army now deep in Georgia, there were increasing fears for the saftey of Macon. Although Kell would have preferred remaining, Nathan insisted that Blanche be brought to a safer locality. Also, he had valuable papers which he would entrust to no one else. In the middle of September, Kell, his wife, and son left for Thomas County to stay with McIntosh relatives and the Spaldings.

On the first anniversary of her son's death, Blanche wrote in her journal:

> It comforts me to see my Husband so resigned, yet it reproaches me too, that I am not as much so—he realizes the Sin, the temptations, the evil, our little boy has been spared, he feels God's goodness and mercy, in transplanting these sweet blossoms of our married life to a purer dearer home, while I think only of my loss.[33]

In Macon a raid or a general movement of Sherman's army was expected daily. Nattie was now the only lieutenant in his company and would have to lead his men in their next battle. Nathan could sense the tension under which his son had left him: "His heart seems much subdued and he talks with the confidence of a Christian." Eight hundred Confederate soldiers had encamped on the grounds of Sylvan Lodge and were "destroying the fences and timber and desolating the place very much."[34]

From Thomas County the Kells went to Liberty County, and at Savannah Kell offered his services to Captain Tattnall. Tattnall responded hopelessly: "My son, it would only be to shoulder a musket and go by my side. There seems no work for us to do; the Navy has done all it could, and you have done your share."[35] Nevertheless, he said he would contact Kell if he were needed.

In the city, although the price of food had doubled, Kell was able to obtain supplies of beef and bread. They arrived at Walthourville in a downpour on November 21. After getting settled, Blanche wrote her father of their experience:

> We are marooning indeed and in truth I wish you could see our roughness. The old house has no sashes, and the wooden shutters must be open these cold days to give us any light—a kind neighbor lent us a bed, and our bed clothing was in the basket we brought—so we sleep very comfortably, all three of us in one bed. Then the same lady lent us each a cup and plate, and a bowl and pitcher to use in our room, and we have one chair and the trunks, and we are doing very well. . . . We brought 10 loaves of bread from Savannah and 15 lbs. of meat, and I had some of the tea Mr. Kell brought in, and a paper of coffee, and the little tin can of sugar so we can hold out a week or longer, and by that time maybe Mr. Kell will be able to get us some hominy, etc. He had the offer of a hog this morning but thought it cost too much to get it. I have since thought it best to write to Mr. Price to get us meal and hominy in Sav., so we will soon be supplied and you must not worry about us.[36]

They were visited by Margery Kell, who—since there was no room in their house—stayed with a neighbor, Mrs. Bryan. Baillie also came to see them and was afterward impressed into the defense of Savannah while trying to rejoin his regiment.

In early December, with Sherman's army approaching, Kell—desperate for the safety of his wife and son—brought them back to Thomas County. Ironically, Macon had turned out to be safe after all, but the prospect of getting there seemed dim with all transportation disrupted. As for Kell, he was impatient to get into the action, believing that "he and every other man ought to be doing something."[37] Orders had finally arrived directing him to "proceed to Richmond, Va., *without delay*, and report to Flag Officer John K. Mitchell, Commanding, for duty."[38]

Kell made three attempts to leave Thomas County but was

frustrated by lack of transportation and the movements of the Federals. Many of the railroad tracks had been cut by raiders, and the roads were filled with refugees. Finally, he was forced to "impress" a "dilapidated cloth-covered wagon" in Thomasville and, with family and nurse inside, proceeded to Albany, a journey of two days and nights. Nearing Albany in the middle of the night, they met a carriage sent by Nathan Munroe. Early the next morning they reached Albany and traveled by train from there to Macon.

With his family secure at Sylvan Lodge, Kell left for Richmond on the morning of December 23. The journey was difficult and dangerous. In Sparta, Georgia, he spent a "sad and gloomy" Christmas, while at Sylvan Lodge Blanche again turned to her journal:

> A sad sad Christmas! . . . thank Heaven My Darling would not leave me elsewhere than here—Oh God, how I thank thee for my Darling Husband and his precious love. . . . Johnny has been happy today. Santa Claus came, with all that he could bring these *hard times* and it does not take much to make him happy—so sweet and easily contented is his disposition.

And a week later on New Year's Eve:

> It is *nine* years ago this night of the year, since my beloved wrote me his first letter, offering me as he said "a heart never before won by woman." I had many loves then but I thank God for the choice I made! . . . I have had tenderness and comfort from the One to whom I gave a happy girl's heart, which did not know *how to love*, as the more sorrowful wife has since learned. I *thought* I loved you then Darling. I *know* I love you *now*.

15

DEFEAT

As Kell made his way to Richmond, he had good cause to fear for the safety of his mother and sister in Liberty County. They had remained there in an unsuccessful attempt to sell their corn and, being so near Savannah, could hardly avoid an encounter with the enemy. As Sherman's army approached, Margery, Mary, and Mrs. Bryan were stranded at the home of Isaac Aiken near Walthourville. Aiken and the younger women of the household had left in haste after being warned that the Yankees would soon be upon them. (The older women—it was reasoned—were not likely to be molested.) Except for a few Negroes and old people in the neighborhood, the three women were alone. Before leaving, Aiken had buried Margery's silver and had ordered his Negro boy to take care of the women.

On December 23 the sounds of hoofbeats and men's voices were heard in the Aiken yard; the Yankees had arrived. Entering the house, they told the frightened women that they were searching for firearms and demanded keys to trunks. They began dumping the contents on the floor, and—although Margery "stood over them and saw they took nothing"—one soldier took three silver forks from the dining room, and another took "a nice little pen knife" from Mary. Otherwise, they "behaved very well."[1] Identifying themselves as men of Kilpatrick's cavalry, they assured the women that they had nothing to fear from Federal cavalry but that the ten thousand infantrymen at Midway "would take and destroy everything." The cavalrymen then rode off.

Early on Christmas morning, a group of mounted infantry came "rushing into the Yard." They immediately entered the house and searched every room and closet, after which they turned their attention to food and valuables. To the terrified women, they seemed a "horrid set of deamons [*sic*]." They made no uncivil remarks, however, and only demanded food. All of Mrs. Bryan's meat was taken, but Margery had earlier hidden hers with her corn in a small log house in the stable yard, and this was not found. For the three women the experience was a nightmare. Margery later wrote: "I could not keep from crying all the time they were racing about the house. Mary looked as if she was cut out of stone and Mrs. Bryan talked and cried. . . ."[2] The soldiers left at sundown but returned in the morning and remained the entire day. In an effort to discover where valuables were hidden, the soldiers put a rope around the neck of an old Negro and threatened him with hanging; he finally "told all he knew." Mrs. Bryan's trunks were taken from their hiding place and their contents "trampled and disused," although only towels and handkerchiefs were taken. The Negroes were told they could have the silk dresses, but—when they made no move to take them—their own best clothes, tobacco, and sugar were seized. (One soldier, however, took no part in the looting.) All of the vacated homes were ransacked, and two were burned. All the poultry and livestock found were taken away. The soldiers then gave the "country people" permission to strip the houses of those who had fled, thus completing the devastation.

A few days after the Federals had left—the cavalry to McIntosh County and the infantry to Savannah—Margery wrote in desperation, hoping to somehow get a letter through to Brooks County: "Starvation stares us in the face if we cannot go. . . . Our Negroes do not support us and we must make an effort to do so ourselves."[3]

In Brooks County Charles Spalding set out by buggy to rescue Margery and Mary. Halfway to Walthourville he learned that if he continued his horses were likely to be seized by either Confederate or Union cavalry; reluctantly, he turned back. A few days later he was able to make rail connections to Doctortown in Liberty County and had the Confederate commander there send in a flag of truce on behalf of the women. Spalding himself sent in a reliable man with "mules and cart and a large basket of provisions."

The women were safe but becoming desperate. Another party of Yankee cavalry had come to the house asking for meat and bread. They had, however, "behaved very civilly." As the homes had been "stripped of provisions," they were forced to search the woods for hidden corn, but, by the time a Confederate colonel and five soldiers arrived with a flag of truce, they had all left. Three weeks of effort by Charles were finally rewarded. On January 13, with a mule cart for the women and a wagon and "old foundered horse" for the baggage, the group left. The roads were in a sorry condition ("all under water") and the wagon broke down, but five days later they arrived at the Retreat.

Margery had heard no news of Baillie in weeks, and she feared he had been captured. The thought of her son in a Northern prison camp—"without even one blanket"—tormented her. The disastrous fall of Savannah had convinced Margery that the war was lost.

> I am in despair and think the Confederacy is lost. O if Georgia had done her duty as noble Virginia, how different would our prospects be, but she has fallen far short and must reap the results.[4]

On December 31 Kell arrived in Richmond and was given the command of C.S. Ironclad *Richmond* of the James River Squadron. Kell had already been warned about ironclads. William Evans, now at Charleston, had written him, "This Ironclad work is a horrible business, a kind of nondescript vessel with nothing about her like a ship except the battery."[5] Actually, the *Richmond*, although no *Alabama*, was far better suited for a new type of naval warfare. She had been commissioned in the summer of 1862 and been commanded by Lieutenant William H. Parker during engagements on the James River in 1864. Covered with five inches of iron and armed with four seven-inch rifle guns, she was sturdy but slow, limited to a speed of six knots.[6] She made up one-third of the squadron (except for a few torpedo and gun boats); Flag Officer Mitchell commanded the *Virginia* and Commander Thomas R. Rootes the *Fredericksburg*. The three vessels lay off Chaffin's Bluff, about nine miles below Richmond and in sight of the Federal positions. Before reporting to his new command, Kell spent four days with Colonel Sims and Tadie in Richmond and sized up the city as being "without doubt the securest spot in the Confederacy."[7]

Aboard the *Richmond*, Kell's quarters consisted of what had formerly been two staterooms. He had an efficient steward and meals were good: genuine coffee and sugar, fresh bread and butter, meat, vegetables, and, occasionally, even turkey.[8] Feeling conspicuous in the elegant new uniforms he had brought from England, Kell purchased material for a suit and overcoat but found that tailoring would be too expensive.

Within a few weeks of Kell's arrival, the squadron took the offensive. On the evening of January 23, Mitchell directed the three ironclads, with six gunboats and two torpedo boats, down the river. Their objective was to destroy the large Union supply base at City Point. (Rear Admiral David D. Porter had left a reduced Federal squadron when he went to participate in the Fort Fisher operations.) Lashed on either side of the *Richmond* were the gunboats *Drewry* and *Beaufort*, with the torpedo boat *Wasp* in tow. The Union batteries above Dutch Gap gave the alarm, but the squadron arrived at Trent's Reach without mishap. *Richmond*, *Virginia*, and the gunboats anchored, while the *Fredericksburg* sought to find a way through the obstructions before them. Mitchell felt jubilant when this vessel made it through, but when his *Virginia* attempted it, she became grounded. By 3:30 a.m. the *Richmond* and two gunboats had also run aground. It was impossible to make any further move until flood tide lifted the stranded vessels free. Mitchell ordered the *Fredericksburg* recalled so that she at least would be clear of the Union batteries.

For several hours the grounded vessels received the full force of the batteries. The *Drewry*, lashed alongside the *Richmond*, was blown to pieces and the *Scorpion* badly damaged by the same explosion. Aboard the *Richmond* the shock was "terrific," but, although struck almost constantly, she was at such an angle that most of the projectiles ricocheted off her casements. The Union monitor *Onondaga*, and several gunboats which had been down the river, moved up in the morning to join the fight but were not aggressive in their attack.[9] At about 11:20 a.m. the grounded craft succeeded in getting afloat, and they retired up the river to their former positions. Surprisingly, only one man in the expedition had been killed and eight wounded. Kell had been on his feet "constantly day and night."[10]

On his forty-second birthday, spent on the near-frozen James River, Kell thought of the Confederate soldiers in the trenches and considered himself fortunate. To his great delight, he was summoned soon afterward to Richmond on a twenty-four-hour leave. Captain Semmes had arrived in the capital and had requested to see Kell. He had a letter and present (a smoking cap) from Blanche, with whom he had visited briefly in Vineville. Blanche and her father had been delighted with Semmes, who praised Kell as his "right hand" during their long association.[11] Blanche's letter brought welcome news: Kell's mother and sister were safe at the Retreat with the Spaldings.

Since boarding the Richmond, Kell had been drinking James River water, and it soon brought on an attack of dysentery. He wrote: "It is all I can do to keep out of the hands of the Doctors and the Hospital, which I should dread away from home."[12] His health unimproved, Kell was finally relieved of his command but ordered to remain in Richmond. Leaving the *Richmond* when he did, he missed a final opportunity to serve under Raphael Semmes. (Semmes, promoted to rear admiral, replaced Mitchell as commander of the James River Squadron and would serve until the evacuation of Richmond; then he would destroy his ships and organize his sailors into a military unit.) For the next few weeks, Kell received every attention from Tadie and the Colonel. He enjoyed an occasional ride on the horse Bob Minor put at his disposal. But for Kell, there was new cause for concern over Blanche. Her poor health continued, and she was pregnant again.

As March began and preparations for the evacuation of Richmond were in evidence, Kell could still find reason for optimism: "I think and hope when the entire Seaboard is given up the Cause will be strengthened and our forces concentrated out of reach of their gunboats and Ironclads."[13] Letters to Vineville now had to be hand carried.

In the middle of March, Kell accompanied the Simses to Danville, believing that the change might benefit his health. They boarded at a home next to the family of General William J. Hardee, enabling Kell to obtain the latest war news sent by telegraph to the General. On March 24, Captain Sydney S. Lee, in Richmond, sent a dispatch to Kell; it would be Kell's last from the Confederate government. He was granted a leave of absence until May 1, at which time he was to "report in writing" the condition of his health.[14] When Kell appeared at Sylvan Lodge, Blanche almost fainted at his unexpected arrival and the shock of seeing him so wan and pale. He was burning with fever.

Kell was in Vineville when the report came that Lee's army had surrendered. The day before the surrender of Macon (to General James H. Wilson), Kell, accompanied by his servant boy, boarded the crowded train for Hawkinsville in Pulaski County. There he was taken into the home of Colonel Nightingale, an old friend and neighbor from the coast, and nursed by Mrs. Nightingale.

The victorious Federals swept through Macon after the surrender of the city's defenders—mostly old men and boys—on April 20. First to be seized was the nearly completed ammunition factory at Vineville. Then soldiers began rushing into yards and houses demanding food. Ten parties were fed breakfast at Sylvan Lodge before the family was able to eat. Blanche tried to locate Confederate General William W. Mackall to secure protection for their home, but learned that the General was a prisoner and "like a sore headed bear." Returning home, she was met by her nurse, accompanied by a heavily bearded Yankee officer. The nurse said to Blanche, "Missis, I told this soldier you and old Marster wanted somebody to stay in the house for the soldiers were troublesome." The officer, a lieutenant colonel of cavalry, raised his hat and said politely, "Madam,

I am very sick and in need of quiet. Your servant boy told me he thought you would take me in." Impressed with the officer's appearance and manner, Blanche answered, "I would like to have an officer and a gentleman protect us in my father's house; he is old and an invalid and there is only my little son and myself." The colonel, forcing a smile, said he hoped he would fill her requirements.[15]

The officer was Colonel Henry Harnden, commanding the First Wisconsin Cavalry. Blanche would later recall that they had no regrets about taking him into their home: "He was a gentleman." Harnden's surgeon, quartermaster, chaplain, and orderly were in constant attendance on him; they petted little Johnny and were courteous to the adults. No mention was ever made of the war. Nathan Munroe invited Colonel Harnden to dine with them, and he readily accepted. One morning Harnden politely handed Blanche the newspaper brought him by his orderly. (The regular Macon newspaper had discontinued operation, but the military were printing a daily paper.) Blanche gasped in disbelief as she read: "General Orders No. 20, punishable with death." Harnden quickly explained, "The soldiers are getting very disorderly and many complaints are being made of them. If they enter a private dwelling, especially a bedroom, and are identified, they are to be shot." "How very strict your discipline," said Blanche. "Yes, necessarily," he replied.[16] Not long afterward, Colonel Harnden suddenly left Vineville on a secret mission, which—it was later learned—was to apprehend Jefferson Davis.[17]

On April 25 the "shocking" news of Lee's surrender was learned at the Retreat and gave Margery Kell "quite a sick time." She was glad the war had ended but feared for the safety of her sons. Evelyn was "thankful" that Lincoln was dead and hoped that Secretary Seward would also die, believing it would result in "better terms with the Yankees."[18] On May 16, in Macon, Kell signed his parole papers authorized by General Wilson.[19]

When Harnden's regiment left Macon, Blanche and Kell were at the Varner's home in Sunnyside. While the Federal cavalry rode north to Atlanta, three horsemen reined in at the Varner home. Hearing the clatter of hoofs, Blanche ran to the window and, in the moonlight, saw three Yankee soldiers arguing with her uncle. She could hear them plainly. When asked how many men were in the house, Mr. Varner replied, "My overseer and myself." But the soldiers had seen another man—"a big officer"—and they demanded to know his whereabouts. In a frenzy of terror, Blanche told her husband to attempt escape out the window, but he refused and asked her to leave him. Although his navy revolver had been stolen and he had no other weapon, when a saber was banged against the door Kell opened it and went out. The men demanded to see his parole. "What business have you with my parole?" Kell asked indignantly, but reached into his breast pocket for it. Reacting immediately, a soldier raised his saber to strike him, but Blanche was quicker and—although seven months pregnant—threw herself in front of her husband. Forgetting her fear, she spat out, "How dare you enter this house! General Orders No. 20 say such an act is punishable with death! I left Macon three days ago. Colonel Harnden, Quartermaster Kinney, and Doctor Robinson were in my father's house, and the regiment is passing now." And, turning, she addressed the servants gathered in the hallway. "Tell Lege to go on the McDonough road and ask the Colonel of the Regiment to come here to me, to Mrs. Kell."

As the soldier lowered his saber, Blanche noticed that the faces of the three cavalrymen were filled with "abject fear." One of them said, "Oh, Madam, we were not going to your room. All we wanted was to see the parole." And, indicating Mr. Varner, he continued, "If that damned Old Puppy had told us that his parole was right we would not have come in." The three men agreed together that the lady had "pluck," and if "all had been like her the South could not have been whipped so easy." After Kell had countermanded Blanche's order to Lege, the soldiers demanded silver, watches, and other valuables. The servants replied that "Old Mistis" had sent the silver to Macon. Blanche had three watches in her pocket—her own, her father's, and her husband's—and all three were ticking. In her excited state they seemed so noisy that she feared the soldiers would hear them, but she was not approached. They scorned her uncle's broken silver watch.

An hour after the three had galloped off, a group of officers arrived and politely requested feed for their horses. When asked if there had been trouble, Mr. Varner replied, "Some robbers and scoundrels have been here trying to intimidate us." The officers promised protection in return for feed for their horses and a meal for themselves. These were provided, after which they went to sleep on the porch floor. But for those in the house there was little sleep that night. As Blanche recalled: "We passed a very sleepless night being afraid to trust our enemies too implicitly."[20]

For the Kells, the war had ended at last.

16

THE SAILOR TURNS FARMER

With the war at an end, Kell was faced with important questions, for as a former officer of the *Alabama* he was considered no better than a "pirate" to many in the North. Should he leave the country? How could he provide for his family? Kell's decision was to remain in Georgia and farm—unless compelled to flee.

Still in South Georgia with her daughters, Margery Kell —although grateful that her family had been spared—had no illusions about the future. She was utterly destitute, without even a dollar in negotiable currency. There was no way of knowing the condition of the property in McIntosh County, or even whether they could claim it as theirs. And to Margery the political situation looked equally bleak, "having such an enemy as Andy Johnston [*sic*] to rule us."[1] Mary preferred leaving the country to submitting to Yankee rule, but, lacking the means, she suggested purchasing a small farm and selling its produce.[2]

Margery and Mary were realistic enough to understand that in order to live they would have to sell whatever remained of their property. The old days were gone. After learning of the "Yankee rules and regulations concerning the Negroes," the women realized that the plantation system was forever destroyed. As Mary put it, "We have never been able to make a good crop when the Negroes worked for us for nothing but their support—and what means have we of paying them *any* wages—high or low? It would be the maddest sort of speculation to attempt it of course and nothing but ruin before us."[3]

At the first opportunity, Kell's mother took the oath of allegiance in Quitman, believing it would protect her property and bring assistance from the Federals. She and Mary advised Donny to follow the example of "great and good Genl. Lee" and to forget the idea of leaving the country. To Margery, emancipation could be lived with, and there was even cause for optimism:

> Everyone (except Charles) has made bargains with their Negroes to go on working, . . . the bargain that all seem to make is to give the Negroes the half of everything planted and the Negroes to pay half the plantation expences, for instance they feed the animals and pay for half of all that is bought. You have nothing to do with their expence if you feed them the first year which most planters will have to do. You deduct their feed from their share of the crop of corn so there is no risk. Very few planters in the old system ever cleared half of the crop after paying all expenses—and the half of the crop divided among all of the workers would not amount to much.[4]

Margery advised Donny to rent a farm near the Varners in Sunnyside, as his health would benefit and Blanche could be near her father. Then, too, she recalled that Kell had "always had a turn for farming."

Baillie returned to Georgia early in June[5] and, when it was safe to do so, left the Retreat for McIntosh County. He found Rushland in good condition, but the Grove had been broken into—apparently by a local white man—and all the furniture removed. At the Ridge he found a Union regiment encamped and its officers living in the Kell house, but they assured him they would be leaving the area later in the fall. Baillie immediately made arrangements for securing oxen and plows and hiring freedmen to plant a cotton crop at Rushland.

Kell and Blanche had returned to Vineville early in June, and on July 13, 1865, a son was born there. To the family it seemed almost as though Munroe had returned. Old Mammy expressed it best: "I feel strange when I look at him; I feel like God done let Munroe come back."[6] When it came time to name the baby, Kell expressed his choice: "As connected with my last dream of glory and from personal friendship and affection, I would like to name him Raphael Semmes."[7]

When Blanche had recovered, they returned to Sunnyside, and Kell continued to benefit from fresh air, quiet, and rest. Admiral Semmes, living in Mobile, acknowledged the honor bestowed upon him by his former "luff":

> We have known each other long and well and under trying conditions, and I shall always esteem it a privilege to call you my friend. . . . I think you will act wisely in building yourself a log cabin and going to farming. . . . I shall be very happy to stand sponsor for your boy, but do not doubt that you will administer to the little fellow all the discipline he may require as he grows up.

Semmes had no intention of following the example of General Lee:

> I would not accept a pardon if offered me, as I infer by doing this I would imply that I had done wrong in taking up arms, whereas I shall always be proud that I used my feeble powers to prevent the consolidation and therefore the destruction of the government formed by your ancestors and mine.[8]

Kell's decision to settle in Spalding County was based only partially on the "bracing" effects of its climate. More practically, it was because the Varners had generously offered as much of their land as Kell could use, rent-free. The old couple, with no children of their own, were anxious to have their favorite niece and her family as neighbors. As for Blanche, the hills and fields reminded her of her childhood and of the "old playground" of little Boysie and Dot. However, sharing the Varner home would not be a permanent arrangement. The Kells wanted a home of their own. An agreement was worked out. At a cost of $1,000—most of it a gift of the Varners—Kell purchased several acres of adjacent land on which were two log cabins.[9] These were moved together to form a temporary dwelling while additions were being built. Although Kell admitted that the land was "indifferent," he believed it would "yield sufficient to live upon, and being in a healthy section of country with fine water and delightful fruit," would make a "desirable summer residence." It would also mean the realization of a long-held dream:

> To have a home and my family with me is what I have longed for since I became a married man and God grant I may now enjoy it with as much gratitude, in a Log cabin as though it was a palace.[10]

Blanche was in Vineville in late December when frightening news came: Semmes had been arrested. Horrified, she immediately had her husband summoned from Sunnyside and begged him to leave the country, taking her and the children with him. He refused, saying, "Captain Semmes may need me. Send for the Rector of the Church. I want our child baptized today.[11] Later, Kell received a communication from Semmes asking him to be ready to testify in his behalf should he be needed. The summons never came—nor was Kell ever bothered by the authorities—and Semmes was eventually released without a trial.

As the year 1865 came to an end, Blanche turned to the journal she had left untouched for a year:

> And we have the prospect of *a home—the first* really ours in all our married life—how happy should I be! and how happy I am tho' the bitter will come with the sweet and I am soon to leave loved Sylvan Lodge forever—where I spent my happy childhood! . . . Every inch of the soil is holy ground to me! but I must give it up! and thank God for a humble little cottage now building at "Rocky Knoll" John's home and mine.[12]

By the first of the year Kell had engaged four freedman for planting and had acquired two mules and a pony for plowing. His arrangement, which he considered "a liberal contract," was to furnish and feed the stock, provide all farm implements, feed the freedmen, and give them a third of what they produced.[13]

Margery Kell, enjoying good health, was able to view the changes in her life philosophically:

> I have always thought the working class were the happiest people in the world and altho' we are not exactly those, we have a great deal that we never did before and it makes us sleep soundly and eat hearty and keeps us in good health—so you see I am not inclined to think poverty a great evil.

Margery felt strongly that she could never go back to the Grove to live: "I hate to see the place. I look back on my life there as living in another world, or at least another country." The old home was rapidly falling into decay, with no buyers and only the former slave quarters and small parcels of land being rented to freedmen. The house at the Ridge had been sold (at $1,000) for much less than its value. Margery pictured the entire coastal region as made "desolate"; its planters were being ruined by "advancing to the Negroes, and making nothing."[14] They themselves were reduced to living on the "pityful [*sic*] rents" which Baillie collected from the Negroes, and even this was a risky affair.

On April 30, 1868, Kell and his family moved into the one completed room of Rocky Knoll. Two months later, Hettie arrived and moved into a second completed room; she began to teach the children of the neighborhood, using Mr. Varner's wheat house as a classroom.

As the months and years went by, the Kells were but little concerned with politics or national affairs. They were too far removed, and life on a farm had its own challenges. There was pleasure for the children in their animal pets; Blanche once again had her favorite St. Bernard and Newfoundland dogs and Kell his terriers. There were lean years, such as one in which Kell lost a dozen bales of cotton and had to use the rest of the crop to pay the debts. But the garden and animals could always be counted on to provide food for the family.[15]

If Kell had a longing for the ocean, he kept it to himself, although he would delight his family and neighbors with sea stories and reminiscences. Once when his servant was driving him, Kell absent-mindedly called out, "Port your helm!" The bewildered Negro had no idea what was expected of him until Kell, laughing, corrected himself, "Ben, drive to the left." He had been daydreaming of a fox hunt with Brown Wallis in the cork forests of Spain.[16]

On December 7, 1867, a baby girl—Margery Baillie—was born at Rocky Knoll. It was some time after this that the Kells received a welcome visit from Raphael Semmes. Greeting Blanche, Semmes told her, "I'm glad to see you again to congratulate you on so safely anchoring my friend Kell." Presenting her three children, Blanche replied, "Admiral, these are the anchors." She jokingly referred to the fact that although her husband had been a stern disciplinarian on the *Alabama*, he let her and the children have their own way in everything. To this Semmes replied, "Oh, my dear little Madam, a man can take a ship to sea, a man-of-war at that, and never be able to control a woman and a parcel of children and never try to. Kell disciplined finely, and I could not have had the ship I did without him."

Blanche also spoke of her husband's "sectional pride and prejudice," which brought the reply, "He has fifteen or more years longer to live to feel as I do; I am at least fifteen years his senior. Give him that long to grow reconciled to things as they are."[17]

Kell never saw his former commander again, although several letters arrived for little "Semmes" Kell before the death of the Admiral in 1877. When *Service Afloat* was published in 1869, Semmes had a copy mailed to his namesake, inscribed "To the little Admiral from the Admiral."

Generous, uncomplaining Nathan Munroe never lived to enjoy the house—"Chestnut Grove"—he was having built next to Rocky Knoll. On May 3, 1868, he died, after hours of intense suffering. To Blanche the loss of her father was a "heartbreaking, desolating stroke." To help combat her despondency and restore his own health, Kell decided to take his family to Halifax. Dick Armstrong had settled there with other Confederates in exile, including naval officers Josiah Tattnall, George T. Sinclair, and John Taylor Wood. In the summer of 1868 the Kells sailed by passenger steamer to Halifax, where they engaged a girl as nurse for the children. After several days in the city, they went by stage to the village of Musquodoboit on Petpeswick Bay. Adults and children alike delighted in the scenery, ocean air, and seafood. Kell had seen many places during his years at sea, but none seemed more beautiful to him than Acadian country.[18] In two months he gained thirteen pounds and almost completely recovered his health. After their stay in the country, the Kells spent two weeks in Halifax at the boarding house used by the Confederate exiles. Dick Armstrong, now married, was profitably engaged in land speculation, and he advised Kell to invest through him in real estate. The profits which Armstrong described were too much to resist, and by 1870 Kell was receiving small dividends on his Canadian investments.[19]

In late 1868, Hendley Varner died, leaving "poor desolate childless old Aunty" to linger on alone for another thirteen months. The death of the Varners brought an estrangement between Blanche and her sister Hattie; the entire Varner estate was left to the Kells, and Hattie tried unsuccessfully to break the will.

Still another death occurred on October 17, 1870: that of Margery Kell. During her last illness, at the Spalding home, she told her daughter repeatedly, "John is son *and* daughter to me.... You do not know what he is to me."[20]

There were other heartbreaks. Margery's namesake—little May—died in the summer of 1873. In December of 1881, John Kell, Jr., who had survived diphtheria in 1863, died of consumption. Only a year before, he had received his medical degree from Savannah Medical College.

There were the deaths of old friends: Bob Minor in 1871 and Dr. Fahs in 1873. In the fall of 1873, Kell had received a telegram from Selma, Alabama; Fahs was seriously ill and desired to be with his old friend during his recovery. Kell wired that he should come at once. Before he reached his destination, however, Fahs (accompanied by his wife and brother) had a relapse, and the doctors in Atlanta urged him to remain there. He refused, saying, "If I must die, I would rather die with Kell." On the morning of November 17 he was brought by train to Sunnyside and carried on a bed into the Kell home. Nine hours later he was dead.[21]

But, despite death, there was the joy of new life as Kell's family grew. Five more children were born and would live to comfort their parents in old age: Hendley Varner, born in 1869; Sarah Tabitha in 1871; Hester Estelle in 1873; Evelyn Spalding in 1875; and Mary Carolyn in 1877. Each new baby was received into the "sanctuary for rearing [the] young—in God's faith and to His glory!"[22]

In March of 1874, Blanche's close friend, Mary (Day) Lanier,[23] was living at Sunnyside while her husband was in Baltimore. One day at Rocky Knoll, she received a letter from her husband which contained a poem he had written for her; it was "My Springs." Later that summer, Sidney joined his wife and children to become a temporary neighbor of the Kells. Lanier would spend hours with the children, walking up and down the roadside playing his flute. The Kell boys made their own "flutes" from swamp reeds and, in imitation, would march in a file behind the poet. In all directions were fields of ripening corn, and Lanier loved to wander along the paths that went through the fields. One day, following his usual walk, he came into the Kell's sitting room, sprawled upon the sofa, and began to speak of the beauty of the corn; he longed to express it in verse. In the days that followed, Lanier could be seen sitting on a crosstie of the railroad, almost surrounded by the waving fields of corn, writing on scraps of paper on his knee. Later that fall he revised and polished what became one of his best known poems—"Corn."[24]

As his family grew, Kell's world came to center increasingly on his farm and the little community of Sunnyside. His sisters were frequent guests and would eventually (with Charles and Evelyn Spalding) make Sunnyside their home. Baillie came, too, but would settle permanently only after years of restless discontent and inability to make a life of his own. For his sisters and brother, Kell now held the role so long maintained by Margery as leader of the clan. He accepted this position as a matter of course, knowing that his mother had expected it of him.

17

THE *ALABAMA* LEGEND

During her career of twenty-two months, the *Alabama* became an emotion-stirring legend, not only in the South, but throughout the English-speaking world. Until his death in 1877, Raphael Semmes served as articulate defender of C.S.S. *Sumter* and *Alabama*, and most Southerners—including Kell—felt that *Service Afloat* said all that was necessary on the subject. The lengthy book covered far more than the cruises; it included descriptions of peoples and places and Semmes' defense of his actions during the war. For most Northerners there was much to disagree with, and Semmes' references to "howling Demos," "Demoniac" Yankees, and "gloomy, saturnine fanatics" were hardly intended to placate them. The emotions aroused by the Confederate raiders were revived during the *Alabama* Claims arbitration in 1871; the proceedings clearly showed the extent of the damage to Northern commerce done by the raiders and, most notably, the *Alabama*. Northerners' accounts of the naval war could be equally bitter. For example, Admiral David D. Porter contended, after reading Semmes' book, that it "embraced not an account of one act of bravery or generosity, but only records of burning, sinking, and destroying, worthy of the buccaneers."[1]

At his Sunnyside farm, Kell was satisfied to avoid the controversies as long as Semmes was alive to answer the critics. But after the death of his captain, Kell automatically became spokesman for C.S.S. *Alabama;* as senior surviving officer he could not evade this responsibility. However, he was a reluctant speechmaker and disliked writing. As he explained, his life was one of "deeds and duty, not words."[2] Lacking Semmes' flamboyant temperament, Kell spoke always of "duty" and "honor," content to let his dead commander receive the praises. Nevertheless, he was pleased with recognition of his own achievements. To his family and friends (and eventually to all who knew him) he was "Captain Kell," and it was a title he felt in good conscience he had earned.

Kell's first attempt at writing for publication came a few years after the war. The editor of *Burke's Weekly for Boys and Girls* (published in Macon) persuaded him to write a brief account of the *Alabama-Kearsarge* battle. The article appeared anonymously under the title, "A Yarn from Uncle Bob's Log; or A True Tale of the *Alabama*." The account emphasized that Captain Semmes had unknowingly engaged an enemy "disguised" with "armor of mail." In his article, Kell repeated Semmes' explanation why he had taken on a stronger opponent: "Had our captain known that she was protected by chain armor he would not have risked the lives of his gallant crew, or the loss of his noble little ship, by giving battle to an iron-clad!"[3] Kell would repeat this contention many times. The charge that the *Alabama's* captain knew the *Kearsarge* was protected by chains reflected unfavorably on Semmes' judgement and veracity, and nothing could provoke Kell to anger quicker than anything critical of Semmes or the ship he loved so well. When later he took up his pen to challenge a Northern account of the *Alabama-Kearsarge* fight, he stated his reason for doing so:

> My great commander sleeps. His caustic pen is silent to the malice of his foes. I hold it my sacred duty to his memory and to history to refute false statements against him or the gallant ship he commanded.[4]

However, Kell could be sensitive to the point of wild exaggeration when he believed that his ship had been disparaged. One day his daughter Tibbie told him that her school history book mentioned the sinking of the *Alabama* by the *Kearsarge*. He asked her, "Did the history tell you that the *Alabama* sank the *Hatteras*, almost twice her size, off Galveston, sent her to the bottom in thirteen minutes, and saved every soul on board?"[5] When Tibbie replied no, he said angrily, "It is a one-sided untrue history, and you shall not study it!" And, turning to Blanche: *"Destroy that book!"* Some months later, when another daughter came to him with the same story, Kell demanded to know why Blanche had not destroyed the book. She answered: "Well, my senior officer, it is too nice a book to burn up, and I have been reared with such reverence for books if you will allow me I will give it to my little butler for a Christmas present." Kell then muttered that a "lying history" was more suitable for Blanche's butler than for their children.[6]

Semmes was always spoken of with "pride and pleasure" at the Kell home. The "luff" gave him only praise: "He was the most fearless man I ever knew, and I loved him for it." And, to a news reporter, Kell said, "[Captain Semmes] was a man of the quickest insight, the greatest firmness and the most reckless daring. He was never imprudent, but he was absolutely without fear."[7]

Throughout the 1880's and early 1890's, Kell was drawn into correspondence concerning published accounts relative to the *Alabama*. On July 2, 1881, an article by a "W. E. Howard"—who claimed to be "late of the Confederate Steamer *Alabama*"—appeared in the Philadelphia *Weekly Times*. Howard referred to Kell as "a very able man," but his comments on other officers and the ship itself were not only uncomplimentary but filled with inaccuracies.[8] Kell wrote to the Editor of the *Times*, denouncing Howard as an imposter, and soon afterward the newspaper published an article by Oliver J. Semmes in defense of his father.[9]

By the 1880's a new generation of Southerners wanted to know more about the now legendary *Alabama*. Reporters traveling to Sunnyside to interview the old sailor could always be assured of a good story. Alfred Branham and other reporters, writing as they did for the benefit of a Southern audience, portrayed the *Alabama* as the underdog wooden ship versus the powerful "iron-clad" *Kearsarge*. Kell was described as a modest, retiring man, who had little to say of his own role as "luff" of the *Alabama*.

The old veteran had become almost completely bald, with only dark brown locks around his temples, and his long beard had turned golden gray. His complexion—tanned and ruddy—marked him as a man who spent most of his time out of doors. At one hundred and seventy-five pounds, he remained in robust physical condition.

In April of 1884 Kell attended the annual reunion of the Association of the Army of Tennessee, held in New Orleans. He had been asked to deliver an address, "The Navy of the Confederacy." Both he and Matt O'Brien, now a resident of New Orleans, spoke on the *Alabama-Kearsarge* fight, after which O'Brien presented his senior officer with a gold-headed cane on behalf of the Association. Kell was elected an honorary member, the fourth to be so recognized.

That same year an article in the New York *Sun*[10] repeated a story told to Colonel J. Schuyler Crosby by a "Sir John Burgoyne" in Florence, Italy, a few years earlier. Burgoyne claimed to have taken the first lieutenant of the *Alabama* on a tour of the *Kearsarge* sometime prior to the battle. According to the account, this officer had later identified himself to Burgoyne. Kell wrote a letter hotly denying that he had ever set foot aboard the *Kearsarge:*

> [Lord Burgoyne] lays me liable for great temerity in permitting Capt. Semmes unknowingly to engage an iron clad, for certainly the battle would not have taken place had that fact been divulged, nor would there have been an opportunity for the brilliant imagination of Lord Burgoyne in picturing that tragic scene after the sinking of the Alabama when he pulled into the boat Capt. Semmes and a little later the first officer of the Alabama, his friend of the "table d'hote" and fellow visitor to the Kearsarge.[11]

Kell was disturbed enough to write to the Reverend Tremlett in London, asking him to inquire about "Lord Burgoyne"; Tremlett, however, could offer little information.[12] Soon, Dick

Armstrong wrote a blistering letter to the *Sun*, containing what was perhaps the last word on the Burgoyne story: "I think I can trust my memory so far as to state that Lieutenant Kell did not leave the side of the *Alabama* from the day she entered Cherbourg until she steamed out of the port—in fact, was not on shore at all."[13]

When *The Century Illustrated Monthly Magazine* began its series of feature articles on the Civil War, written by participants on both sides, Kell was asked to contribute. (Armstrong had already refused to write the article, believing that to do so would be a discourtesy to Kell.) Kell at first declined, claiming that "Admiral Semmes' book was enough for history and the world,"[14] but changed his mind when his "home circle" pointed out that the article would be a valuable contribution to the history of the "Lost Cause." Kell was advised by the editors of *Century* to "view the events in a historical spirit and consider the lapse of time that has intervened." When they received his manuscript and noted contradictions between his and other versions of the *Alabama-Kearsarge* fight, Kell would concede only that his "*wording*" might be at fault but that his facts were correct.[15]

Kell's "Cruise and Combats of the 'Alabama' " appeared in the April, 1886 edition of *Century* (and was later included in volume IV of *Battles and Leaders of the Civil War).* It dealt chiefly with the *Alabama-Kearsarge* battle and, unlike Semmes' account, was devoid of bitterness and recrimination. Public response to the article was enthusiastic, and circulation had to be increased by a third to meet the demand. Kell received letters of congratulations from old and new friends, and from strangers.

Although Kell was pleased with the reception given his article, he was indignant at the two articles which accompanied it. They were: "Life on the 'Alabama' " by an alleged member of the crew and "The Duel Between the 'Alabama' and the 'Kearsarge' " by the surgeon of the *Kearsarge.* Kell and Dr. Galt both discredited Surgeon Browne's account of the fight as being mere hearsay, contending that the surgeon of a war vessel would be at his station in the cockpit of the ship, waiting to receive the wounded.[16] The implications of the other article, however, were far more serious; it presented a picture of the *Alabama's* crew as mostly drunkards and cutthroats, and included such derogatory statements as, "The poor show we made with the *Kearsarge* . . . disposed of the glory we achieved in burning defenseless merchantmen. . . ."[17] The article was soon expanded into a book.[18] If "Haywood" had really been a member of the crew as he claimed, the *Alabama* legend was irreparably damaged. If he was a fake, then he would have to be exposed.

As the surviving *Alabama* officers launched a blistering attack against "Philip Drayton Haywood," the truth soon became apparent. Haywood was actually a clever imposter who had completely deceived the *Century* and Houghton, Mifflin editors. In the first place, there had been no "Haywood" among the crew,[19] although even Kell conceded he might have shipped (or written) under a different name. However, Haywood gave himself away. In an autobiographical sketch published in the *Century*,[20] he made claims that had no basis in fact. In the first place, he claimed he had been warranted a midshipman in the British navy and assigned to the frigate *Swiftsure* in 1853. (There is no Haywood listed among the promotions and appointments in the Royal Navy for 1853 and 1854;[21] there was no vessel named *Swiftsure* in the British navy until 1870, and that was an ironclad.)[22] He claimed to have been wounded in the attack against Sebastopol while aboard the *Britannia*—there is no Haywood listed among the casualties of this ship during the engagement—and to have served as a lieutenant aboard the *Redoute*. (No ship of this name was commissioned in the British navy during the period of Haywood's claims.)[23]

The men who had sailed on the *Alabama* had no difficulty proving Haywood to be a liar and impostor. In an interview, Kell proved conclusively that Haywood had never been on board the *Alabama*. In the first place, none of the crew had been allowed ashore at Terceira, yet Haywood had written of the crew defying the authorities there. He had described the troublemaker, George Forrest, as tall and powerful, with "considerable manly beauty," while Kell remembered him as "a short, thickset fellow with dingy yellowish hair . . . positively ugly." Haywood had also claimed that the sailors had been paid by the month, a statement which Kell believed was alone sufficient to expose him: "In no branch of naval service are the men paid by the month. Merchantmen and war vessels alike pay at the end of a voyage or cruise." Kell had much more to say about Haywood's article and book; in contrast to Haywood's representation of the *Alabama*'s crew, Kell gave an entirely different picture:

> I never saw a better crew. I had served in the United States navy twenty years, and the discipline on the Alabama was superior to that of most men of war. Admiral Semmes was a stern disciplinarian and would have nothing but the most perfect order on board. The achievements of these men belie the charge that they were rogues and habitual drunkards. They must have been well drilled and watchful at all times to have accomplished what they did. We did not know at what moment we might sight a prize or fall in with a hostile man of war. It was my duty to see that the crew and ship were in order at all times and I believe I did so. When the men were allowed to go on shore some of them did get tipsy, and once we had considerable trouble with a party of them, but these were the usual incidents of the service and occurred no oftener on the Alabama than on the best regulated man of war. Our crew very seldom got on shore as we only went to port when compelled to do so. Instead of many riotous liberty days, such as Haywood describes, we had on our entire cruise, I think, only five 'liberty days' at all, and two of these were on barren coasts where there was no whisky. When we took a prize and found whisky on board it was the first thing destroyed. I can bear witness to the pluck, subordination, and general good character of the crew. They all seemed to feel a pride in the success of the Alabama and served her with a devotion such as I never before saw displayed by seamen. Such a thing as mutiny was never suspected by the officers, nor do I believe it was ever contemplated by any of the crew. They were brave, active, cheerful fellows, responsive to every call of their officers and always 'spoiling for a fight', not among themselves, but with the enemy.[24]

It was an enterprising reporter for the Philadelphia *Weekly Times* who discovered Haywood's real identity. In a feature article, headlined "A Literary Criminal," the reporter presented the results of his investigation. He had been in contact with Kell and was able to point out Haywood's most obvious errors pertaining to the *Alabama's* cruise. He also noted various discrepancies between the book and the article. Finally, he identified the bogus sailor as James Young of Philadelphia, a skilled engraver with a long criminal record under various aliases. Before writing his exposé, the reporter located "Haywood" at his Philadelphia home and found his appearance identical to the description of "J. H. Horton," forger, found in a Pinkerton wanted bulletin. "Horton" had drawn a sketch of himself for the detectives, which was located in their files. Young, alias "Haywood" and "Horton," told the reporter of his being paid $200 for his *Century* article and $600 by Houghton, Mifflin for the book he had written in only ten days. He was already under contract to write another book of his "adventures."

The editors of the Century Company and Houghton, Mifflin were, to say the least, dismayed. The latter company took immediate steps to have Haywood's book suppressed, while the *Century Magazine*, in its issue of March, 1887, announced that "P. D. Haywood", "from his own admission . . . was not a seaman on the Confederate cruiser though at the time the article was accepted he assured us he was." The disclosures seemed to be a victory and vindication for the *Alabama*.

His *Century* article established Kell as the foremost authority on the *Alabama*. In late 1886 he was questioned by Professor Henry A. Scomp of Emory College regarding the drinking habits of the officers and men aboard his ship. Scomp was researching material for his history of the "liquor traffic" and temperance movement in Georgia. Scomp's letter reached Kell at a time when the old sailor was anxious to refute Haywood's misrepresentations about the *Alabama*'s crew. Kell's reply—a brief discussion of the use of wine and other spirits aboard the *Alabama*—repeated the facts he had stated earlier concerning the ship's crew and their having been "compelled to keep sober."[25]

In March of 1891, when John A. Cockerill, editor of Pulitzer's New York *World*, wanted some feature articles on the *Alabama*, he remembered the *Century* articles and thought of Kell. Cockerill suggested that Kell write several articles based on "reminiscences, anecdotes, and striking incidents" of the *Alabama*'s cruise, including the *Kearsarge* battle.[26] Kell agreed and signed a contract to write six articles for $50 each. Two of the articles were written and published,[27] but the series was never completed. With his natural aversion to writing, Kell regretted the assignment, and—after Cockerill left the *World* that same year—he felt under no obligation to live up to the contract. The next year, however, Kell contributed an article to *The Sunny South* (November 26, 1892), which described the *Alabama*'s visit to Table Bay in South Africa.

In 1892 and 1894 two articles by *Kearsarge* veterans appeared in the Northern press and caused an outraged Kell to challenge the veracity of the writers. The first, written by former Paymaster J. Adams Smith, appeared in the *Washington Post* (September 22, 1892)[28]; it had received high praise from the Secretary of the Navy. Kell's rebuttal was chiefly directed at Smith's contention that the *Alabama* had fired after displaying the white flag. Restating the position he took in his *Century* article, Kell claimed that the *Alabama* had *not* fired after surrendering, and he called Smith an "untruthful vilifier" for stating the contrary. According to Kell, it was the *Kearsarge* that had acted treacherously, having fired into the *Alabama* as she was sinking.[29]

The second article, written by Austin Quinby, former marine corporal, appeared in the Boston *Journal* (February 11, 1894). Once again came the charge that the *Alabama* had fired after hauling down her colors, and once again Kell issued a denial. Kell was so incensed at the *Journal* article that in a letter to his son-in-law he wrote: "I am fully persuaded that the present generation of Yankees must die out before the truth can be told in that quarter doing justice to the gallant little Alabama against her iron clad antagonist the Kearsarge."[30]

Kell eventually realized that a book of recollections would be a lasting contribution to the "Lost Cause" as well as to his loved ones. He began to record his reminiscences "for the pleasure of . . . family and friends" and as a record of "the truth of history."[31] The book would feature the cruises of C.S.S. *Sumter* and *Alabama*. For several years Kell wrote sporadically, but he eventually chose to narrate to his wife, mostly from memory or after referring to his collection of letters. Retelling the pleasant episodes of the past was always a pleasure for Kell. For Blanche, however, the job of transcribing her husband's conversation was not easy. She confided to her son-in-law:

> Capt. Kell is a difficult person to write after—especially Reminiscences. He often stops short in the very middle of a sentence and flies wide of the subject to tell something else suggested by the train of thought and so loses the thread of narrative. But I think what he writes bears always the stamp of his true and honest nature.[32]

Although the manuscript was finished before 1895, it was not published until shortly before Kell's death in 1900. After her husband suffered a serious stroke in 1895, Blanche had to assume more and more of his responsibilities, including that as defender of the *Alabama*. Ironically, the "enemy" most damaging to the legend would be neither Yankee nor bogus sailor, but an officer of the famous raider. The Judas would come from within.

Late in 1895, while Kell was still recovering from his stroke, Arthur Sinclair's *Two Years on the Alabama* was published. Sinclair, fifth lieutenant on the *Alabama*, had been working on his book for several years, and he had occasionally written Kell, Armstrong, and other officers for information. By the middle of 1894, however, Armstrong was having second thoughts about Sinclair. For one thing, Sinclair was telling people that he had been promoted to commander, for "conspicuous gallantry," but that the war had ended before his commission came through. In a letter to Mrs. Kell, Armstrong revealed his contempt for his one-time shipmate, accusing him—among other things—of being utterly irresponsible. Regarding Sinclair's competence while an officer aboard the *Alabama*, Armstrong wrote:

> Quietly ask Captain K[ell] why he assigned S[inclair] to my Division as Supernumerary during the fight and gave Sinclair's junior—Bulloch—command of the 3rd Division? . . . 'Pears to me somehow that when S[inclair] was on deck your husband was up and dressed in his room.[33]

Sinclair's book again raised the question of whether Semmes knew he was about to fight an "ironclad." Sinclair stated that a day or so before the *Alabama-Kearsarge* battle, the French port admiral at Cherbourg had informed Semmes that "an officer detailed to visit the Kearsarge . . . had reported the fact of the chain-armor arranged on the ship, and strongly advised Semmes not to engage her . . ."[34] And yet, Semmes had always maintained that he had been unaware of the chain plating and that Winslow had been guilty of a "cheat" in "disguising" the fact. Kell, too, had consistently stated that his commander would never have risked his ship or the lives of his men had he known of the advantage held by the *Kearsarge*. In 1883 he had told a news reporter, with some bitterness, why he believed the *Alabama* had lost the battle:

> There were but two things that prevented our whipping the Kearsarge; our powder, which had been exposed to all kinds of weather for two years, was bad, and the Commander of the Kearsarge, a Southern man, by the way, resorted to a miserable trick to prevent injury to his vessel. He ironplated her with heavy cable chains and covered the armor with a thin sheeting of plank to hide the deception.[35]

In his *Century* article, Kell had again presented his defense of Captain Semmes' judgment in offering battle to the *Kearsarge:*

> Captain Semmes felt the more keenly the delusion to which he fell a victim (not knowing that the *Kearsarge* was chain-clad) from the fact that he was exceeding his instructions in seeking an action with the enemy; but to seek a fight with an iron-clad he conceived to be an unpardonable error. However, he had the satisfaction of knowing she was classed as a wooden gun-boat by the Federal Government; also that he had inspected her with most excellent glasses, and so far as outward appearances showed

she displayed no chain armor. At the same time it must be admitted that Captain Winslow had the right unquestionably to protect his ship and crew. In justice to Captain Semmes I will state that the battle would never have been fought had he known that the *Kearsarge* wore an armor of chain beneath her outer covering.[36]

Before reading Sinclair's book, Kell received a letter from a daughter of Semmes, imploring him to speak out in defense of his captain. According to Anna Semmes Bryan, "The account given by Mr. Sinclair reflects great discredit on the judgment and discretion of the dear dead."[37] A few weeks later, after Blanche had read the book to him, Kell dictated a letter to Sinclair which pointed out what he considered "grievous errors as to history":

> Capt. Semmes says in his book, in his official reports to Mr. Mason and the Secretary of the Navy and has said in my presence that he would never have undertaken so unequal a combat and he did *not* know it. The look of astonishment on his face when he saw the shell strike the K[earsarge]—and fall off in the water—proved his ignorance of the fact when he told me to "try solid shot." Another error, your pronouncing the fuses etc. *good* when certainly one in three failed to explode at our last target practise at the prize ship Rockingham. When I reported to Captain Semmes the deterioration of both powder and fuses and we overhauled magazine and shell room when Capt. Semmes sent for me to talk over the fight he was contemplating I reminded him of these facts but he seemed to think our chances fair notwithstanding, not dreaming we were to fight an ironclad![38]

In reply, Sinclair assured Kell that he had no intention of reflecting upon the judgment and wisdom of their "dear old leader." However, he refused to retract what had been contradicted by Kell. Instead, he explained further:

> I remember, so well, a Lieut. coming on board our vessel from the French Admiral and with his compliments reporting that upon visiting the 'K' in the "offing" for the purpose of supplying her with fresh provisions he had observed the improvised armor,

> and strongly advised Semmes not to offer her battle. Now my *opinion* is that Semmes having *already* given out to the world his determination to make the fight, clung to his judgment. Nor can I now (even at this late date) see that he erred—suppose that shell, planted in her stern post had exploded. Who can doubt the result. In regard to the practice at prize ship Rockingham I do not remember that the shell failed to explode in many cases (as you state) but the damage to this vessel was serious enough, had it been the 'K', to bring her colors from the peak.[39]

Admitting that he had written his book from memory, Sinclair invited Kell to call attention to errors for correction in later editions. However, for Kell the correspondence was ended. He did not publicly condemn Sinclair or his book, as he believed this would only give publicity to the charges; he hoped that his own book, when published, would substantiate the facts given in Semmes' *Service Afloat*. There was no further communication with Sinclair, whose name forever remained anathema in the Kell home.

Armstrong had a great deal to say privately about Sinclair and his book. In a confidential letter to Mrs. Kell, he denounced *Two Years on the Alabama* as "a trash pile of rubbish," calling it a "pirated edition" of Semmes' book. In Armstrong's opinion, Sinclair was guilty of an unpardonable transgression: "Sinclair did not have soul enough to appreciate the dignity of the service and mission of the Alabama!"[40] Armstrong considered Sinclair's excessive praise of the *Alabama's* officers merely an attempt to discount their adverse criticism of his book. Like Kell, Armstrong did not publicly denounce *Two Years on the Alabama* as he feared the publicity would only help its sale. Instead, he marked his copy of the book with comments and corrections for the benefit of his family and close friends. Armstrong advised that Semmes' heirs sue Sinclair for libel and have *Service Afloat* reissued as soon as possible.[41] Armstrong, still in self-imposed exile in Nova Scotia, explained why he wanted nothing derogatory written about Semmes:

> With regard to the little Malay pilot episode I have a perfect

> recollection of all the circumstances, but as these reflect discredit upon Captain Semmes I should strongly advise that no mention whatever be made of the affair.[42] I find no mention whatever made of this and other happenings of a like nature by that contemptible plagiarist Sinclair. I think we should not mention anything which would derogate from the fame of Semmes. In giving this advice I feel that I am very charitable for of all the officers of the Alabama I was probably the most harshly treated by S[emmes] and yet if I should ever write of or about my war service I feel now that to his faults I should be blind. Not perhaps that I love Semmes less but the reputation of our ship the more.
>
> The 'Alabama' of all the ships that ever floated perhaps enjoys the most world-wide celebrity and everything written about her will be read with avidity and criticized with severity—knowing this I have not had the temerity to enter the lists as a historian, and have hitherto withstood the solicitations of my friends to put my pen to paper.

Armstrong never wrote his book, for he recognized his own shortcomings as a writer of history: "I am too utterly prejudiced for an historian and have too good a memory to forget or to forgive."[43]

Not long after Kell's death, Dr. Galt would make a statement that would add credibility to Sinclair's most damaging charge against Semmes. Galt wrote Blanche that "the officers [of the *Alabama*] did know or hear the *K[earsarge]* was chain clad." Although not one to destroy letters, Blanche confided to a daughter that she had "*suppressed*" Galt's. In 1912, W. Breedlove Smith, Semmes' former Secretary, revealed in an interview that the *Alabama's* officers "had heard rumored" that iron anchor cables had been placed to protect the engines of the *Kearsarge*.[44] Blanche, however, remained unconvinced by disclosures on this most sensitive issue. She told her daughter: "I know your Father and Capt. S[emmes] did not know it."[45]

18

ADJUTANT GENERAL

In the fall of 1884, after years of "profitless farming" by her husband, Blanche felt compelled to seek a political appointment for him, as she knew he would not take the initiative himself. The recent election of Grover Cleveland as President gave her cause to believe that Kell might benefit from the new Democratic administration. She asked George W. Wood, a family friend and neighbor, for help in securing for Kell the position of "Custom House Officer" in Atlanta. Wood was requested to contact the governor or "*any prominent* Atlanta men" on Kell's behalf. Blanche, faced with the problem of educating six children, explained: "We have been almost buried in the country for twenty years past and my husband knows very few prominent men—and was never one to push himself forward in any way."[1] Not long afterward, Wood and other citizens of Sunnyside formed a committee and wrote a petition on behalf of their distinguished neighbor. In it they suggested that Kell be elevated "either by the suffrage of our citizens or by Presidential appointment to any important office under the immediate control of the United States government." This, they explained, would be a "reward for his unswerving devotion to the true principles of government, as held by the Democratic party," and for service to "the whole country."[2] Copies of the resolutions and proceedings of the meeting were sent to newspapers in Griffin, Macon, Savannah, and Atlanta. Kell was pleased with the gesture, as he considered a man's neighbors best qualified to test the "true ring of the metal."[3] However, no offer was forthcoming.

In the spring of 1886, Blanche decided to make another attempt to secure a place for her husband. This time she appealed to Henry W. Grady, editor of the Atlanta *Constitution*, asking him to write to her husband regarding a position. Not long afterward Kell received an invitation from Grady to attend the unveiling of a statue of Benjamin H. Hill in Atlanta. Jefferson Davis was to be the guest of honor. In his invitation, Grady revealed the depth of his feelings for Kell: "I have always admired you and loved you for your gallantry in the cause for which my father gave his life, more than you have ever suspected."[4] In addition to sentiment, Grady had political reasons for desiring Kell's presence at the ceremony. As prime mover behind John B. Gordon for the governorship, Grady was anxious to win the support of the Confederate veterans. Later, on May 9, Gordon announced his candidacy, and Grady took personal charge of the campaign. When the Democratic Convention met in Atlanta on July 28, it nominated Gordon on the first ballot. Even before the nomination, Kell was being considered by Gordon supporters as a possible Commissioner of Agriculture. It was Grady and Evan P. Howell, also of the *Constitution*, who advised Kell to petition Gordon for the position of Adjutant General, a "place of dignity" more to Kell's liking. In August Grady reported to Kell, confidentially, that Gordon had concurred, and the appointment was practically certain.[5] The *Constitution* was not alone in its support of Kell. A number of prominent citizens from Bibb and Spalding counties also added their influence.

On November 16 Governor-elect Gordon offered Kell the position, and he accepted at once. The $2,000 yearly salary would be of great help in supporting his family and educating the children.

On the first day of the new year, 1887, Kell left Sunnyside to assume his new office: "Adjutant General, Inspector, and Keeper of Public Buildings." For the time being, he would board in Atlanta and return to Sunnyside to spend Sunday with his family.

Kell's predecessor in office—Colonel John A. Stephens—claimed to have relinquished the position because of "failing eyesight." Stephens had told Kell that the job was "nothing," that he had spent only two days of the month at his office, signing paychecks and collecting his own.[6] Such a "system" was not to Kell's liking, however, nor is there reason to believe that Governor Gordon would have been satisfied to have a passive chief of staff. Although the first and fifteenth days of the month—when he signed the paychecks of the watchmen, porters, and workmen—were his busiest, Kell maintained a full work week. As Adjutant General, he was head of the Georgia Volunteers (the state militia) and chairman of the Military Advisory Board, which met at least once a year to discuss military matters. Although as Adjutant General he had the rank of colonel of cavalry, he still preferred to be addressed as "Captain" Kell.

In May of 1887 when a Grand Reception for the Governor and his staff was held in Macon, Kell appeared in his new gray uniform. Also on the Governor's staff as colonels were the Quartermaster General (Charles H. Olmstead of Savannah) and the Judge Advocate General (John S. Candler of Decatur). A new governor was authorized to appoint aides-de-camp, and twenty-two of Gordon's appointees were also present in their dress uniforms.

His new responsibilities and the daily company of other men gave Kell a new lease on life. He soon came to love Gordon, and he delighted in being a "right hand" to the Governor, as he had been to Semmes. The four years under Gordon—"Gordon's time," as he later referred to them—were among the happiest of his life. Gordon had a "boyish way" about him and, when with Kell, would affectionately put an arm across his shoulder. Blanche asked her husband what he would do if the Governor ever hugged him, and he answered, "Oh, I expect I would hug him back, like another boy."[7]

Despite his new position, Kell remained a sailor at heart. Once, as he came down the Capitol steps, he was asked by a stranger where Governor Gordon could be found. Without hesitation, Kell replied, "He's aloft." The startled landsman could only say, "Good God! Is he dead?" As Kell later explained to his wife, "aloft" was his natural way of indicating that the Governor was just above where they were standing.

Beginning in 1889, an "accommodation train" made it possible for Kell to leave his home in the morning and return each evening. Although it took an hour and ten minutes each trip, Kell was delighted to again spend evenings with his family. He would tell them of people he had met and new friends made each day, which showed that he was once more "a man amid other men." Kell was on friendly terms with the leading Georgians of the new generation, but his heart was still with the Old South. He expressed his feelings in a letter to Georgia historian and orator Charles Colcock Jones:

> Words can not express my feelings of gratitude to you for the clear, patriotic and forcible manner in which you placed before your hearers, the incomparable superiority of the virtue, wealth and integrity of the old South to that which some are pleased to term the New South.[8]

To another "comrade" of the "Lost Cause" he wrote:

> Although a quarter of a century has passed, my heart leaps into quick action when the days of the Confederacy are talked over; the cause was lost, but the principle for which we fought will brighten as the years roll on, and the name of the Confederate soldier will be the synonim [*sic*] for valor, honor and patriotism.[9]

In the summer of 1890, as his second two-year term was drawing to a close, Governor Gordon wrote to his probable successor on behalf of his Adjutant General. Gordon explained that Kell—"thoroughly faithful and conscientious"—not only needed the job but deserved it.[10] Kell's reappointment by the next governor was not a matter of course, however, and he had at least one rival for his position. It was necessary for Kell to seek support among the members of the Military Advisory Board and the officers of the Georgia Volunteers. Their support was readily forthcoming, including that of the distinguished Charles C. Jones, and Kell was reappointed by Governor William J. Northen. (In 1894 and 1896 Kell would be reappointed by Governor William Y. Atkinson and in 1898 by Governor Allen D. Candler.)

As he entered old age, Kell's health steadily failed. Any

change of water or climate affected his stomach, and he became easily fatigued. The trip into Atlanta became so tiring for him that he had to rest and take a glass of malt before going to his office.

On October 14, 1895, Kell returned home exhausted by added duties related to the Atlanta Piedmont Exposition. Early the next morning—on their thirty-ninth wedding anniversary—Blanche was awakened by the sound of abnormally heavy breathing. To her dismay, she found her husband unconscious on the floor by the bed. Numb with despair, Blanche hurried to a son's room to tell him that his father was dying. The "terrified children" with great difficulty lifted Kell into bed, and doctors were summoned. Although the doctors despaired of his recovery, Kell regained consciousness. Seeing his family standing over his bedside, he asked: "Where am I? What is the matter? I'm like Tom Watson,* don't know where I'm *at*." Dr. Anthony's face brightened, and he turned to Blanche, saying, "The Captain is *all right*. I didn't know the Captain had that much fun in him." He then said to Kell, "We'll try and keep you in the *middle* of the road. You're a little sick with the Atlanta Exposition overwork, but you'll soon be well."[11] During the next ten days, it was still uncertain whether or not Kell would recover. The newspapers, in fact, reported that he was dying. When the crisis had passed, it was apparent that Kell would never regain his health. The fact that he lived at all seemed a miracle to Blanche. The doctors told her that Kell had been stricken with "congestive apoplexy" and had been in a comatose condition.[12]

After one particularly restless night during his convalescence, Kell asked Blanche if he had been "wild in his sleep." When she answered that he had, he explained, "I fought the fight between the *Alabama* and the *Kearsarge* more vigorously if possible than before, and you remember the night in Vineville when I had the same experience and frightened you so."[13]

After almost three months of convalescence, Kell had recovered sufficiently to resume his duties in Atlanta. Blanche at first thought it best for him to resign, but she was persuaded that his health would benefit from a continued "active life

*Thomas E. Watson (1865–1922), Georgia Populist.

spent among men." On January 6, 1896, Kell and Blanche left for Atlanta; they would board at a rooming house near Kell's office, and Blanche would look after her husband when he was not at work. When Blanche saw him welcomed by the capitol staff, she realized more than ever how much being Adjutant General meant to him. She confessed, "I never realized how much of his heart was there nor how susceptible he is to all the love and adulation he receives."[14] They remained in Atlanta a week, but because Kell was still not strong, the days spent in the city were reduced to three or four. Following doctors' advice, Blanche made certain that her husband ate nothing after 4 or 5 p.m.; a glass of malt and a few crackers or bread made up his last meal of the day. Blanche later credited this practice with prolonging Kell's life.[15]

Kell was in no condition to carry on the increased duties of Adjutant General, Inspector, and Keeper of Public Buildings. Even before his stroke, his duties had had to be lightened by two full-time assistants. Captain Oscar J. Brown, of the regular army, had taken over all military duties, and William E. Hatchett, a capitol guard, had been detailed by Governor Atkinson as a clerk in Kell's office.

In June of 1896, Kell was well enough to attend the reunion of Confederate veterans held at Richmond. It was now Captain Brown, however, who rode beside Governor Atkinson in the parade; Kell, with other infirm Confederate naval veterans, was provided with a carriage. At the Grand Reception, a colonel on the staff of Governor Atkinson, kissing Kell's hand, told him: "You are to me the greatest Georgian now living."

In December of 1897, the Georgia legislature honored Kell by increasing the rank of Adjutant General to that of a brigadier general. Six state employees sent him his general's commission, framed in silver, with the message, "We will ever love you while you live and when you are no more on this earth we will love and cherish the memory of one Georgia has honored herself in honoring."[16]

Early in 1898, Governor Atkinson, on the advice of his Military Advisory Board, appointed Colonel William G. Obear (previously Inspector General of Rifle Practice) as "Assistant"

Adjutant General, replacing Hatchett. The Board considered it more appropriate to have an experienced military man in the office, thereby allowing Captain Brown to spend more time inspecting the militia. The duties of Adjutant General were especially critical after war had been declared with Spain. When Captain Brown returned to his regular army command, he was replaced by Captain J.B. Erwin until the end of the war. In May Obear became "Acting" Adjutant General.

Although now a mere figurehead, Kell was still a person of great prestige and popularity throughout the state. There were many who regarded him as an expert on naval affairs. But Kell's views concerning Cuba and the sinking of the *Maine* were typical contemporary jingoistic sentiment. In news interviews he was freely quoted:

> I hate the Spaniards so that my opinion may not be an impartial one, but they are a treacherous people and my belief is that there was treachery in the case in some way. I hope that there will be a thorough investigation. . . . Yes, I would drive every Spaniard off the island if I had my way. We ought to have been at it long ago. We would sink or drive away every ship they have. It would be a short engagement and the most deadly ever known. It would not last long. We have the best fighters in the world. No other people can whip us. We could hardly whip each other in our own war. . . . If I were twenty years younger I would be in the war if one comes, and if I can only get a little stronger I shall go anyway, if war is declared. This country has had abundant provocation for war and I think there ought to be a fight to teach the Spaniards a lesson or two and at the same time to show the world that Americans have not forgotten how.[17]

Although he tried to continue his weekly trips into Atlanta with Blanche during 1899, Kell had lost interest in affairs there. It was home and family that he loved. Meeting strangers had become a burden to him, and Blanche tried to shelter him from all new and trying situations. The officials of the Central Georgia Railway also tried to help; in July of 1899 they issued a directive: henceforth, train number 105 was to stop "on flag" to take on Atlanta-bound passengers at Sunnyside, and two other dailies were directed to let off Kell or members of his family coming from Atlanta.[18]

Despite "electric battery" and "water cure" treatments and the constant attention of his family, Kell's health continued to worsen. Blanche still thought it good for him to go into Atlanta occasionally, but for most of his last year—1900—he was too weak to endure the trip.

A final satisfaction for Kell was seeing the book which was his legacy to his family and beloved South. In March of 1900 Blanche had found a publisher—the Neale Company—and three months later the first copy off the press was sent to her. Mr. Neale had written on the flyleaf James Barron Hope's poem "Our Heroic Dead':

> A King once said of a prince cut down
> 'Taller he seems in death.'
> And this speech holds true for now as then
> 'Tis after death that we measure men.
> And as mists of the past are rolled away,
> Our heroes who died in their tattered grey
> Grow taller and greater in all their parts,
> Till they fill our minds as they fill our hearts.
> And for those that lament there's this relief,
> That glory sits by the side of grief.

The last interest taken by Kell, in something other than his family circle, was for the welfare of William Crawford, one of the *Alabama*'s sailors. He urged Blanche to do her utmost with Dr. Galt to have Crawford admitted to the Virginia Soldier's Home.[19]

On the morning of October 5, 1900, as Blanche was writing a letter, her husband called her to his bedside. She asked if he wished her to send for their son Semmes, and he answered yes. Throughout the day he appeared weary but not in pain. Often he looked "lovingly and wistfully" into the faces of his wife and children. Then, at 7:30 p.m., uttering only a slight sigh, he closed his eyes and folded his hands upon his breast. He could no longer hear the sounds of weeping. He was making a final voyage on an unknown sea—homeward bound.

Notes

Notes for Chapter I

1. New York, 1900, p. 123.
2. Alfred Iverson Branham, *Story of The Sinking of The Alabama, '290': Interview with Captain John McIntosh Kell, Given Forty-Six Years Ago, June, 1883* (Atlanta, 1930). Interview, which originally appeared in two Georgia newspapers and a London periodical, was published as a pamphlet in 1930.
3. F. H. Richardson, "Incidents in the Career of the Alabama." Newspaper clipping [1886] in Blanche Kell Scrapbook owned by Mrs. Evelyn McLemore of Darien, Georgia.
4. W. J. Scott, "An Hour's Talk with a Sea Captain." Newspaper clipping in Blanche Kell Scrapbook owned by Munroe d'Antignac of Griffin, Georgia.
5. The Scotch form of the name was Mackintosh More.
6. *The Revolutionary Records of the State of Georgia*, ed. Allen D. Candler (Atlanta, 1908), I, 37.
7. Lachlan McIntosh (1725–1806) gained notoriety by his duel with Button Gwinnett (a signer of the Declaration of Independence). Gwinnett was mortally wounded.
8. *Georgia Revolutionary Records*, I, 348–356.
9. Letter from Judge Thomas Kell of Baltimore to Margery Kell, December 14, 1840; copied on Kell and Nisbet Family Genealogical Chart, Duke University.
10. *Collections of the Georgia Historical Society* (Savannah, 1901), V (Part 1), 66, 92, 99; *Georgia Revolutionary Records*, I, 145; II, 116, 477, 538, 539, 547, 553.
11. James Stacy, *History of the Midway Congregational Church, Liberty County, Georgia* (Newman, Georgia, n.d.), p. 31.
12. The estate left by John Kell included an island, plus 1300 acres of Liberty County mainland, four lots in Sunbury, seven Negroes, *L60*, and assorted livestock. Will, dated November 26, 1784; executed December 13, 1784. d'Antignac Collection.
13. Charles C. Jones, Jr., *The Dead Towns of Georgia*, in *Collections of the Georgia Historical Society* (Savannah, 1878), IV, 213–215.

14. Franklin Bowditch Dexter, *Biographical Sketches of the Graduates of Yale College with Annals of the College History* (New Haven, 1912), VI, 138.
15. John Kell composed his own book (dated January 1, 1808, Savannah). d'Antignac Collection.
16. Alexander A. Lawrence, *James Moore Wayne; Southern Unionist* (Chapel Hill, 1943) pp. 14–16.
17. Commission, dated November 12, 1810, Milledgeville, Georgia, in John Kell Folder, Georgia Department of Archives and History (Atlanta).
18. Nisbet-Kell Genealogical Chart.
19. Sarah Harriet Butts, *The Mothers of Some Distinguished Georgians of the Last Half of the Century* (New York, 1902), p. 158.
20. Marriage contract, dated October 28, 1816. d'Antignac Collection.
21. E. Merton Coulter, *Thomas Spalding of Sapelo* (University, Louisiana, 1940), p. viii.
22. *The Aristocratic Journey*, ed. Una Pope-Hennessy (New York, 1931), p. 234.
23. Frances Anne Kemble, *Journal of a Residence on a Georgian Plantation in 1838–1839* (New York, 1863), pp. 80–81.
24. Goulding (1810–1881) is reported to have invented a sewing machine which was used by his wife before Elias Howe's machine was patented. Bertha Sheppard Hart, *Introduction to Georgia Writers* (Macon, 1929), p. 308; Lucian Lamar Knight, *Georgia's Landmarks, Memorials and Legends* (Atlanta, 1914), II, pp. 225–227.
25. *Sapelo* (Philadelphia and Macon, 1877), pp. 158–159.
26. *Records of Darien Presbyterian Church, 1822–1862.* Typewritten copy at the Georgia Historical Society, Savannah. It is recorded that Mrs. M. S. Kell, a communicant, was "Dismissed," but no reason is given.
27. John Kell died of a probable heart attack at the Grove, November 10, 1827.
28. The 1820 McIntosh County Census report shows that John Kell owned sixty-eight slaves; in the 1830 Census the number is down to thirty-seven slaves of Margery Kell. Georgia Census Records (microfilm), Georgia Department of Archives and History.
29. John McIntosh Kell, *Recollections of a Naval Life* (Washington, 1900), pp. 8–9.
30. Margery Kell to Kell, Nov. 23, 1838. Kell Papers, Duke University. All letters footnoted, unless otherwise cited, are from this collection.
31. Kell, pp. 8–9.
32. The record number of appointments is due to there being three Secretaries of the Navy that year: James K. Paulding, George E. Badger, and Abel P. Upshur. According to one 1841 appointee, each Secretary "exercised his power in providing for his friends, and the Navy was so filled up with Midshipmen that, in order to employ them, it was necessary to crowd the steerages . . . far beyond their capacity. It took some years to overcome the inconvenience that this crowding produced." Samuel R. Franklin, *Memories of a Rear-Admiral* (New York, 1898), p. 15.
33. Edward M. Steel, Jr., *T. Butler King of Georgia* (Athens, 1964), p. 36.
34. Kell, p. 9.
35. Record Group No. 45, National Archives.

Notes for Chapter II

1. Herman Melville, *White Jacket* (New York, 1850), p. 269.
2. Secretary Spencer had been the means of his son's receiving an appointment as acting midshipman in 1841; he wanted to expose Philip to the discipline aboard a man-of-war. The boy had gained a reputation in college for rebelliousness and contempt for authority. Before the *Somers* episode, he had been in trouble on two other ships (for forgery and drunkenness), but his father's and uncle's influence had saved him from dismissal. A court of inquiry vindicated Mackenzie, and he was afterward acquitted of charges of murder, oppression, and illegal punishment. During and after the trials, Mackenzie was the center of much controversy (James Fenimore Cooper wrote articles bitterly attacking him), and he never again commanded a ship.
3. Park, Benjamin, *The United States Naval Academy* (New York, 1900), pp. 426–428.
4. Thomas H.S. Hamersly, *Complete Army and Navy Register* (New York, 1888), p. 480.
5. Kell to Secretary of the Navy, Sept. 28, 1841. Record Group No. 45. National Archives.
6. Kell to Margery Kell, Nov. 14, 1841. d'Antignac Collection.
7. James C. Tily, *The Uniforms of the United States Navy* (New York, 1964), pp. 89–94.
8. Nov. 14, 1841. d'Antignac Collection. While in New York City, Kell visited another of his many cousins, Maria Jane McIntosh (1803–1878). During the two decades before the Civil War, her novels were popular in both the United States and England. Hart, *Georgia Writers*, pp. 287–291.
9. Nov. 23, 1841. Record Group No. 45. National Archives.
10. *Dictionary of American Naval Fighting Ships* (Washington, 1963), II, 387.
11. Kell to Margery Kell, Dec. 1, 1841, in "Life and Letters of John McIntosh Kell," unpublished manuscript of Blanche (Munroe) Kell. Kell Papers. Duke University. (Whenever available, I have referred to the originals of all letters used by Mrs. Kell in her manuscript, since her editing often distorts.)
12. Kell to Margery Kell, Jan. 1, 1841.
13. Daniel Ammen, *The Old Navy and The New* (Philadelphia, 1891), p. 34.
14. Benjamin, pp. 56–57, 60.
15. Melville, p. 164.
16. Kell, "Journal of a Cruise in the U.S. Ship *Falmouth*," [1842–1843], Kell Papers.
17. Benjamin, p. 92.
18. Kell to Margery Kell, Feb. 14, 1842.
19. "Reminiscences of the Old Navy," *The United Service* (Philadelphia, 1882), pp. 487–488.
20. *Ibid.*, p. 482.
21. Melville, p. 403.
22. Kell to Margery Kell, Sept. 2, 1842.
23. Melville, pp. 34–35. Samuel R. Franklin, who was a midshipman aboard the *United States* at the same time that Melville was an ordinary seaman,

corroborates that reefers were sometimes punished by "mast heading"—being ordered up the masthead. Page 30.

24. Kell to Margery Kell, July 30, 1842. Blanche Kell MSS.
25. Kell to Margery Kell, July 30, 1842; Aug. 27, 1842.
26. Kell to Hetty Kell, Apr. 14, 1843.
27. Kell, pp. 13–14. It being the summer fever season, Kell and Commander McIntosh probably found Margery Kell's family at their summer home at the Ridge, three miles north of Darien, or in Liberty County.
28. *Ibid.*, p. 14.
29. Kell to Margery Kell, July 10, 1843.
30. McIntosh to Kell, Oct. 11, 1843. Contained in "Records of General Court-Martial and Courts of Inquiry of the Navy Department, 1799–1867." Microfilm Copy No. M–273, Roll No. 65. National Archives.
31. General Orders. "Journal of a Cruise in the U.S. Frigate *Savannah,* Andrew Fitzhugh Esq. Commanding," Kell Papers.
32. *Savannah,* 1708 tons; *Falmouth,* 705 tons.
33. Kell to Margery Kell, Sept. 23, 1843. d'Antignac Collection.
34. A large squadron was kept in the Pacific to protect American commerce and whaling and to guard American interests in Mexican-held California.
35. Walter Colton, *Deck and Port* (New York, 1850), pp. 72–73. The "pollywogs," or "greenhorns," were customarily lathered from a tub of grease and tar and "shaved" with a ship's scraper.
36. Kell to Margery Kell, Jan. 17–29, 1844. Blanche Kell MSS.
37. *Ibid.*
38. In October, 1842, Commodore Jones had on his own initiative (as a result of an erroneous war report) seized Monterey, California. A day later he realized his mistake and withdrew. To conciliate Mexico, Jones was relieved of command in January, 1843. However, he continued to cruise the Pacific, apparently unaware of his recall until later that year. When he returned to the United States, he was charged with disobedience of orders but was eventually restored to full command.
39. Kell to Margery Kell, Feb. 15, 1844. Blanche Kell MSS.
40. Colton, *Deck and Port*, p. 230.
41. Franklin, p. 43.
42. Kell, pp. 16–17.
43. Fitch W. Taylor, *A Voyage Round the World, and Visits to Various Foreign Countries, in the United States Frigate Columbia* (New Haven and New York), II, pp. 317–318.
44. The incident is revealed in a letter from Elizabeth P. Fahs to Blanche Kell, April 19, 1863. Kell told his naval friend, Dr. Charles F. Fahs, who told Mrs. Fahs. There is no other mention of the "finger" in letters or papers. Several other sources tell of robbing "Pizarro" of fingers or toes. Ammen, p. 309; William H. Parker, *Recollections of a Naval Officer* (New York, 1883), pp. 179–180. In 1871 a visiting scientist found that all the bones to the wrist were gone. He wrote, "I was permitted to slice off a bit [of silk] as a relic. I very soon threw it away, however, on being told by . . . an English Roman Catholic clergyman attached to the cathedral for many years, that he believed a great many skeletons and no inconsiderable number of silk cloaks, had been doing duty for the memory of the great Pizarro, since the Conqueror was accredited

to have been deposited here." Thomas J. Hutchinson, *Two Years in Peru, with Exploration of Its Antiquities* (London, 1873), I, p. 310.

45. Kell to Margery Kell, July 15, 1844.
46. Kell, pp. 17–18.
47. The disaster occurred during ceremonies held on the Potomac River, February 28, 1844. Secretary of State Abel P. Upshur was among those killed.
48. Kell to Margery Kell, July 15, 1844. Dallas was given a funeral with honors and buried near Lima, but three years later his body was exhumed and returned to the United States.
49. Melville, p. 346.
50. Kell to Margery Kell, Nov. 14, 1844.
51. *Ibid.*
52. Kell to Margery Kell, Apr. 23, 1845. Blanche Kell MSS.
53. Kell, p. 22.
54. Letter of Lieut. Neil M. Howison, May 15, 1845. Court-Martial Proceedings.
55. Colton, *Deck and Port*, p. 299.
56. Kell to Margery Kell, Nov. 8, 1854. Blanche Kell MSS.
57. Nov. 8, 1845. Blanche Kell MSS. Kell and other officers took a five-day trip to the Kilauea crater, which Kell always remembered as one of the "unforgotten pleasures" of his life.
58. Kell, p. 26. A missionary blamed the evil influences on English ships-of-war and "all the American whale ships that have touched at this port for a few years past." He praised the conduct of the officers and crews of American men-of-war. Rev. Henry T. Cheever, *The Island World of the Pacific* (New York, 1856), pp. 352, 355.
59. Kell to Margery Kell, Nov. 19, 1845. Blanche Kell MSS.
60. Kell to Margery Kell, Apr. 21, 1846. Blanche Kell MSS.
61. Kell, *Savannah* Journal. Article 41 of the Act of Congress (1800) provided that "a court-martial shall not, for any one offense not capital, inflict a punishment beyond one hundred lashes."
62. Franklin, p. 66.

Notes for Chapter III

1. The authorities replied that they had no gunpowder with which to return the salute.
2. Doc. No. 4, House of Rep., 29th Cong., 2nd Sess., p. 648.
3. *Ibid.*, pp. 645-646.
4. *Ibid.*, p. 644.
5. There is no evidence that Kell was one of the landing party; he probably witnessed the flag-raising from the *Savannah.*
6. Doc. No. 4, House of Rep., 29th Cong., 2nd Sess., p. 647.
7. Prior to Sloat's arrival at Monterey, a group of insurgents, chiefly American immigrants to California, had raised the Bear Flag at Sonoma, declaring an independent California republic. Captain John C. Frémont of the United States Topographical Engineers assumed ex-officio command of these forces.
8. John Charles Frémont, *Memoirs of My Life* (Chicago, 1887), I, 542.

9. Fred Walpole, *Four Years in the Pacific in Her Majesty's Ship Collingwood, from 1844 to 1848* (London, 1849), II, 215.
10. Frémont, I, 533.
11. Allan Nevins, *Frémont: Pathmarker of the West* (New York, 1939), p. 288.
12. Frémont, I, 534.
13. Walter Colton, *Three Years in California* (New York, 1850), p. 21.
14. Walter Colton (1797–1851) was a professor of moral philosophy and an editor before entering the U.S. Navy as chaplain in 1830. The administration of Colton at Monterey was noted for its fairness and humanity.
15. Nevins, p. 290.
16. Hubert H. Bancroft, *History of California* (San Francisco, 1886), V, 255–257.
17. Sloat disavowed Stockton's proclamation.
18. Kell underlined "*President James Polk's Proclamation*. . . ." Kell, *Savannah* Journal.
19. Kell to Margery Kell, Sept. 19, 1846.
20. Colton, *Three Years in California*, pp. 59–60; 71. The keeping of crews beyond their term of enlistment if public service so required was authorized by an act of Congress (1837). They were to be paid by additional one-fourth of their wages.
21. George W. Ames, Jr., "Gillespie and the Conquest of California," *California Historical Society Quarterly*, XVII, No. 4, Part I, pp. 335, 341. The Americans suffered four killed and six wounded in the encounter. A naval officer described Captain Mervine as "an officer who has never enjoyed any degree of favor among officers who have sailed with him; . . . he seems hasty, & without much judgement, exceedingly suspicious and impetous, and . . . much puffed with conceit & self importance. . . ." "Naval Conquest in the Pacific; The Journal of Lieutenant Tunis Augustus Macdonough Craven, U.S.N.,'" ed. John H. Kemble, *California Historical Society* Quarterly, XX, No. 3, p. 216.
22. Werner H. Marti, *Messenger of Destiny* (San Francisco, 1960), p. 90.
23. Craven Journal, pp. 218–220.
24. Bancroft, V, 380–381.
25. Colton, *Three Years in California*, p. 152. Extortion and threats had been used against the Californians, such as tying a child at the stake and threatening to shoot him unless the father delivered up a certain number of horses. *A Navy Surgeon in California, 1846–1847; The Journal of Marius Duvall*, ed. Fred B. Rogers (San Francisco, 1957), p. 72.
26. Kell, pp. 30–31.
27. Pages 76–77.
28. Kell, p. 33. Duvall, who was surgeon, states: "None were wounded on our side, the enemy having fired too high." Kell states that one American was wounded.
29. *Ibid.*, p. 34.
30. Bancroft, V, 383.
31. Duvall Journal, pp. 94–95.
32. *Ibid.*, p. 97.
33. Sept. 5, 1847.

Notes for Chapter IV

1. In 1850 the U.S. Naval Academy offered a four-year course.
2. Benjamin, p. 172. A monument was erected at the school to honor Shubrick, Pillsbury, and two passed midshipmen who drowned when the brig *Somers* capsized off Vera Cruz on Dec. 8, 1846.
3. Franklin, p. 88.
4. Benjamin, pp. 174–175; 180.
5. Parker, p. 119.
6. Benjamin, p. 161.
7. Pages 118, 121.
8. Page 89.
9. Kell, pp. 37–38.
10. Franklin, p. 93.
11. Parker, p. 119.
12. Franklin, p. 88.
13. Two of the duelists—Francis G. Dallas and Walter W. Queen—were eventually reinstated.
14. Kell to Margery Kell, Apr. 14, 1848.
15. Benjamin, pp. 181–183, 185. After the hanging in effigy incident, the ringleaders were apprehended and arrested for insulting a superior officer. Their defense was that a professor was not superior to a midshipman, but was simply a citizen employed by the Navy. As a result, the professors demanded and received commissions as officers and a pay raise.
16. Kell to Margery Kell, Apr. 14, 1848.
17. Parker, p. 125. In later years, Franklin remembered Morgan, Gwinn, and James Armstrong as having been on the Board. Franklin, p. 94.
18. Page 95.
19. Abercrombie repeated the course but again failed the examination; he was dismissed from the service on August 28, 1849. Hamersly, p. 16.
20. Benjamin, pp. 426–428. Kell claimed that he was number 27 in his class; it may be that he ranked number 27 in his section (1847–1848) of 94. Kell, p. 39. Since Kell was later court-martialed, but reinstated, it is also possible that he was officially dropped in the numerical ranking of his class.
21. Secretary of Navy to Kell, July 10, 1848. Record Group No. 24, National Archives.
22. Oct. 6, 1848. Record Group No. 45, National Archives. Kell's orders to report to the *Albany* were dated September 26, 1848, but he did not receive them until October 18.

Notes for Chapter V

1. Midshipmen received $400 per year; passed midshipmen, $750.
2. Kell to Margery Kell, Oct. 27 or 28, 1848.
3. *Dictionary of American Naval Fighting Ships*, I, 21. The *Albany* had a tonnage of 1064; she was 147 feet, 11 inches long, with a speed of 13 knots.

4. Phelps, "Reminiscences," p. 25. The *Albany* was lost at sea in 1854.
5. Eggleston to Blanche Kell, Dec. 28, 1909. Printed in *Confederate Veteran* (Nashville), XVIII, No. 2, p. 61.
6. Page 104.
7. My narrative is based on the testimony given in the Court-Martial proceedings, July 20–Aug. 4, 1849, unless otherwise cited. Nothing concerning the passed midshipmen was recorded in the log of the *Albany* (Record Group No. 45, National Archives).
8. Randolph later denied using the word "arrest"; however, testimony indicates that he said "arrest" while highly agitated.
9. Kell in his *Recollections* (pp. 39–40) incorrectly states that he was the *first* to be given the order to light the lieutenant's candle and that the "three other passed midshipmen in like manner refused to obey the order and were also suspended."
10. Several years earlier Reid had been obliged to leave the bedside of a dying brother, on Randolph's order, at a time when he himself was ill and unable to perform his official duties. Although Reid considered Randolph's conduct towards him to be discriminatory, it is unlikely that Randolph was fully aware of the circumstances.
11. Only a few years earlier, Navy Chaplain Walter Colton had written: "The illegality of an order, though it may mitigate the offense, cannot for a moment justify disobedience. Such a doctrine would make every man a judge in his own case, and overthrow discipline. He must obey the order, and seek redress at its proper source." Colton, *Deck and Port*, p. 7.
12. The brief conversation between Kell and Randolph, as remembered many years later, is found in Branham Interview, 1883. It is doubtful, however, that Kell would have responded without a "sir," even under these circumstances.
13. The strict discipline aboard the *Albany* is seen in the record of floggings aboard that vessel. During 1849, 189 men were punished for the usual infractions (disobedience, fighting, drunkenness, and skulking), plus others, such as "calling orderly a damned liar," "neglect to report a shoal of whales when on lookout," "giving prisoner in his charge a lighted cigar," "doubling grog while on sick list," and "growling and talking during the time of working ship." Doc. No. 26, Executive Documents, 1st Sess., 31st Cong. (1849–50), VII, 67–71.
14. William B. Preston served from Mar. 8, 1849, until July 22, 1850.
15. Kell to [Mary] Kell, June 4, 1849.
16. Kell to Mary Kell, June 12, 16, 1849. d'Antignac Collection.
17. Secretary of the Navy to Kell, July 3, 1849. Record Group No. 45, National Archives.
18. A Court of Inquiry attributed the capsizing to want of weight in the brig and consequent loss of stability. Semmes was exonerated of negligence.
19. Raphael Semmes, *Service Afloat and Ashore During the Mexican War* (Cincinnati, 1851), pp. 97–98. This should not be confused with Semmes' other *Service Afloat*, which concerns his Civil War career.
20. Robert C. Rogers, "Some Reminiscences of Philip Spencer and the Brig 'Somers,'" *The United Service* (July, 1890), IV (New Series), 32–33.

21. Scott Interview.
22. Blanche Kell MSS.
23. Scott Interview.
24. Semmes, *Service Afloat*, p. 123. Semmes' Letter Book (1848–1858), Library of Congress, p. 114, mentions only that he served as Counsel for the accused passed midshipmen.

Notes for Chapter VI

1. Kell, p. 41.
2. In 1850 the estate was valued at $10,000, the livestock at $550, and machinery and farm implements at $100. Agricultural Census for 1850, Twenty-second District, McIntosh County, Georgia. Duke University.
3. After completing three years at Princeton, Baillie transferred to the Kentucky Military Institute, receiving his B.A. in 1852.
4. Kell, p. 43.
5. Berrien (1781–1856) practiced law in eastern Georgia before becoming a U.S. Senator in 1824. He served as Attorney General in President Andrew Jackson's first cabinet, but resigned in 1831. He was returned to the Senate as a Whig in 1841 and served until 1852. He was a political moderate until 1850, when he came out against the compromise of Henry Clay.
6. Kell, p. 44.
7. While in Washington Kell made several visits to the Capitol building, where he listened to some of the great debates on Clay's compromise bill.
8. No correspondence has been located which would indicate an official review of the court-martial and its sentence. One unofficial letter from Senator Berrien to Secretary Graham (dated Sept. 26, 1850) merely mentions "the young midshipmen Kell and Hopkins." *The Papers of William Alexander Graham,* ed. J. G. de Roulhac Hamilton (Raleigh, 1957–1961), III, 403.
9. Clarke died while in the service, in 1855; Hopkins resigned soon after his reinstatement; Roe distinguished himself in the Union Navy during the Civil War and eventually became a Rear Admiral. Hamersly, pp. 147, 357, 613.
10. Kell to Spalding, Oct. 23, 1850. d'Antignac Collection. This was Kell's last contact with Spalding, who died on January 4, 1851.
11. Kell's arrival in Charleston in late December coincided with that of Jenny Lind, the "Swedish Nightingale." He attended one of her concerts, an event he considered one of the "greatest musical privileges" of his life. Kell, p. 46.
12. Frank M. Bennett, *The Steam Navy of the United States* (Pittsburgh, 1896), p. 104. The *Susquehanna,* nine guns, was 250 feet long, weighed 2213 tons, and required a complement of 300 men.
13. Kell to Margery Kell, July 1, 1851. Blanche Kell MSS.
14. Kell to Margery Kell, July 27, 1851.
15. Kell, p. 61.
16. Francis L. Hawks, *Narrative of the Expedition of an American Squadron to the China Seas and Japan. . . .* (New York, 1857), pp. 234, 239, 366.

17. Kell to Margery Kell, June 2, 1856. Blanche Kell MSS.
18. In the U.S. an anti-Aulick faction had succeeded in having him replaced by Perry. After Aulick's return, he was exonerated of any misconduct. Edward M. Barrows, *The Great Commodore* (New York, 1935), pp. 213–214.
19. Kell to Margery Kell, Sept. 23, 1852.
20. Charles Lee Lewis, *Admiral Franklin Buchanan* (Baltimore, 1929), pp. 126–127.
21. Kell to Margery Kell, Feb. 22, 1853. d'Antignac Collection.
22. Taylor (1825–1878) was well known during his lifetime as a traveler, translator, and man of letters.
23. Bayard Taylor, *India, China and Japan* (New York, 1855), p. 288.
24. *Ibid.*, pp. 321–322.
25. Matthew Calbraith Perry (1794–1858), a brother of Oliver H. Perry, was already an officer of distinction at the time of the Japan Expedition. William E. Griffis, *Matthew Calbraith Perry* (Boston, 1887).
26. William H. Hale, "When Perry Unlocked the 'Gate of the Sun,' " *American Heritage* (April, 1958), IX, No. 3, p. 95.
27. Many of the notes taken (including those of Bayard Taylor) were later incorporated into Perry's official account. At least two members of the expedition (J. W. Spalding and Midshipman Glenn Sproston) ignored Perry's orders, and their accounts of the expedition were later published separately.
28. A Japanese account said of the American ships: "The name of boat is steam ship or fire wheel ship. . . . She don't care a tempest, heavy rain nor violent waves, she runs as quick as a dragon in swimming." Hale, p. 19.
29. Letter [Garret R. Barry], July 14, 1853, in *Proceedings of the Massachusetts Historical Society* (April, 1886), 2nd Ser., II, 260–261.
30. Kell to [?], Oct. 16, 1853. Blanche Kell MSS.
31. Although they gazed in wonder and delight at the miniature railway and other presents, the Shogun's court was actually well informed, having seen copies of the *Illustrated London News,* which carried the story (complete with pictures) of the expedition when it was being fitted out.
32. *The Opening of Japan; A Diary of Discovery in the Far East, 1853–1856, by Rear-Admiral George Henry Preble, U.S.N.* ed. Boleslaw Szczesniak (Norman, 1962), p. 327.
33. William Jones Boone (1811–1864) was the first Protestant Epsicopal bishop of the diocese of Amoy, China. He was appointed a medical missionary in 1837 and finally died in China.
34. "The Georgia Episcopal Institute and Christ College".
35. Emma Wray to Blanche [1854].
36. *Preble Diary*, p. 330.
37. Emma Wray to Blanche, Apr. 30, 1854.
38. Kell was 31 in 1854.
39. Apr. 30, 1854.
40. *Ibid.*
41. The account of the *Susquehanna*'s cruise to Nanking is found in Exec. Doc. No. 22, 35th Congr., 2nd Sess., VIII, 64–84.

42. *Ibid.*, p. 78.
43. Kell, p. 71.
44. Exec. Doc. No. 22, p. 79; Kell, pp. 74–75.
45. June 24, 1854.
46. Kell, p. 65.
47. July 28, 1854.
48. Letter copied by Emma Wray in her letter to Blanche, Sept. 30, 1854.
49. Ringgold eventually recovered from his physical and mental breakdown and was restored to duty.
50. *The Macon Daily Telegraph*, May 7, 1912.

Notes for Chapter VII

1. A sketch of Nathan Munroe's life is found in the Blanche Kell MSS; it was published as a pamphlet in 1911.
2. Stephen Elliott (1806–1866) was the first Protestant Episcopal bishop of Georgia; elected in 1840, he served until his death.
3. *The Southern Business Directory and General Commercial Advertiser* (Charleston, 1854), I, 221.
4. Henry Kollock Reese, Kell's cousin, became pastor of the Macon church in October, 1854. Oliver J. Hart, *The History of Christ Church Parish, Macon, Georgia, 1825–1925* (Macon: 1925), p. 29.
5. d'Antignac Collection.
6. All of the events hereafter described, unless otherwise cited, are found in Blanche Kell MSS. The conversations were recalled by Mrs. Kell many years afterward and should not be taken literally.
7. When told of the remark years later, Kell said: "The old gentleman should not have expected a man who had met his fate, his destiny, to be talkative."
8. Kell to Secretary of the Navy, July 8, 1855. Record Group No. 45. National Archives.
9. Sept. 23, 1855.
10. Kell's commission was approved and authorized by Congress on July 24, 1856.
11. Kell to Secretary of Navy, Nov. 24, 1855. Record Group No. 45, National Archives.
12. Dec. 7, [1855].
13. Dec. 12, 1855.
14. At the request of Blanche Kell, her husband's love letters were buried with her when she died in 1917.
15. *Letters from the United States, Cuba, and Canada* (London, 1856), II, 14.
16. Kell to Margery Kell, Apr. 25, 1856. Blanche Kell MSS.
17. Kell, p. 100.
18. John Anthony Winston (1812–1871), planter, was governor of Alabama from 1853 to 1857.
19. Kell to Margery Kell, Apr. 14, 1856; Kell to Margery Kell, Apr. 25, 1856. Blanche Kell MSS.
20. Kell, p. 102.
21. James McQueen McIntosh (1828–1862), an 1849 graduate of West Point,

became a Brigadier General in the Confederate Army; he was killed at Elkhorn in 1862. His brother, John Baillie McIntosh (1829–1888), became a Brigadier General in the Union Army.

22. Kell to Margery Kell, July 31, 1856. Blanche Kell MSS.
23. Charles Spalding (1808–1887) attended West Point. Evelyn Kell, a cousin, was his second wife. In 1856 he was a state representative.
24. Kell to Margery Kell, July 31, 1856. Blanche Kell MSS.
25. Mary Kell to Blanche, Aug. 1 [1856].
26. Blanche to Tabitha Munroe, Sept. 14, 1856.
27. Blanche to Tabitha Munroe [1856]; Blanche to Nathan Munroe, Nov. 23, 1856.
28. *Ibid.*
29. Kell, p. 104.
30. Blanche to Tabitha Munroe [1856].
31. Blanche to Tabitha Munroe, Dec. 2, 1856; Hettie Kell to Blanche, Sept. 4, 1857.
32. Blanche Kell MSS.
33. Blanche to Tabitha Munroe, Jan. 31, 1857.
34. Blanche to Tabitha Munroe, April 21, 1857.
35. John Elliott Ward (1814–1902), born at Sunbury, Georgia, was a lawyer, diplomat, and politician, who served in the Georgia Legislature and as U.S. District Attorney for Georgia. In 1854 he was elected mayor of Savannah. In 1856 Ward was president of the National Democratic Convention at Cincinnati which nominated James Buchanan. Two years later he was appointed by the President as envoy extraordinary and minister plenipotentiary to China, but left China after the election of Lincoln in 1860. Ward was disappointed with the secession of Georgia and took no part in the war. In 1866 he moved to New York City to practice law.
36. May 18, 1957.
37. Harriet Hutton to Blanche, July 28, 1857.
38. The store ship *Supply*, launched in 1846, was 547 tons, with four guns. Kell's order was dated Oct. 17, 1857.
39. Kell to Secretary of the Navy, Oct. 25, 1857. Record Group No. 45, National Archives.
40. Kell to Blanche, Oct. 25, 1857. Eugenius Aristides Nisbet Papers, Duke University. Henry Ward Beecher (1813–1887) had been minister of the Plymouth Church since 1847. He reportedly preached to a congregation averaging about 2500 persons. For all Beecher's fame, Kell noted that the collection plate had "more coppers than silver on it."
41. Kell to Blanche, Oct. 28, 1857.
42. Kell to Margery Kell, Oct. 31, Nov. 16, 1857.
43. McIntosh to Commodore French Forrest, Nov. 24, 1857.
44. Dec. 14, 1857. d'Antignac Collection.
45. Kell to Blanche, Dec. 25, 1857. d'Antignac Collection.
46. Jan. 11, 1858.
47. Nathan Munroe to his daughters, Aug. 8 [1858]. d'Antignac Collection.
48. Telegram, John Hutton to Henry K. Reese, Aug. 4, 1858. d'Antignac Collection. A letter was sent the same day by the Reverend Bragg.

49. Aug. 8 [1858]. d'Antignac Collection.
50. Blanche Kell MSS.

Notes for Chapter VIII

1. Aug. 21, 1858. d'Antignac Collection.
2. Aug. 24, 1858. d'Antignac Collection.
3. Blanche to Nathan Munroe [Jan., 1860].
4. Private Journal of Blanche Kell, 1863–1873. d'Antignac Collection.
5. Margery Kell to Kell, Sept. 12 [1858]. The estate ("Rushland") covered 470 acres, including pine land. In 1860 it was valued at $2,500. Agricultural Census for 1860, McIntosh County, Georgia. Duke University. The slave census for the year shows that Baillie Kell was the owner of 98 slaves. Slave Census, 1860, McIntosh County, Georgia. (microfilm copy) Georgia Dept. of Archives.
6. While on an exploring expedition, the *Water Witch* had veered toward the Paraguayan side of the Parana River in an effort to avoid shoals, thus coming under fire. One American was killed. On Dec. 8, 1857, President Buchanan denounced the attack as "unjustifiable" and demanded satisfaction. James B. Bowlin was appointed commissioner to work out a settlement of the demand for $500,000, an apology, and damages to the family of the sailor killed on the *Water Witch.*
7. Oct. 21, 1858. Blanche Kell MSS; Kell, pp. 115–116.
8. Carlos Antonio Lopez (1792–1862) became dictator of Paraguay in 1844.
9. Kell to Blanche, Nov. 18, Dec. 25, 1858; Jan. 2, 1859. Blanche Kell MSS.
10. Diary of Charles F. Fahs, covering cruise of steamer *Water Witch* to Paraguay, Sept. 2, 1858 to May 1, 1859. Library of Congress.
11. Jan. 11, 1859. Blanche Kell MSS.
12. Kell to Margery Kell, Jan. 13, 1859.
13. Negotiations took place from Jan. 27 to Feb. 1 at Asuncion. Lopez agreed to apologize and to pay the family of the dead seaman; the larger settlement was to be left for later arbitration. Although repeated efforts were made by the U.S. to collect even a token amount, nothing was ever paid by Paraguay.
14. Kell to Blanche, Feb. 6, 1859. Blanche Kell MSS. Dr. Fahs was presented to President Lopez in Asuncion. He described him as a "very short and exceedingly fat gentleman of seventy-two years; he has a very mild and rather intelligent face, and we were all most agreeably disappointed in him, for we have been taught to regard him as a cruel and heartless tyrant, all of which his looks and what we have heard of him here, entirely deny." Fahs Diary, Feb. 10, 14, 1859.
15. Feb. 17, 1859. Blanche Kell MSS.
16. Kell to Blanche, Feb. 23, 1859. Blanche Kell MSS; Kell, p. 128.
17. Kell to Blanche, Mar. 6, 1859. Nisbet Papers.
18. Kell to Blanche, July 5, 1859.
19. As commandant of the Navy Yard, McIntosh had the rank of flag officer. His executive officer was Commander Eben Farrand.
20. Kell to Blanche, Sept. 5, 1859.
21. Sept. 22, 1859. d'Antignac Collection.

22. Blanche to Nathan Munroe, Oct. 23, 1859.
23. Nov. 6, 1859.
24. Kell to Margery Kell, Nov. 15, 1859; Margery Kell to Kell, Nov. 5, 1859.
25. Nov. 22, 1859. The provisions of Thomas Spalding's will are found in Coulter, pp. 299–300.
26. Hettie Kell to Blanche, Dec. 26, 1859.
27. Blanche to Nathan Munroe, Jan. 21, 1860. Blanche Kell MSS.
28. David Glasgow Farragut (1801–1870), as a Federal naval officer, would capture New Orleans and win the battle of Mobile Bay.
29. John Henry Winder (1800–1865) commanded Barrancas Barracks, Florida, 1858–1860; as a Confederate general he would command all prisons in Alabama and Georgia.
30. Stephen Russell Mallory (1813–1873). a resident of Pensacola from 1858 –1860, became Confederate Secretary of the Navy in 1861.
31. Blanche Kell MSS.; Minor to Blanche, Nov. 7, 1862.
32. John Newland Maffitt (1819–1886) was born at sea between Dublin and New York; he entered the navy as a midshipman in 1832 and became a lieutenant in 1843. In 1858 he was assigned to the Cuban station and commanded the steamer *Crusader* at the time of secession. During the war he would command the *Florida*, one of the most successful of the Confederate cruisers; he would also serve on blockade-running duty.
33. Blanche Kell MSS; Blanche to Tibbie (Kell) Nisbet, Feb. 27, 1913. Nisbet Papers.
34. Nathan Munroe to Blanche, Feb. 29, June 28, 1860.
35. Blanche to Nathan Munroe, Aug. 12, 1860.
36. Kell to Blanche, Nov. 29, Dec. 2, 1860.
37. Dec. 2, 1860.
38. Dec. 11, 1860.
39. Kell to Margery Kell, Dec. 14, 1860; Kell to Blanche, Dec. 15, 1860.
40. *Official Records of the Union and Confederate Navies in the War of the Rebellion* ("1st Series," 27 vols.; "2nd Series," 3 vols.; Washington, D.C., 1894–1922), 1st Ser., IV, 44. Hereafter cited as *ORN*.
41. 208 voted for secession, 89 against.
42. Kell to Secretary of the Navy, Jan. 18, 1861. Record Group No. 45. National Archives. Kell's resignation was accepted on Jan. 23.
43. Morris would command C.S.S. *Florida* from early in 1864 until the capture of that vessel in October, 1864. *Register of Officers of the Confederate States Navy, 1861–1865* (Washington, 1931), p. 138. Hereafter cited as *CSN Register*.
44. New York Sunday *World*, Apr. 19, 1891.

Notes for Chapter IX

1. Kell, pp. 134–135.
2. Mary Kell to Kell, Jan. 28 [1861].
3. Kell to Margery Kell, Jan. 30, 1861. Bishop retired from the service May 8, 1861.
4. Kell was still bitter toward Randolph as is evident by written references

to his "old *friend*," the "chivalrous" Captain Randolph. Randolph had resigned from the U.S. Navy on Jan. 14, 1861. *CNS Register*, p. 160.

5. Kell to Margery Kell, Jan. 30, 1861.
6. Record Group: Adjutant General File; Letters Received, 1860–1865. Georgia Dept. of Archives and History.
7. Josiah Tattnall (1795–1871) had a distinguished record of service dating back to the War of 1812. A few years before the war, at a banquet in Boston, Tattnall exclaimed: "Palsied be the hand of him who attempts the dissolution of this glorious Union." *Memoir and Correspondence of Charles Steedman, Rear Admiral, U.S.N.* ed. Amos Laurence Mason (Cambridge, Mass., 1912), p. 300.
8. Branham Interview, 1883.
9. Aeneas Armstrong would drown on January 26, 1865, when his steam packet boat collided with another steamer on the James River. *CSN Register*, p. 5.
10. Built in 1856, the *Everglade* was 122 feet, with a tonnage of 406 burden. *Dictionary of American Fighting Ships*, II, 564–565.
11. Blanche to Nathan Munroe, Feb. 24, 1861.
12. Emma M. Maffitt, *The Life and Services of John Newland Maffitt* (New York, 1906), p. 222. When Maffitt inspected the *Savannah* and the other three "tugs" comprising the Georgia Navy, he condemned them as fit only as "provisional guard-boats."
13. James D. Bulloch, *The Secret Service of the Confederate States in Europe* (New York, 1884), I, 143.
14. Henry C. Wayne to Morris, Feb. 25, 1861. Letterbook, A.G.O. Navy. Georgia Dept. of Archives and History.
15. Charles Morris to Henry Wayne, Feb. 26, 1861. Letterbook, A.G.O. Navy. Georgia Dept. of Archives and History.
16. Kell to Nathan Munroe, Mar. 14, 1861; Kell to Blanche, Feb. 28, 1861. Blanche Kell MSS.
17. Feb. 27, 1861.
18. Munroe d'Antignac, *Georgia's Navy* (Griffin, 1945), p. 9.
19. Nathan Munroe to Blanche, Mar. 6, 1861.
20. Kell to Nathan Munroe, Mar. 14, 1861, Blanche Kell MSS.
21. Blanche to Nathan Munroe, Mar. 15, 1861.
22. William H. Russell, *My Diary North and South* (Boston, 1863), p. 156. Tattnall's "Mosquito fleet" was ineffectual during the battle of Port Royal, South Carolina, Nov. 7, 1861.
23. Kell to Nathan Munroe, Mar. 22, 1861. Blanche Kell MSS.
24. Blanche to Nathan Munroe, Mar. 30, 1861.
25. Richard Fielder Armstrong (1842–1904) graduated from Annapolis in 1861.
26. Kell to Blanche, Apr. 11, 1861. Blanche Kell MSS.
27. Blanche to Nathan Munroe, Apr. 13, 1861.
28. Nathan Munroe to Blanche, Apr. 11, 1861.
29. Kell, pp. 142–144. Blanche expressed great delight in her husband's "maiden speech."
30. Naval War Records. National Archives.
31. Nov., 1863.

Notes for Chapter X

1. *Naval Duties and Discipline, with the Policy and Principles of Naval Organization* (New York, 1865), pp. 48–66.
2. Kell to Margery Kell, June 9, 1861.
3. May 20, 1861.
4. Semmes, pp. 123–124. Naturally, Semmes' selection of his executive officer depended on availability, seniority, and experience.
5. The *Sumter*, built in 1859, was a screw-steamer of about 500 tons burden; she was 184 feet long. *Dictionary of American Naval Fighting Ships*, II, 569.
6. "The Cruise of the Rebel Ship 'Sumter' " in *Harper's Weekly* (New York, Aug. 16, 1862), p. 525.
7. Semmes, p. 125.
8. Blanche to Wingfield Nisbet, Dec. 7, 1910. Nisbet Papers.
9. Page 42.
10. Galt to James Dana Miller, Dec. 27, 1900. d'Antignac Collection.
11. James M. Morgan, *Recollections of a Rebel Reefer* (Boston, 1917), p. 129.
12. Page 42.
13. Semmes, p. 454.
14. [Hettie] Kell to Blanche, July 22, 1861; Blanche to Nathan Munroe, Sept. 19, 1861.
15. Oct. 22, 1861. Blanche Kell MSS.
16. Hettie Kell to Blanche, Feb. 27 [1862].
17. Margery Kell to Blanche, Mar. 13, 1862.
18. Nathan Munroe to Blanche, Apr. 9, 1862. On Feb. 18 Myers and Thomas Tunstall left Gibraltar to secure coal at Cadiz; at Tangier, at the instigation of the U.S. consul, they were arrested by the Moroccans and turned over to American authorities. They were brought to the U.S. in shackles and imprisoned at Fort Warren. This event became a minor version of the Mason and Slidell affair.
19. Randolph Spalding died Mar. 17, 1862, three months after his resignation as colonel of the 29th Regiment Georgia Volunteer Infantry.
20. Wallis to Blanche, July 4, 1891. Nisbet Papers.
21. Kell, p. 176.
22. *The Illustrated London News.* Feb. 1, 1862.
23. Blanche Kell MSS.
24. *Ibid.* After a visit to the *Warrior* on Feb. 17, Semmes expressed Chapman's sentiment: "With this single ship I could destroy the entire Yankee fleet blockading our coast. . . . "*ORN*, 1st Ser., I, 741.
25. H. S. Hobson, *The Famous Cruise of the Kearsarge* (Bonds Village, Mass., 1893), p. 138.
26. *ORN*, 1st Ser., I, 666.
27. *Sumter* Journal, p. 527. The *Sumter* was disarmed and sold at auction on Dec. 19, 1862; she later became a blockade runner under the name *Gibraltar.* Not long after the war, she foundered in the English Channel.
28. Kell, p. 177.
29. Semmes to Kell, Apr. 10, 1862. Naval War Records. National Archives.
30. Kell to Blanche, June 18, 1862; Kell, p. 178.

31. Kell to Margery Kell, June 17, 1862.
32. June 18, 1862.
33. *Ibid.*

Notes for Chapter XI

1. So called because it was the 290th vessel launched at the Laird Shipyard (on May 15, 1862).
2. Butcher had been first officer on a Cunard steamer.
3. Bulloch, I, 238. Bulloch's official correspondence concerning the building and launching of the *290* is in *ORN*, 1st Ser., II.
4. *ORN*, 1st Ser., I, 773.
5. New York Sunday *World*. Apr. 19, 1891.
6. Aug. 12, 1862.
7. Richardson Interview, 1886. The *Alabama* cost the Confederacy *L47,500* and an additional *L13,437* for equipment. Semmes was given a "cruising fund" of *L20,000*. Bulloch, I, 62; II, 275.
8. The *Alabama* was 211½ feet long, weighing 1050 tons, with a breadth of 32 feet and 14 foot draft. She had two horizontal 300-horsepower steam engines. *Dictionary of American Naval Fighting Ships*, II, 494.
9. *ORN*, 2nd Ser., III, 193.
10. *ORN*, 1st Ser., I, 785.
11. [John Latham], *Narrative of the Cruise of the Alabama, and List of Her Officers and Men, By One of the Crew* (London, 1864), pp. 4–5.
12. Richardson Interview, 1886.
13. *ORN*, 1st Ser., I, 785.
14. [Author identified only as A.M.G.], "The Pride of Mr. Laird's," *Blackwood's Magazine* (Sept., 1963), p. 218. The sailor is identified as William Pengelly.
15. *ORN*, 1st Ser., I, 786.
16. Kell, p. 187.
17. *ORN*, 1st Ser., I, 807.
18. Semmes, pp. 427, 453.
19. Depositions in Exec. Doc. No. 282, 42nd Congr., 2nd Sess., pp. 425–430.
20. *ORN*, 1st Ser., I, 815–816.
21. *Ibid.*, 787.
22. Richardson Interview, 1886.
23. Semmes would increase the quota "upon such other occasions as excessive fatigue or exposure warranted." A supply of brandy was kept in the ship's dispensary under the surgeon's charge. Henry A. Scomp, *King Alcohol in the Realm of King Cotton* (1888), pp. 561–562.
24. *ORN*, 1st Ser., II, 735.
25. New York Sunday *World*, Apr. 19, 1891.
26. *ORN*, 1st Ser., I. 794.
27. Scott Interview.
28. Kell, p. 193; Wallace P. Reed, "Gallant Captain Kell: The Terror of the Seas," "*The Sunny South* (Mar., 1900). According to this exaggerated account, Semmes intended to train his guns on the city and demand a ransom.

29. Kell, p. 194. *ORN*, 1st Ser., I, 796–797.
30. Scott Interview.
31. Pengelly Journal.
32. Kell, p. 196.
33. New York Sunday *World*, May 3, 1891.
34. Latham, p. 7.
35. Semmes, pp. 511–513.
36. Pengelly Journal.
37. Unknown to Semmes, the crew collected *L17*, hoping Forrest could induce a vessel to take him off the island.
38. Richardson Interview, 1886.
39. Anderson to Mrs. Edward C. Anderson, Dec. 22, 1862. Edward Clifford Anderson Papers. Southern Historical Collection. University of North Carolina.
40. Blanche Kell MSS. Sartori remained true to his word in his first report of the *Ariel's* capture (Dec. 9). However, his report to Secretary of the Navy Welles (Dec. 27) omits the earlier statement that "[Semmes'] whole course . . . was most considerate to all the passengers on board." *ORN*, 1st Ser., I, 579.
41. *ORN*, 1st Ser., I, 815–816.
42. Blanche Kell MSS.
43. Margery Kell to Blanche, Nov. 9, 1862.
44. Sims married Sarah Lois (Tadie) Munroe on Dec. 10, 1862. His career in Confederate service included appointment as Inspector and Agent for Railroad Transportation, C.S.A., and lieutenant colonel, Quartermaster Dept.
45. Nattie enlisted in the 66th Regt. Georgia Inf. He was promoted to first lieutenant of his company in November of 1864.
46. Blanche Kell MSS.

Notes for Chapter XII

1. *ORN*, 1st Ser., II, 721.
2. Kell, p. 208. Galveston was recaptured by Confederate General John B. Magruder on Jan. 1, 1863. The Banks expedition was diverted to New Orleans.
3. Bulloch, I, 266. The *Hatteras*, 210 feet long with a 34 foot beam, weighed 1,126 tons. Her battery consisted of four 32-pounders, one 30-pound Parrott gun, and one 20-pound rifle gun. *ORN*, 2nd Ser., I, 100.
4. *ORN*, 1st Ser., II, 18.
5. Kell, p. 208. According to Blake, the ships were from 25 to 100 yards apart, but Semmes believed that they were from 150 to 400 yards apart.
6. The casualties on the *Hatteras* were two killed, five wounded. One *Alabama* sailor was slightly injured.
7. Accounts of the *Hatteras-Alabama* fight used: Kell, pp. 208–209; Semmes, pp. 543–548; *ORN*, 1st Ser., II, 18–19, 21, 683–684; [George T. Fullam], *The Cruise of the Alabama, from Her Departure from Liverpool*, July 29, 1862 (London, 1864).
8. John Cameron, *Our Tropical Possessions in Malayan India* (London, 1865), pp. 274–275.

9. Kell, p. 186.
10. *Ibid.*, p. 209.
11. Semmes, p. 553.
12. Yonge became an informer for the United States authorities in England.
13. Kell, p. 210.
14. *ORN*, 1st Ser., II, 725.
15. Arthur Sinclair, *Two Years on the Alabama* (Boston, 1896), pp. 133–135, 217–228.
16. *Ibid.*, p. 234.
17. Kell to Louisa Tremlett, May 20, 1863. Confederate Museum.
18. Maffitt, p. 400.
19. Semmes, pp. 454–455.
20. Galt to James Dana Miller, Dec. 27, 1900. d'Antignac Collection.
21. Blanche Kell MSS.
22. W. E. Howard, "The *Alabama's* Loss," *Philadelphia Weekly Times*, July 2, 1881. This article has so many factual errors that it cannot be considered a reliable source.
23. George DeWhiting to Kell, May 24, 1894.
24. Blanche Kell MSS.
25. Sinclair, p. 290.
26. New York *Herald*, July 9, 1864.
27. Semmes, p. 123.
28. Kell, "Cruise and Combats of the '*Alabama*,' " *Battles and Leaders of the Civil War* (New York. The Century Co., 1884, 1887, 1888), p. 603.
29. Richardson Interview, 1886.
30. Newspaper clipping, n.d., n.p., in Blanche Kell Scrapbook.
31. New York *Herald*, July 9, 1864.
32. The *Agrippina* failed to keep her rendezvous here, so Semmes was obliged to take on coal from one of his prizes.
33. Among these was the *Conrad*, taken on June 20, 1863. Semmes commissioned her as a cruiser, renaming her *Tuscaloosa*. Lt. Low was designated as her captain, with four officers and ten seamen.
34. Kell to Blanche, July 27, 1863.
35. *ORN*, 1st Ser., II, 758.
36. Kell, pp. 223–225.
37. *South African Advertiser & Mail* (Aug. 19, 1863; Apr. 23, 1864) in Edna and Frank Bradlow, *Here Comes the Alabama* (Cape Town, 1958), pp. 49, 69.
38. Newspaper clipping, n.d., n.p., in Blanche Kell Scrapbook.
39. *Cape Argus* (Aug. 6, 1863) in Bradlow, p. 22.
40. Some of these pictures later appeared in *The Illustrated London News*, Oct. 10, 1863.
41. While at Saldanha Bay, Engineer Simeon W. Cummings accidentally shot himself while returning from a hunt. Kell read the funeral services over the grave, provided by a Boer in a private cemetery.
42. *ORN*, 1st Ser., II, 760–761; 765–767.
43. *Ibid.*, p. 764. Commander Samuel Barron in Paris, on learning that Semmes' health was failing, intended to replace him with Commander Thomas J. Page. *ORN*, 2nd Ser., II, 653.
44. Dudley Taylor Cornish, *The Sable Arm* (New York, 1956), p. 149. Mont-

gomery was a former "jayhawker" and intimate of John Brown in Kansas.

45. [June, 1863].
46. July 5, 1863.
47. Blanche Kell Journal. Mar. 27, 1864.
48. *Ibid.*
49. Blanche to Tibbie (Kell) Nisbet, Feb. 27 [?]. Nisbet Papers.
50. Oct. 6, 1863. d'Antignac Collection.
51. Mar. 27, 1864.
52. Mary Day, a godchild of Nathan Munroe, married Sidney Lanier in 1867.
53. Blanche Kell MSS.
54. *ORN*, 1st Ser., II, 707–708; 762, 764.
55. *Ibid.*, 562.
56. Cameron, p. 273.
57. *Ibid.*, pp. 276–279.
58. Richardson Interview, 1886.
59. *ORN*, 1st Ser., III, 674, 671.
60. Ezra Bartlett to George Barlett, June 14, 1864. Boston Public Library.
61. *ORN*, 1st Ser., III, 664.
62. *Battles and Leaders*, IV, 607.
63. The armament on the *Kearsarge* consisted of two 11-inch Dahlgrens, a rifled 30-pounder, and four 32-pounders. She carried 162 officers and sailors, as compared to 144 on the *Alabama*.
64. It would have been difficult for the Confederates to see the iron chains that Captain Winslow had had slung along the sides of the *Kearsarge* over a year earlier. They were boxed over with boards which stood out at right angles from the ship's sides. The controversy over whether or not Semmes knew about this extra protection is discussed in Chapter XVII.
65. Branham Interview, 1883.
66. Blanche to Wingfield Nisbet, Dec. 7, 1910. Nisbet Papers.
67. Kell, p. 245.
68. *ORN*, 1st Ser., III, 677.
69. *Ibid.*, 1st Ser., II, 598.
70. *Ibid.*, 1st Ser., III, 651.
71. Newspaper clipping, n.d., n.p., Blanche Kell Scrapbook.

Notes for Chapter XIII

1. Sinclair, pp. 275–276.
2. All times indicated should be considered approximate because of conflicting reports.
3. Manet's painting is on display at the John G. Johnson Art Collection in Philadelphia.
4. The author has been unable to positively identify this photograph, which was among those later sold by Rondin as souvenirs of the fight. Evidently his most popular photos were those of the *Kearsarge* and her officers, as these are found in published accounts of the fight.

5. New York *Herald*, July 9, 1864. This source is used whenever the author is sure that the sailor was a reliable eyewitness. Oddly, however, Semmes states that he himself delivered the speech from a gun carriage.
6. Semmes, p. 756.
7. New York *Herald*, July 9, 1864.
8. Journal of Austin Quinby, Marine Corporal on U. S. S. *Kearsarge*, 1862–1864. Peabody Museum, Salem, Mass.
9. *ORN*, 1st Ser., III, 79.
10. Accounts vary from 10:57 to 11:10.
11. Joseph Adams Smith, *An Address Delivered before the Union League of Philadelphia* (Philadelphia, 1906), p. 23.
12. New York *Herald*, July 9, 1864.
13. "A Survivor [John F. Bickford] Recalls the *Kearsarge* Fight," *Boston Evening Transcript*, June 21, 1922.
14. Henry McConnell, "A Naval Battle," *Philadelphia Weekly Times*, July 4, 1885.
15. News clipping, n.d., n.p., in vol. 8, Scrapbook. Nisbet Papers. University of North Carolina.
16. *Battles and Leaders*, IV, 612.
17. Branham Interview, 1883.
18. Blanche to Arthur Sinclair, Jan. 15, 1896. d'Antignac Collection.
19. Kell, p. 247
20. New York, *Herald*, July 9, 1864
21. *ORN*, 1st Ser., III, 651.
22. Sinclair, pp. 280–281.
23. McConnell Account.
24. [John M. Browne], "The Kearsarge and the Alabama," *The Overland Monthly*, Feb., 1875, p. 107.
25. Hobson, p. 114.
26. *The Times*, n.p. [June, 1893].
27. News clipping, n.d., n.p., in Blanche Kell Scrapbook.
28. *Battles and Leaders*, IV, 609; Bulloch, I, 286.
29. *Ibid.*, p. 921.
30. Bulloch, I, 279.
31. New York *Herald*, July 9, 1864.
32. Quinby Journal.
33. *Boston Journal*, Feb. 11, 1894.
34. Estimated at 370.
35. At President Lincoln's request, the shell was later removed from the sternpost, still imbedded in a large piece of oak timber.
36. *Boston Evening Transcript*, June 21, 1922.
37. After the fight Bickford counted thirty-five patches in his pocket, all taken by him from shells used at his gun.
38. *Boston Journal*, Feb. 11, 1894.
39. Gowin—who had an arm amputated—died within the week, becoming the only fatality on the *Kearsarge*.
40. McConnell Account.
41. New York *Herald*, July 9, 1864.
42. William Wainwright Journal. Blount Library. Mystic Seaport, Connecticut.

43. William P. Brooks to Kell, 1886. Blanche Kell MSS.
44. *Ibid.*
45. This remark has also been attributed to Kell.
46. Bulloch, I, 283.
47. New York *Herald*, July 9, 1864.
48. Sinclair, p. 281.
49. New York *Herald*, July 9, 1864.
50. Branham Interview, 1883.
51. *Battles and Leaders*, IV, 610.
52. New York *Herald*, July 9, 1864. The sailor states that when the men saw the colors down "most of them turned round on their officers" enraged, and several ran aft to Captain Semmes with drawn cutlasses. Semmes convinced them they were sinking and "he did not wish any more lives to be lost." Sinclair's account (p. 277) corroborates this.
53. According to one *Kearsarge* sailor, the men on the *Alabama* ran up the white flag in the main rigging and the Confederate flag in the fore rigging simultaneously. However, a misunderstanding may have been caused by the Confederate ensign, which—when hanging limp—closely resembled a white flag of truce. The officers of the *Alabama* denied that two shots were fired after surrendering. However, *Alabama* sailors, when brought aboard the *Kearsarge*, claimed that two junior officers disobeyed Semmes order to cease firing, a charge denied by both Semmes and Kell. Lieutenant Armstrong, commanding the Blakely gun, was—after the war—credited with firing the first and last shots from the *Alabama*.
54. Hobson, p. 116, Aboard the *Deerhound*, when Semmes was asked why the *Kearsarge* had fired after he had surrendered, he said: "Because, seeing two of her sails still up, I think they supposed it was an enticement for them to come near, and if this had been done the *Alabama* would have boarded her; so till we struck the sails the firing did not cease." *The Spectator*, July 9, 1890, p. 83.
55. Branham Interview, 1883.
56. New York *Herald*, July 9, 1864.
57. Branham Interview, 1883. Sinclair's inaccurate version of this incident has King talking to Kell, begging forgiveness for the trouble he had caused during the cruise. Sinclair, p. 283.
58. *Boston Evening Transcript*, June 21, 1922.
59. Branham Interview, 1883.
60. The log of the *Alabama*, along with Semmes' private papers and the chronometers taken from prizes, had been deposited on shore before the fight. Mars was picked up by one of the *Kearsarge* boats but jumped overboard and was rescued by a French pilot boat.
61. Kell later claimed that he and Engineer O'Brien were the last to leave the ship.
62. Kell, p. 250.
63. Branham Interview, 1883. The *Alabama* sank at 12:50, about 20 minutes after firing had ceased.
64. Kell, p. 250.
65. Kell, *Century* Article, p. 920; Kell, p. 250.
66. Blanche Kell MSS.

67. There is no truth to the story later told by Captain Evan P. Jones of the *Deerhound* that Kell put on a crew hat and shouted to a *Kearsarge* boat that Semmes had drowned.
68. It is uncertain whether the chain covering had any effect on the outcome of the fight. In his official report, Winslow wrote that one shot and two shells—32-pounders—struck the chains, and in all three cases the chain was cut through. *ORN*, 1st Ser., III, 63.
69. *The Spectator*, July 19, 1890, p. 83.
70. *Boston Evening Transcript*, June 21, 1922.
71. Wainwright Journal.
72. Francis B. C. Bradlee, "The *Kearsarge-Alabama* Battle," in *Historical Collections of the Essex Institute* (Salem, Mass., 1921), LVII, 220.
73. *Boston Journal*, Feb. 11, 1894. Most of the stories told by *Alabama* sailors to their captors were exaggerated accounts of the fight. For example, some reported that as many as fifty men had been killed. Actually, only nine were killed, twenty-one wounded, and ten drowned.
74. Hobson, p. 137.
75. *Ibid.*, pp. 138–139.
76. New York *Herald*, July 14, 1864. Surgeon Browne found no wounds on Robinson, thus discrediting sailors' reports that he had shot himself to avoid capture.
77. Hobson, p. 139.
78. McConnell Account.
79. News clippings, n.d., n.p., in Quinby Journal.
80. *ORN*, 1st Ser., III, 61.
81. Browne, *Overland* Article, p. 109. One story claims that the officers of the *Kearsarge* wanted their "gallant enemy," Semmes, to escape so he would not be hanged for treason or piracy. *Thirty Years of Colonial Government*, ed. Stanley Lane-Poole (London, 1889). This story is not plausible. Winslow was severely upbraided by Secretary of the Navy Welles for allowing the *Deerhound* to escape.
82. Hobson, pp. 118–119.
83. The *Alabama* sailors were paroled by Winslow, that same day, to the annoyance of Secretary Welles.
84. *ORN*, 1st Ser., III, 667.

Notes for Chapter XIV

1. Privately, Semmes placed the blame for his defeat on faulty powder and fuses and the "awful disparity . . . between the enemy's guns and my own." *ORN*, 1st Ser., III, 664.
2. London *Times*, June [21?], 1864.
3. June 20, 1864. Blanche Kell MSS.
4. Branham Interview, 1883.
5. June 21 [1864]. d'Antignac Collection.
6. The pistols and ivory piece are owned by Mrs. Evelyn (Kell) McLemore of Darien.
7. Kell to Blanche, July 27, 1864. d'Antignac Collection.
8. Miles Freeman was taken to the United States aboard the *Kearsarge* and spent the remainder of the war imprisoned at Fort Warren.

9. Three *Alabama* officers (Bulloch, O'Brien, and Smith) served on C.S.S. *Shenandoah.*
10. d'Antignac Collection.
11. July 11, 1864.
12. Chapman had served as executive officer aboard C.S.S. *Georgia.*
13. It was delivered Oct. 4, 1864.
14. July 10, 1864. Confederate Museum.
15. Richard W. Corbin, "Letters of a Confederate Officer to His Family in Europe During the Last Year of the War of Secession." *The Magazine of History with Notes and Queries* (New York, 1913), No. 24, p. 11.
16. Morgan, p. 189.
17. Branham Interview, 1883. Captain Edwin A. Garrish of the *Rockingham* and his family (among the last prisoners taken by the *Alabama)* were also aboard.
18. Morgan, pp. 189–190.
19. Welles to Rear Admiral S.P. Lee, July 26, 1864. *ORN,* 1st Ser., X, 307. The U. S. legation at London and the U. S. Consul at Halifax kept authorities informed of Kell's movements.
20. d'Antignac Collection.
21. *ORN,* 1st Ser., X, 316–317.
22. *Dictionary of American Naval Fighting Ships,* II, 519. Weighing 284 tons, the *Flamingo* was 270 feet long and had a crew of 45 men.
23. Frank E. Vandiver, *Confederate Blockade Running Through Bermuda, 1861 –1865* (Austin, 1947), p. 137.
24. Kell, pp. 262–263.
25. [Aug. 2] 1864. d'Antignac Collection. Kell also wired the family of Midshipman Anderson in Savannah, telling them that their son was alive and well. A report had reached them earlier that he had been decapitated during the battle with the *Kearsarge.* Kell, p. 261; Morgan, pp. 199–200.
26. Aug. 3, 1864.
27. Blanche Kell MSS.
28. Aug. 20, 1864.
29. Mallory to Kell, Aug. 8, June 10, 1864. d'Antignac Collection. The commission is in the form of a letter.
30. Kell, p. 265.
31. The C.S.S. *Shenandoah* raised havoc with the U. S. whaling fleet in the Arctic before learning that the war had ended. Waddell then sailed his ship to England and surrendered it to British authorities on Nov. 6, 1865.
32. Blanche Kell MSS.
33. Sept. 29, 1864.
34. Nathan Munroe to Blanche, Sept. 17, 20, 1864.
35. Kell, p. 266.
36. Nov. 23, 1864.
37. Blanche to Nathan Munroe, Dec. 4, 1864.
38. d'Antignac Collection. Kell's orders, dated November 28, were directed to Walthourville and probably reached Kell there.

Notes for Chapter XV

1. Margery Kell to "Children," Dec. 29 [1864].
2. *Ibid.*
3. *Ibid.*
4. Margery Kell to Blanche, Jan. 19 [1865].
5. Oct. 27, 1864.
6. *Dictionary of American Naval Fighting Ships,* II, 561–562.
7. Kell to Blanche, Jan. 4, 1865.
8. Kell to Blanche, Jan. 11, 14, 1865.
9. The Union Commander, William A. Parker, was relieved of his command and court-martialed for his failure to take aggressive action.
10. Kell to Blanche, Jan. 26, 1865. Kell's official reports on the expedition are in *ORN,* 1st Ser., II, 673–674; 689–690.
11. Blanche Kell MSS.
12. Feb. 1, 1865. Blanche Kell MSS.
13. Kell to Blanche, Mar. 8, 1865.
14. d'Antignac Collection.
15. Blanche Kell MSS. The conversations were recalled by Mrs. Kell many years after they occurred.
16. *Ibid.*
17. See Henry Harnden, "The Capture of Jefferson Davis" in *War Papers Read Before the Commandery of the State of Wisconsin, Military Order of the Loyal Legion of the United States* (Milwaukee, 1903). Harnden received $3,000 for his role in Davis's capture.
18. Evelyn Spalding to Kell, Apr. 26 [1865].
19. d'Antignac Collection.
20. Blanche Kell MSS.

Notes for Chapter XVI

1. Margery Kell to Kell, May 15 [1865].
2. Mary Kell to Kell, May 15 [1865].
3. [Mary] Kell to Kell, June 23 [1865].
4. Margery Kell to Kell [1865].
5. Baillie was paroled at Hillsboro, North Carolina, on May 3, 1865.
6. Blanche Kell Journal. Dec. 31, 1865.
7. Blanche Kell MSS.
8. *Ibid.*
9. Blanche to Nathan Munroe [1865].
10. Kell to Margery Kell, Sept. 13, 17, 1865.
11. Blanche Kell MSS. Raphael Semmes Kell was baptized on December 28, 1865.
12. Dec. 31, 1865.
13. Kell to Evelyn Spalding, Jan. 11, 1866.
14. Margery Kell to Kell, Feb. 27, 1866; Dec. 15 [?].
15. In 1870 the Kell farm had an estimated value of $3,000, with 180 acres of improved land and 200 acres of woodland. The produce for that year included 500 bushels of Indian corn, 100 bushels of oats, 9 bales of

cotton (at 450 lbs. each), and 25 pounds of wool. Ten years later the farm was valued at $2,400, with 120 acres under cultivation. The produce for the year included 100 bushels of Indian corn, 240 bushels of oats, 53 bushels of wheat, 16 bales of cotton, 60 bushels of sweet potatoes, 130 gallons of molasses, 20 bushels of apples, 100 bushels of peaches, and 50 cord of wood. *U.S. Agricultural Census, 1870 and 1880, for Africa District, Spalding County* (Duke University).

16. Blanche Kell Mss; Kell, p. 296.
17. Kell, p. 276.
18. Kell, pp. 288–289.
19. Armstrong to Kell, Oct. 4, 1870; Aug. 29, 1874.
20. Evelyn Spalding to Kell [1870].
21. Kell, p. 290.
22. Blanche Kell Journal, Apr. 29, 1873.
23. The Kells had attended the wedding of Sidney Lanier and Mary Day at Christ Church in Macon on December 19, 1867.
24. Aubrey H. Starke, *Sidney Lanier* (Chaper Hill, 1933), p. 182; Kell, p. 297.

Notes for Chapter XVII

1. David D. Porter, *The Naval History of the Civil War* (New York, 1886), p. 604.
2. Kell, p. 5; Blanche Kell MSS.
3. The author has been unable to determine the date of issue of *Burke's Weekly* containing Kell's article; it was sometime between 1869 and 1871.
4. Kell to Editor, Atlanta *Constitution* [1892]. Blanche Kell Scrapbook.
5. Actually, the two ships were about evenly matched in size and tonnage. The *Alabama* had a decided advantage in her two pivot guns, the 100- and 68-pounders, plus the fact she had eight guns to the six of the *Hatteras.* In 1886, Kell admitted that the *Hatteras* "had only a slight advantage in size and was apparently about . . . equal in strength." Richardson Interview.
6. Blanche Kell MSS.
7. Branham Interview, 1883.
8. For example, he refers to the surgeon—David H. Llewellyn—as "Alford" and incorrectly states that Lieutenant Sinclair joined the *Alabama* at Cherbourg.
9. "Semmes and His Ship," Sept. 24, 1881.
10. Dec. 8, 1884.
11. Kell to Editor, *Macon Telegraph and Messenger,* Dec. 10, 1884.
12. Tremlett to Kell, Jan. 1, 1885.
13. Kell, pp. 298–299.
14. *Ibid.,* p. 290.
15. Kell to Clarence C. Buel (of the *Century* editorial staff), Jan. 23, 1886.
16. Kell, p. 292; Richardson Interview, 1886. Browne had written an account earlier, which appeared in *The Overland Monthly* for February of 1875.
17. *The Century Magazine* (April, 1886), p. 910.
18. Philip D. Haywood, *The Cruise of the Alabama, by One of the Crew* (Boston, 1886).

19. Roster of the *Alabama's* officers and crew in Sinclair, pp. 243–352.
20. July, 1886, pp. 464–465.
21. *Colburn's United Service Magazine, and Naval and Military Journal* (London), editions of 1853–1854.
22. Sir William Laird Clowes, *The Royal Navy* (London, 1903), VII, 24.
23. Haywood also claimed to have been a soldier in India during the Sepoy Mutiny and a lieutenant in the Chinese Navy during the Taiping Rebellion.
24. Richardson Interview, 1886.
25. Scomp, pp. 561–562.
26. Cockerill to Kell, Mar. 26, 1891.
27. Apr. 19, May 3, 1891.
28. The substance of Smith's account is also found in his *An Address Delivered before the Union League of Philadelphia* (Philadelphia, 1906).
29. Kell to Editor, Atlanta *Constitution* [1892]. Blanche Kell Scrapbook.
30. Kell to Wingfield Nisbet, Feb. 16, 1894. Nisbet Papers.
31. Kell, pp. 5–6.
32. Blanche to Wingfield Nisbet, n.d. Nisbet Papers.
33. Aug. 1, 1894.
34. Sinclair, p. 261.
35. Branham Interview, 1883.
36. Kell, *Century Magazine*, p. 921.
37. Dec. 30 [1895].
38. Jan. 15, 1896. d'Antignac Collection.
39. April 7, 1896. The prisoners of the *Rockingham* aboard the *Alabama* during the target practice noted that of twenty-four shells fired only seven took effect.
40. Dec. 10, 1895. d'Antignac Collection.
41. *Service Afloat* was reprinted in 1900 by P. J. Kenedy of New York.
42. No evidence has been uncovered which would unravel this mystery. Semmes' journal for Dec. 21, 1863, merely records "taking a Malay pilot. . . ." *ORN*, 1st Ser., II, 791. It is also known that Semmes used a pilot on leaving Singapore.
43. Armstrong to Blanche, Mar. 24, 1897, Feb. 8, 1898.
44. *The Daily Picayune* (New Orleans). Sept. 29, 1912.
45. Blanche to Tibbie (Kell) Nisbet, July 19, 1901. Nisbet Papers. Soon after the battle, Confederate Flag Officer Samuel Barron, in Paris, wrote, "I had heard of an iron sheating of 1 ½ inches thickness about her machinery." Nonetheless, he added, "Until after the battle neither [Semmes] nor I knew anything of the complete protection given to her vital sections by the chain armor she wore," *ORN*, Ser. 1, III, 649. Further evidence on the controversy is that given by Frederick M. Edge *(An Englishman's View of the Battle Between the Alabama and the Kearsarge.* New York, 1864, p. 12). According to Edge, who spoke with wounded *Alabama* sailors in Cherbourg after the battle: "[Semmes] spoke about [the chain covering] to his officers and crew several days prior to the 19th of June, declaring that the chains were only attached together with rope yarns, and would drop into the water when struck with the first shot."

Notes for Chapter XVIII

1. Nov. 24 [1884]. Nisbet Papers.
2. Petition, dated Dec. 29, 1884.
3. Kell to George W. Wood, Dec. 29, 1884.
4. Grady to Kell, Apr. 26, 1886. d'Antignac Collection.
5. Grady to Kell, July 27, Aug. 20, 1886. d'Antignac Collection; Kell, pp. 303–304.
6. Blanche to Tibbie (Kell) Nisbet, Nov. 13, 1899. Nisbet Papers.
7. Blanche Kell MSS.
8. June 5, 1889.
9. Kell to Dr. A. C. Smith, June 22, 1888. Archives of Newman (Ga.) Daughters of the Confederacy.
10. Gordon to William J. Northen, Aug. 19 [1890]. Dept. of Archives. Atlanta.
11. Blanche to Tibbie (Kell) Nisbet, June 23, 1902. Nisbet Papers.
12. Newspaper clipping, n.d., n.p., Blanche Kell Scrapbook.
13. Blanche Kell MSS.
14. Blanche to Tibbie (Kell) Nisbet [1896?]. Nisbet Papers.
15. Blanche Kell MSS.
16. *Ibid.*
17. Newspaper clippings, n.d., n.p., in volume 8, Scrapbook, in Nisbet Family Papers, Southern Historical Collection. University of North Carolina; d'Antignac Collection.
18. d'Antignac Collection.
19. Crawford died before his application was approved.

SELECTED BIBLIOGRAPHY

Manuscript Sources

BOSTON PUBLIC LIBRARY
Letter of Ezra Barlett, June 14, 19, 1864

CONFEDERATE MUSEUM (RICHMOND)
John McIntosh Kell Folder (letters of Kell to Miss Louisa Tremlett)

DUKE UNIVERSITY
Agricultural Census. Georgia. McIntosh County. 1850, 1860; Spalding County. 1870, 1880
Blanche Kell Scrapbooks (contain newspaper clippings)
Eugenius Aristides Nisbet Papers
John McIntosh Kell Papers
"Journal of a Cruise in the U.S. Ship Falmouth"
"Journal of a Cruise in the U.S. Frigate Savannah"
Kell and Nisbet Families Genealogical Chart
"Life and Letters of John McIntosh Kell." Unpublished manuscript by Blanche Munroe Kell

GEORGIA DEPARTMENT OF ARCHIVES AND HISTORY (ATLANTA)
Georgia Census Records. McIntosh County. 1830–1860. (includes Slave Census Records) Microfilm
John Kell Folder
John McIntosh Kell Folder
Letterbook, A.G.O. Navy
Record Group: Adjutant General File. Letters Received, 1860–1865

GEORGIA HISTORICAL SOCIETY (SAVANNAH)
Records of Darien Presbyterian Church, 1822–1862 (typewritten copy)

LIBRARY OF CONGRESS
William H. Cushman Papers
C.S.A. Papers. Navy Dept.
Diary of Charles F. Fahs, covering cruise of steamer *Water Witch* to Paraguay, Sept. 2, 1858, to May 1, 1859. 1 volume
Raphael Semmes Letter Book, 1848–1859. 1 volume

MYSTIC SEAPORT (CONNECTICUT), G. W. BLUNT WHITE LIBRARY
Charles A. Pool, "Journal of the Cruise of the U.S.S. Kearsarge in Search of Rebel Privateers"
William Wainwright Journal (Cruise of the U.S.S. *Kearsarge*)

NATIONAL ARCHIVES
Record Groups 24 and 45 (1841–1861)
Records of General Courts Martial and Courts of Inquiry of the Navy Department, 1799–1867. Microfilm copy no. M–273. Roll no. 65

PEABODY MUSEUM OF SALEM, MASSACHUSETTS
Journal of Austin Quinby, Marine Corporal on U.S.S. *Kearsarge*, 1862–1864

PRIVATE COLLECTIONS
Collection of Munroe d'Antignac. Griffin, Georgia
Diaries of Blanche Munroe Kell. 1863–1917
Family letters
John Kell Precedent Book
Naval commissions. U.S. and Confederate
Scrapbooks (with newspaper clippings) of Blanche Munroe Kell
Mrs. Evelyn Kell McLemore. Darien, Georgia
Blanche Kell Scrapbook (with newspaper clippings)

UNIVERSITY OF NORTH CAROLINA. SOUTHERN HISTORICAL COLLECTION
Nisbet Family Papers. Vol. 8. Scrapbook
Edward Clifford Anderson Papers

VIRGINIA HISTORICAL SOCIETY (RICHMOND)
John Kirkwood Mitchell Papers

Books and Periodicals

Ames, George W., Jr. "Gillespie and the Conquest of California," *California Historical Society Quarterly*, XVIII, (Dec., 1938).

[A.M.G.] "The Pride of Mr. Laird," *Blackwood's Magazine*, CCXCIV (Sept., 1963).

Ammen, Daniel. *The Old Navy and the New.* Philadelphia: J. B. Lippincott, 1891.

Bancroft, Hubert Howe. *History of California.* 7 vols. San Francisco: The History Co., 1886.

[Barry, Garret R.] "Letter of Purser of U.S. Steam Frigate 'Susquehanna, July 14, 1853," *Proceedings of the Massachusetts Historical Society*, 2nd Series, II (Apr., 1886).

Barrows, Edward M. *The Great Commodore; The Exploits of Matthew Calbraith Perry.* Indianapolis: Bobbs-Merril, 1935.

Benjamin, Park. *The United States Naval Academy.* New York: G. P. Putnam's Sons, 1900.

Bennett, Frank M. *The Steam Navy of the United States: A History of the Growth of the Steam Vessel of War in the U.S. Navy, and of the Naval Engineer Corps.* Pittsburgh: W. T. Nicholson, 1896.

Bowen, George Ferguson. *Thirty Years of Colonial Government; A Selection from the Despatches and Letters of the Right Hon. Sir George Ferguson Bowen*, ed. Stanley Lane-Poole. 2 vols. London: Longmans & Green, 1889.

Bradlee, Francis Boardman Crowninshield. "The *Kearsarge-Alabama* Battle; The Story as told to the Writer by James Magee of Marblehead, Seaman on the *Kearsarge*," *Historical Collections of the Essex Institute*, LVII (1921).

Bradlow, Edna and Frank. *Here Comes the Alabama; the Career of a Confederate Raider.* Cape Town: A. A. Balkena, 1958.

Branham, Alfred Iverson. *Story of the Sinking of the Alabama 290: Interview with Capt. John McIntosh Kell, executive officer of the Alabama, given to Alfred Iverson Branham, forty-six years ago, June, 1883.* Atlanta: Cornell, 1930.

Browne, John M. "The Duel Between the *Alabama* and the *Kearsarge*," *Battles and Leaders of the Civil War*, 4 vols. New York: Century, 1884, 1887, 1888.

______. "The Kearsarge and the Alabama: A New Story of an Old Fight," *The Overland Monthly*, XIV (1875).

Bulloch, James D. *The Secret Service of the Confederate States in Europe; How the Confederate Cruisers were Equipped.* 2 vols. New York: G. P. Putnam's Sons, 1884.

Butts, Sarah Harriet. *The Mothers of Some Distinguished Georgians of the Last Half of the Century*. New York: J. J. Little, 1902.

Cameron, John. *Our Tropical Possessions in Malayan India: Being a Descriptive Account of Singapore, Penang, Province Wellesley, and Malacca; Their Peoples, Products, Commerce, and Government*. London: Smith & Elder, 1865.

Candler, Allen D., ed. *The Colonial Records of the State of Georgia*. 26 vols. Atlanta: Franklin, 1905.

———. *The Revolutionary Records of the State of Georgia*. 3 vols. Atlanta: Franklin-Turner, 1908.

Chapelle, Howard I. *The History of the American Sailing Navy; The Ships and Their Development*. New York: W. W. Norton, 1949.

Cheever, Rev. Henry T. *The Island World of the Pacific*. New York: Harper, 1856.

Clowes, Sir William Laird. *The Royal Navy: A History from the Earliest Times to the Death of Queen Victoria*. 7 vols. London: Sampson Low & Marston, 1903.

Colburn's United Service Magazine, and Naval and Military Journal, 1853, 1854. London: Hurst and Blackett.

Colton, Walter. *Deck and Port; or, Incidents of a Cruise in the United States Frigate Congress to California*. New York: A. S. Barnes, 1850.

———. *Three Years in California*. New York: A. S. Barnes, 1850.

Corbin, Richard W. "Letters of a Confederate Officer to His Family in Europe During the Last Year of the War of Secession," *The Magazine of History with Notes and Queries*, No. 24 (1913).

Cornish, Dudley Taylor, *The Sable Arm; Negro Troops in the Union Army*, 1861–1865. New York: W. W. Norton, 1956.

Coulter, E. Merton. *Thomas Spalding of Sapelo*. Baton Rouge, Louisiana: Louisiana State University Press, 1940.

Craven, Tunis Augustus Macdonough. "Naval Conquest in the Pacific; The Journal of Lieutenant Tunis Augustus Macdonough Craven, U.S.N., During a Cruise to the Pacific in the Sloop of War *Dale*, 1846–49," ed. John Haskell Kemble. *California Historical Society Quarterly*, XX, iii (Sept., 1941).

D'Antignac, Munroe. *Gerogia's Navy, 1861*. Griffin, Georgia, 1945.

Dexter, Franklin Bowditch. *Biographical Sketches of the Graduates of Yale College with Annals of the College History*. 6 vols.

Dictionary of American Biography. 20 vols. & index. New York: Charles Scribner's Sons, 1928–1937.

Duvall, Marius. *A Navy Surgeon in California, 1846–1847; The Journal of Marius Duvall*, ed. Fred B. Rogers. San Francisco: John Howell, 1957.

Edge, Frederick Milnes. *An Englishman's View of the Battle Between the Alabama and the Kearsarge: An Account of the Naval Engagement in the British Channel, on Sunday June 19, 1864*. New York: A.D.F. Randolph, 1864.

Eggleston, J. R. "Letter of J.R. Eggleston to Blanche Kell, Dec. 28, 1909," *Confederate Veteran*, XVIII, ii.

Franklin, Samuel R. *Memories of a Rear-Admiral*. New York: Harper, 1898.

Frémont, John Charles. *Memoirs of My Life*. 2 vols. Chicago: Belford & Clarke, 1887.

[Fullam, George Townley.] *The Cruise of the Alabama, Raphael Semmes, Commander, from Her Departure from Liverpool*, July 29, 1862. London, 1864.

Georgia Council of Safety. *Proceedings of the Georgia Council of Safety, 1775 to 1777. (Collections of the Georgia Historical Society*, vol. V, pt. 1.) Savannah: Braid & Hutton, 1901.

Goulding, Francis Robert. *Sapelo; Child-Life on the Tide-Water*. Philadelphia: Claxton and others, 1877.

Graham, William Alexander. *The Papers of William Alexander Graham*, ed. J. G. de Roulhac Hamilton. 4 vols. Raleigh: State Dept. of Archives and History, 1960.

Griffis, William E. *Matthew Calbraith Perry; A Typical American*. Boston: Cupples & Hurd, 1887.

Hale, William Harlan. "When Perry Unlocked the 'Gate of the Sun,' " *American Heritage*, IX, iii (Apr., 1958).

Hall, Basil (Mrs.). *The Aristocratic Journey; Being the Outspoken Letters of Mrs. Basil Hall Written During A Fourteen Months' Sojurn in American 1827–1828*. New York: G. P. Putnam's Sons, 1931.

Hamersly, Thomas H. S. *Complete Army and Navy Register of the United States of America from 1776 to 1887.* New York: Hamersly, 1888.

Harnden, Henry. "The Capture of Jefferson Davis," *War Papers Read Before the Commandery of the State of Wisconsin, Military Order of the Loyal Legion of the United States.* Milwaukee: Burdick & Allen, 1903.

Hart, Bertha Sheppard. *Introduction to Georgia Writers.* Macon: J. W. Burke, 1929.

Hawks, Francis L. *Narrative of the Expedition of an American Squadron to the China Seas and Japan, Performed in the Years 1852, 1853, and 1854, under the Command of Commodore M. C. Perry, United States Navy.* New York: Appleton, 1857.

Hobson, Henry S. *The Famous Cruise of the Kearsarge: An Authentic Account in Verse of the Battle with the Alabama off Cherbourg, France, on Sunday, June 19, 1864.* Bonds Village, Mass., 1894.

Hutchinson, Thomas J. *Two Years in Peru, with Exploration of Its Antiquities,* 2 vols. London: Sampson Low and others, 1873.

Jones, Charles C. *The Dead Towns of Georgia. (Collections of the Georgia Historical Society,* vol. IV.) Savannah, 1878.

Kell, Blanche Munroe. *Nathan Campbell Munroe; A Brief Sketch of a Beautiful, Unselfish Christian Life.* Sunnyside, Georgia, 1911.

Kell, John McIntosh. "A Yarn from Uncle Bob's Log; or A True Tale of the Alabama," *Burke's Weekly for Boys and Girls.*

———. "Cruise and Combats of the 'Alabama,'" *Battles and leaders of the Civil War,* vol. IV. 4 vols. New York: Century, 1884, 1887, 1888.

———. *Recollections of a Naval Life; Including the Cruises of the Confederate Steamers Sumter and Alabama.* Washington: Neale, 1900.

Kemble, Frances Anne. *Journal of a Residence on a Georgian Plantation in 1838–1839.* New York: Harper, 1863.

Knight, Lucian Lamar. *Georgia's Landmarks, Memorials and Legends.* 2 vols. Atlanta: Byrd, 1914.

[Latham, John.] *Narrative of the Cruise of the Alabama, and List of Her Officers and Men, By One of the Crew.* London, 1864.

Lawrence, Alexander A. *James Moore Wayne, Southern Unionist.* Chapel Hill: The University of North Carolina Press, 1943.

Lewis, Charles Lee. *Admiral Franklin Buchanan; Fearless Man of Action.* Baltimore: Norman & Remington, 1929.

Maffitt, Emma Martin. *The Life and Services of John Newland Maffitt.* New York: Neale, 1906.

Marti, Werner H. *Messenger of Destiny; The California Adventures, 1846–1847, of Archibald H. Gillespie, U.S. Marine Corps.* San Francisco: John Howell, 1960.

Melville, Herman. *White-Jacket; or the World in a Man-of-War.* New York: Harper, 1850.

Miller, Francis T. *The Navies.* ("Photographic History of the Civil War," vol. VI.) New York: Review of Reviews, 1911.

Morgan, James Morris. *Recollections of a Rebel Reefer.* Boston: Houghton Mifflin, 1917.

Murray, Amelia. *Letters from the United States, Cuba, and Canada.* 2 vols. London: John W. Parker and Son, 1856.

National Cyclopaedia of American Biography. 47 vols. and index. New York: James T. White, 1892–1965.

Naval History Division, Navy Dept. Office of the Chief of Naval Operations. *Dictionary of American Naval Fighting Ships.* 2 vols. Washington: U. S. Government Printing Office, 1959, 1963.

Nesser, Robert Wilden. *Statistical and Chronological History of the United States Navy,* 1775–1907. 2 vols. New York: Macmillan, 1909.

Nevins, Allan. *Frémont: Pathmarker of the West.* New York: Appleton-Century, 1939.

Official Records of the Union and Confederate Navies in the War of the Rebellion. Series I, 27 vols.; Series II, 3 vols.; General Index, 1927. Washington: Government Printing Office, 1894–1922.

Parker, William H. *Recollections of a Naval Officer, 1841–1865.* New York: Charles Scribner's Sons, 1883.

[Penhoat, Adm.] "Kearsarge and Alabama: French Official Report, 1864," *The American Historical Review,* XXIII, i (Oct., 1917).

Phelps, Thomas S. "Reminiscences of the Old Navy," *The United Service; A Monthly Review of Military and Naval Affairs,* VII (1882).

Porter, David D. *The Naval History of the Civil War.* New York: Sherman, 1886.

Preble, George Henry. *The Opening of Japan; A Diary of Discovery in the Far East, 1853–1856, by Rear Admiral George Henry Preble, U.S.N.*, ed. Boleslaw Szczesniak. Norman: University of Oklahoma Press, 1962.

Reed, Wallace P. "Gallant Captain Kell: The Terror of the Seas," *The Sunny South* (Mar., 1900).

Register of Officers of the Confederate States Navy, 1861–1865. Washington: United States Government Printing Office, 1931.

Roe, Francis Asbury. *Naval Duties and Discipline, with the Policy and Principles of Naval Organization.* New York: Van Nostrand, 1865.

Rogers, Robert C. "Some Reminiscences of Philip Spencer and the Brig 'Somers,'" *The United Service,* New Series, IV (July, 1890).

Russell, William Howard. *My Diary North and South.* Boston: Burnham, 1863.

Scomp, Henry A. *King Alcohol in the Realm of King Cotton; or, A History of the Liquor Traffic and of the Temperance Movement in Georgia from 1733 to 1887.* Blakely, 1888.

Semmes, Raphael. *Service Afloat and Ashore During the Mexican War.* Cincinnati: Wim. H. Moore, 1851.

———. *Service Afloat; The Remarkable Career of the Confederate Cruisers Sumter and Alabama, During the War Between the States.* New York: P. J. Kennedy, 1900.

Sinclair, Arthur. *Two Years on the Alabama.* Boston: Lee and Shepard, 1896.

Smith, Joseph Adams. *An Address Delivered before the Union League of Philadelphia.* Philadelphia: J. B. Lippincott, 1906.

The Southern Business Directory and General Commercial Advertiser. Charleston: Walker and James, 1854.

Stacy, James. *History of the Midway Congregational Church, Liberty County, Georgia.* Newman, Ga.: S. W. Murray, n.d.

Starke, Aubrey H. *Sidney Lanier; A Biography and Critical Study.* Chapel Hill: University of North Carolina Press, 1933.

Steedman, Charles. *Memoir and Correspondence of Charles Steedman, Rear Admiral, U.S.N.*, ed. Amos Laurence Mason. Cambridge, Mass.: Riverside, 1912.

Steel, Edward M., Jr. *T. Butler King of Georgia*. Athens: University of Georgia Press, 1964.

Taylor, Bayard. *India, China and Japan*. New York: G. P. Putnam, 1855.

Taylor, Fitch W. *A Voyage Round the World, and Visits to Various Foreign Countries, in the United States Frigate Columbia; Attended by Her Consort the Sloop of War John Adams, and Commanded by Commodore George C. Read*. 2 vols. New York: D. Appleton, n.d.

Tily, James C. *The Uniforms of the United States Navy*. New York: Thomas Yoseloff, 1964.

U.S. Executive Branch. Doc. No. 26, 31st Cong., 1st Sess.

———. Doc. No. 282, 42nd Cong., 2nd Sess.

U.S. House of Representatives. Doc. No. 4, 29th Cong., 2nd Sess.

U.S. Senate. Exec. Doc. No. 22, 35th Cong., 2nd Sess.

Vandiver, Frank E., ed. *Confederate Blockade Running Through Bermuda 1861–1865; Letters and Cargo Manifests*. Austin: The University of Texas Press, 1947.

Walpole, Fred. *Four Years in the Pacific in Her Majesty's Ship Collingwood, from 1844 to 1848*. 2 vols. London: Richard Bentley, 1849.

Wesley, Rev. John. *The Journal of the Rev. John Wesley, A. M. Sometime Fellow of Lincoln College, Oxford.*, ed. Nehemiah Curnock. 8 vols. London: Robert Culley, 1909–1916.

Newspapers

Atlanta Constitution

Boston Evening Transcript

Boston Journal

The Daily Picayune (New Orleans)

Griffin News

Harper's Weekly; A Journal of Civilization

The Illustrated London News

London Times

Macon Daily Telegraph

Macon Telegraph and Messenger

New York Herald

New York Sun

New York World

Philadelphia Weekly Times

The Spectator (London)

Washington Post

INDEX

www.ingramcontent.com/pod-product-compliance
Lightning Source LLC
LaVergne TN
LVHW050600110926
847619LV00018B/107